This Is Our Time!

This Is Our Time!

The 2010 **SAN FRANCISCO GIANTS** World Series Champions
The Inside Story: Improbable. Wild. Unforgettable.

CHRIS HAFT & ERIC ALAN

CONFLUENCE BOOKS
ASHLAND, OREGON

Confluence Books is an imprint of White Cloud Press

This book is available in quantity at special discounts for your group or ogranization. For further information contact:
Confluence Books, PO Box 3400, Ashland, Oregon, 97520
Phone: 541.488.6415
email: info@whitecloudpress.com

Photography © 2011 by San Francisco Giants
Cover and interior design by Christy Collins, Confluence Book Services

Printed in the U.S.A.

Library of Congress Cataloging-in-Publication Data

Haft, Chris.
 This is our time! : the inside story of the San Francisco Giants' world championship season—2010 / by Chris Haft and Eric Alan.
     p. cm.
   ISBN 978-1-935952-52-7 (pbk.)
1. San Francisco Giants (Baseball team). 2. World Series (Baseball) (2010) I. Alan, Eric. II. Title.
 GV875.S34H34 2011
 796.357'640979461--dc23
                    2011020613

Mixed Sources
Product group from well-managed forests and other controlled sources
www.fsc.org Cert no. SW-COC-002283
© 1996 Forest Stewardship Council
FSC

Contents

Introduction

Above and Beyond

One Seamless Motion

In the supposedly impossible our greatest triumphs lie. In the absurd, the deepest truth suddenly flashes you with all the rudeness and grandeur of any naked statue. And in a white five-inch sphere, you can see the entire beauty and lunacy of life—especially a sphere thrown, caught and hit in San Francisco in 2010. Wherever and whenever you are now, there's a tale that will still be told to children, grandchildren and strangers on the street by those who were there. There will be laughter, knowing smiles, unforgotten private joy at the outrageous edgy madness of it all. It was a legendary party, and you can still go back and join the free characters who were there. We will take you.

But first we'll take you further back: to New York, to 1954, via grainy footage of a man running, gracefully but almost desperately, towards a wall looming at him. Suddenly, he throws up a gloved hand and makes an impossibly elegant capture of another tiny white sphere, then in one seamless motion, he turns to hurl it back from where it came, in one of the most fluid instances of human motion ever seen.

That man was Willie Mays, the sphere came off the bat of Vic Wertz and the setting was the World Series against Cleveland—the last year the Giants would be baseball's world champions for longer than the lifetime of many. It was a moment that still replays endlessly in memory, like a dream of love's highest orgasmic instant.

Fifty-six years later, Willie Mays sits in a chair facing a million faithful believers—the largest gathering San Francisco has ever seen—while a man who isn't the Pope says he feels like he is and blesses the crowd in Mays' own name. Mays watches with an unfathomable expression as a man right in front of him reaches deep into his pants, ripping out in one swift motion a red thong for the million to see.

Crowds of men and women in false beards go wild. That, too, is mere moments after an accidental Zen master gives a brief, poignant lesson on impermanence.

It's as surreal as any stoner's dream—and yet it's transcendent, with a depth of spirit and accomplishment few ever attain. It's one of the best testaments to the power of human cohesion: to placing group over self, to the grace of equanimity under pressure, to believing in yourself when the world does not. It's irrefutable evidence of how vastly different individuals can create unity by most fully being their wildest selves. It's the San Francisco Giants of 2010, world champions at last, the kind of improbable team that comes along once in a generation to make even the uncaring suddenly emotional. It's the perfect tonic for a difficult time.

It still is. We will indeed take you there.

Temple of a Million Misfits

From within their cathedrals, synagogues and mosques, the high priests of this planet's faith traditions would not, for the most part, agree to place baseball in the same divine category as their own religions. And the men who make their living with that little white sphere are not saints by any means—they're as flawed and crazed as the rest of us—but the sacred is where you find it. And since you can find plenty of wisdom in the story of the 2010 Giants, even if the players didn't plan to place it there, who has the right to deny the sacredness of this saga? And if it culminates in a perfect but accidental social protest against a messy age, which also happens to be the most fun party a wild city's ever seen, doesn't that make it even more sacred? It's certainly as easy to see grace within that combination as it is to see Mother Mary's face in a tortilla.

Jon Miller is not the Pope: Let's get that straight. He's "only" a Hall of Fame baseball announcer, capable of spinning excitement out of the ordinary, finding stories in between pitches, calling forth voices with the mastery of a cartoon voice-over actor. Still, he had that papal feeling, addressing a million gathered believers at the Bearded Church of the Rally Thong, otherwise known as the Giants' 2010 victory celebration.

"This must be what it's like to be the Pope," Miller said to the mass. "To go out at St. Peter's in the balcony, and you look out, and there's hundreds of thousands of people." He paused for a moment to gaze upon the congregation before his voice boomed out again to the local heavens.

"So I'd just like to bless you all in the name of Mays and McCovey, Will Clark, Kruk and Kuip, Lincecum, Cain and Wilson. Amen."

Who better than Miller to give the blessing at the first World Championship parade in San Francisco's history? Who better to place the moment in the context of the others who had previously walked the path, the legends of the Giants' rich faith? Born and raised in the Bay Area, Miller had given magic to the Giants' airwaves for 13 years by 2010—as well as to other national and regional broadcasts for longer than the lifespan of most current players. He'd seen the power and glory of baseball, forever and ever, amen. For a man of that cloth, this moment was the divine pinnacle.

Mike Krukow is not a minister any more than Jon Miller is the Pope. Well, actually he is: He's a mail-order minister who specifically got his license to perform a wedding ceremony at the Giants' hallowed stadium for two Giants fans who had met and found their blessed union there. But primarily he's a Giants announcer filled with vivid stories—some of them publishable—and reverence for the game, long after his own major league pitching career has faded into history. When the Great Spirit said to him, "Grab some pine, meat!" and forced him to ride that bench into retirement, he did not lose an ounce of his faith. He took another seat in the temple—in the broadcast booth alongside his old teammate Duane Kuiper, becoming the Kruk and Kuip so respectfully mentioned by Miller on that holy day.

It wasn't the Bible Krukow referred to when his own turn came at the Bearded Church pulpit, but it was a holy book nonetheless—from his perspective and that of the mass congregation. It was a moment of higher love and community.

"Everybody here today . . . you are not standing alone. You are standing with the person who taught you the great story of the San Francisco Giants." Krukow looked resplendent in the faith's traditional colors of orange and black, a beret perched on his head that would do the city's beat poets proud. "They taught you *right*! They taught you, you had to be *loyal*. You had to love your *team*!" He passionately gave the congregation credit for their part, along with identifying their duty. "You have but one responsibility, and you owe it to the person who taught you the Good Book of the San Francisco Giants. You need to pass this story on! Keep this love alive!!!" It's an oral tradition, this faith, as well as a written one.

As for the other broadcast voices carrying the Giants faith across the air daily, Duane Kuiper hadn't been crucified. Jesus, no! (And young Dave Flemming hadn't yet had time to be.) So why did Kuiper use the celebratory pulpit to talk about 28 years of "torture"? In the best of all Giants years, why did he make that a theme all year, slowly turning it into a positive mantra? No one died for the sins of the Dodgers. At least not directly. Hopefully. Really, you never know about these things. In any case, his sermon's theme was simple: We have overcome. Or as he phrased it, "The torture is . . . OVER!!!" The team has risen.

As for the players themselves, what of their role as bearers of the faith at the celebration? Buster Posey was not intentionally a Zen master, although he was the team's star catcher, cleanup hitter, good shepherd of the pitching staff and a world champion about to claim the league's Rookie of the Year title. But he might as well have been a monk on that celebration stage, staring into the first November day with thoughts of beginning again.

"Let's enjoy this today, tomorrow, for a week, maybe even a month. And then let's get back to work and make another run at it." Just like those monks and their sand paintings—destroyed as soon as they're created to teach the great Buddhist lesson of impermanence—baseball is as impermanent as we are. It was all Posey needed to say, which was fortunate because there were a hell of a lot of speeches to fit in.

"I'm not a man of many words," said ace relief pitcher Brian Wilson, vicar of the Bearded Ones, another of the names used in the blessing by Miller. "I'm not even sure what to say right now," he added, before managing in less than a minute to mention strangely sweet smells in the air, a job offer, supposed medical issues, fans etched in history and a truly shadowy figure who'd recently become legendary.

"I'm kind of having a mini heart attack. I'm not sure what it's from—maybe the electricity in the crowd, maybe the smell of Proposition 19, I'm not sure."

Proposition 19 was California's latest ballot measure to legalize marijuana for recreational use, which had been narrowly voted down the previous day. The election might have been a digression but for those sweet wafting smells and the offer by San Francisco Mayor Gavin Newsom to let Wilson take his job—Newsom having won another office the same day Proposition 19 had failed.

"I'd like to thank the mayor for allowing me to try to take the reins. I don't think I'm up for the job. But . . . I know a man who is. Where's *The Machine*???"

With that dark and foreboding question, Wilson walked away, leaving a crowd to ponder the whereabouts of a strange and wordless figure, seen clad only in a black leather hood and other minimal leather attire, wandering nearly naked in the background of a broadcast—reputedly only seen in the neighborhood on visits to borrow sugar.

(The Machine is a story for a later chapter, where he overlaps with deep faith and Mohawks, beards and the sign of the crossed arms.)

Whatever pitcher Matt Cain thought of The Machine and his whereabouts, the pulpit was not a sanctuary for him, even if his name was now forever ingrained in the blessing. Never mind that he was fresh off one of the calmest and most masterful postseason pitching performances ever seen. Not a single earned run did he allow in the entire postseason; not even an uncomfortable expression crossed his face under the supposed pressure. The mound itself is a comfort zone for him, perhaps a sanctuary. But staring out at the million in the congregation, he acknowledged before giving his own speech of gratitude, "It's a lot more nerve-racking than you might think." The power of a million to smother you, even if it's with adoration, is a vastly humbling and frightening force to face. Love can overwhelm as much as it can overcome.

The dizzying speeches continued with gratitude and celebration expressed in Spanish and English, the speakers giving thanks to God and family, fans and teammates and all the behind-the-scenes members of the Orange and Black Ops teams who had made it possible to chase a little white ball all the way to the top of the world. Even the governor of California, Arnold Schwarzenegger—known better as a sinister film character himself—took the microphone to congratulate the team and to mention the shadowy presence of The Machine.

In the end, it came down to first baseman Aubrey Huff, a.k.a. Huff Daddy, to summarize and complete it all. His gratitude was deepened by a decade of losing on terrible major league teams and by the Giants' willingness to imagine what he could bring when he was home on the couch and jobless before spring. "Nine years of my life in last and fourth place! This organization had the heart to bring me here, to give me a chance." This is the chance we're all looking for—to excel, to be given a context that brings out the best of what the world's never seen within us. "And here I'm in front of you beautiful people, nailing this, world champions!" He paused in apparent wonder, passing the credit and celebration to the assembled masses. "You deserve this as much as I do. Trust me." He chose a gift to give back—one of the strangest and most beloved bits of team clothing.

"I've got a little present for you guys here in San Francisco. I'm sure all of you have heard about the Rally Thong," Huff correctly surmised. "Now this is a family event. I can't skin it all the way. But if you've seen *Zoolander*"—the hit cult film about a dim male fashion model—"I have a special talent just for you!" With that—and with Willie Mays sitting right behind him—Huff reached into the crotch of his pants, digging deep with great flair and drama, until he pulled out San Francisco's most famous underwear from within. "The Rally Thong's going to the Hall of Fame!!" Huff claimed, though the Hall of Fame would later decline it, instead opting for Huff's left shoe. "We'll do it again, baby! San Francisco, I love you! Thank you very much."

And the speeches were over. It was a surreal scene, unfolding under perfect warm blue skies, centered by the players who'd created just enough magic to get by using a deceptively simple formula: *See ball, throw ball, catch ball, hit ball.* It hadn't sunk in then just how much permanent magic might arise from those simple actions. Somewhere in the chain of rising complexity, life begins and climbs its unpredictable divine path. Teams evolve; teams are created. New chapters are written, ever different, ever mysterious.

Baseball is all the Church of Winning on some level. No one can deny that. Few would've come to a parade for the Giants if they'd finished an ugly fourth in a division of five, crawling home saying, forgive me Father, for I have hit into 200 double plays and walked the leadoff man enough to seal my own sorry fate. Lo, I have walked through the Valley of Absent Offense. I have been cast out from the temple due to an inability to move the runner over. Yeah, to hell with spirit, winning is the American way.

And still the deeper story is that it's all the Church of Striving— bearded or clean-shaven, win or lose. It's about putting life on the line and risking all failure, even if the whole world is watching, for the sheer richness of reaching to be the best you can ever be—and not doing so alone or in conflict with the ones next to you, but doing it in harmony, with modesty and a lot of deep laughter and support for each other along the way. That was the 2010 Giants, and that is why the magic has nothing (although everything) to do with baseball. It doesn't matter if you're reading this in the year 2079. It doesn't matter if you hate the game. If you love the wildness of the strong human spirit, if you love finding the great teachings in the stinging mist of champagne spray or if you just love a good party, you will find it here. You may even find it wearing neon orange shoes—at least until league officials complain.

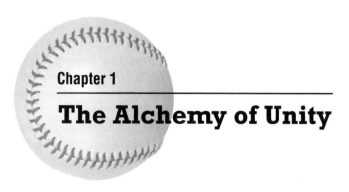

Chapter 1

The Alchemy of Unity

Murphy, Chemistry and Sculpture

Giants clubhouse and equipment manager Mike Murphy has a uniquely deep historical perspective. Murphy has worked for the Giants since 1958—their inaugural season out West after moving from New York—so the time between his hiring and the first San Francisco baseball championship can be measured in complete reinventions of the world, even shifted views of the universe. When "Murph" joined the Giants, the Russians had barely sent Earth's first satellite into orbit; by the time he watched the Giants finally win the 2010 World Series, space telescope scenes of the other edge of the universe were commonplace, and astronomers were beginning to identify potentially habitable planets in distant corners of the sky. The entirety of communications back home had been digitized, and unfathomable inventions were spewing forth with the force and fury of hot lava. Even baseball had gone through eras of strain and rejuvenation.

Throughout that entire age, Murph met nearly every player who wore a San Francisco uniform—more than 1,500 of them—and succeeded in making each feel comfortable, without being overly fawning or businesslike. If a player needed a T-shirt, Murph quickly fetched him one. If one player's uniform pants materialized in another's dressing stall, Murph would help. If a father confessor was necessary, Murph would listen. Details make a team run, and for over half a century, he kept them running as well as anyone. He was a central member of the Orange and Black Ops team behind the scenes, and the way it seemed in 2010, he would still be that central for another thousand years. (Despite a wild rumor to the contrary, he was not, however, The Machine.)

In 2010, the walls of Murphy's AT&T Park office reflected the breadth and depth of his admirers. Of course, the gallery included a signed photo of Willie Mays, the greatest Giant. But there was also still a shot of Dave LaPoint, who spent a single, mostly forgettable season with San Francisco in 1985. From ex-superstars to former scrubs, all were equally welcome in Murph's clubhouse.

Journeymen might be the most astute in rating clubhouse managers, given their experience with so many, and few summarized Murph more succinctly than first baseman/outfielder Mark Sweeney, who played for seven different teams. During his time with the 2006–07 Giants, Sweeney delighted in crowing, "Murph, you're the best!" No one has ever argued.

And no one argues with Willie McCovey, either, when he says, "Once you're a Giant, you're always a Giant." Mike Murphy has spent several decades as the essential keeper of that flame.

Murphy often has visitors. One afternoon in late March 2010, his visitors were equally vintage and two of a kind. Jim Davenport and Joe Amalfitano are two baseball lifers with as much history as Murph himself, true Giants with a combined 108 years in professional baseball. Both are accomplished former infielders and still employed by the Giants as special assistants in player development. During spring training, Davenport and Amalfitano spent all day at minor league camp, hitting fungoes, dispensing advice and teaching fundamentals. A member of the 1958 Giants, Davenport was still adored by fans who had been raised on black-and-white televisions. Amalfitano was in his sixth separate stint with the Giants as a player, coach or instructor—enough to supersede his employment with the Dodgers as a third-base coach from 1983 to 1998 and a senior advisor from 2002 to 2004. Both still looked big league in their sport shirts and slacks, as if their next stop was the first tee at the Masters.

The three mostly talked about going home, since the major leaguers would soon break camp, and the minor leaguers would follow. Before Davenport and Amalfitano said their farewells, though, Murph left them with a thought that would linger.

"This is the most close-knit team I've ever seen," he told them, with the full weight of his historical perspective. Again, no argument. His quiet, simple observation was a prescient one. That chemistry would prove to sustain the Giants throughout a grueling, uncertain yet ultimately supreme season.

That chemistry didn't await the players like the jerseys Murph and his assistants daily hung in their dressing stalls. It wasn't automatic, like the pitching machines spitting spring baseballs in the batting cages beyond Scottsdale Stadium's right-field wall. Natural as chemistry seems, it has to be sculpted, like Rodin working with clay and bronze. As Giants manager Bruce Bochy reflected after the season, "The chemistry thing, I've said this: It doesn't just happen. It happens because you work at it." Relying merely on natural magic is for amateurs and passive ones at that.

Bochy would be far from passive, although he'd often resemble Rodin's "The Thinker" in the dugout during the year—except with a more anxious expression and a larger head. Even in retrospect, he wasn't entirely sure what his role was in creating or sustaining the magic meld between his players.

"That's hard for me to quantify," Bochy said after season's end while describing his aim of an atmosphere with the mindsets of winning and fun. It's a noble, elusive goal. Even in the corporate world, studies show that productivity and fun are directly connected, yet only unlikely masters can remember that and stay loose under pressure.

Thus it was a brilliant beginning when Aubrey Huff, the team's new first baseman/outfielder—contractually appointed to be Savior of the Mediocre Offense—arrived in the Giants clubhouse in February and talked about the team's presumed leader, pitcher Tim Lincecum, whom he had yet to meet.

"I hear he looks like the batboy," said Huff.

Like most good jokes, it had an element of truth. After Lincecum had been first called up from the minors a few years earlier, he was said to have had trouble with a stadium security guard, who couldn't believe a guy looking like Lincecum was actually a player.

Spoken by a less skillful comedian, the joke could've been a toxic beginning. Instead, it was a harbinger of Murphy's prescient vision of oneness.

No matter how bad they are, few teams are wholly toxic on the field and in the clubhouse. Players learn to like each other, if only to survive the duration of the season. Throughout the previous decade of losing, Huff had always found redeeming qualities in his teammates. But he almost immediately sensed something different about the Giants upon reporting to Scottsdale. He could gravitate naturally towards any number of his new teammates.

"Everybody went out of their way to greet me and welcome me," Huff said when the year was over. "I felt really at home from day one. I never felt that comfortable coming into a clubhouse on a new team. From there on, I just felt the same every day," he continued. "You can see the love on this team, I'm sure. I felt that all year with this group of guys."

That love would inspire his own wild leadership on the field, in the clubhouse and in fitting into the San Francisco mold of fitting in nowhere else. The oneness began to form between the castoffs and misfits, the favorite sons and the unknown, the overpaid and the underrated.

Offensive Dismissals

Being a close-knit team guarantees nothing in the win column. Getting along well while losing is forgettable if vaguely admirable. Entering spring, the Giants were a team skeptics found easy to dismiss, despite a pitching staff that was the envy of anyone paying attention. Pitching alone will win a few more games than sheer chemistry, but pitching alone is what many critics felt the Giants had. In many eyes, their offense remained mythical, retired or otherwise off on an extended sabbatical. The defense was considered porous, arthritic, erratic and other nasty synonyms writers were thumbing through their thesauri to find.

It was a reasonable perspective with which to begin an unreasonable year. The team Giants general manager Brian Sabean and others had been diligently building was still as unstable as San Francisco's fault-ridden ground.

Sculpting a steady roster was a greater challenge in 2010 than in 1954. With the shift from contractual slavery to frequent free agency, the game had veered away from the team towards the individual, towards transient winners instead of dynasties. Association between player and team had declined precipitously. General managers such as Sabean—who hadn't even been born in 1954—faced an annual scramble to evolve and create their teams, a challenge their Eisenhower era counterparts would've never imagined. Managers such as Bochy would need more of a meet and greet with new players every spring. More transient players would have to greet each other. Old-timers might call it decline, but it was only a reflection of increased player freedom—and of the rest of society, also shifting restlessly on unstable career ground. In any industry, the days of the lifetime employee were over—except for Mike Murphy, of course.

Bochy didn't have Rodin's luxury of shaping one permanent sculpture, either. With roster and injuries constantly shifting in 2010, he would have to employ 126 different lineups in 162 games, even before his playoff rosters shifted again.

When Bochy looked out onto the spring fields, this is the offensive landscape he saw:

Aubrey Huff, now considered central, was not even a man the team had first sought. Or second sought. To save the condemned offense, the team would've gladly embraced another monster slugger such as Barry Bonds, capable of putting balls in places beyond the edge of dry land. But none of those statistics-minded free-agent sluggers had chosen to come to a cool, cavernous stadium with a reputation as a place where home run statistics die. Hell hath no fury like a suitor scorned, as Shakespeare almost wrote. So the Giants were left to furiously pursue their third choice for a left-handed power hitter: Huff, a quality player despite being sentenced to losing American League teams as a designated hitter, first baseman and outfielder. When the Giants called him, he was none of those things. After a bad year, he was at home without a job offer or even one thong to his name.

In spring, Huff's hitting looked promising, but his defense at first base appeared shaky—not surprising since he had mostly been a designated hitter lately. At least Huff was playing—unlike second baseman Freddy Sanchez, a former batting champion for Pittsburgh whose daily highlight now was playing catch with a member of the athletic training staff. Quietly in the winter—so quietly it wasn't publicly admitted at first—Sanchez had undergone left shoulder surgery for the second time in a year and wouldn't play his first game until May 19.

At shortstop, Edgar Renteria's age (34) and dreadful 2009 season inspired little confidence among outsiders. In the first year of a two-year, $18.5 million deal inflated by a high demand for competent shortstops, Renteria endured elbow and shoulder injuries and hit a career-low .250 in 124 games—miserable for a man who had once been one of the game's finest hitters. Yet players and coaches alike revered Renteria for multiple reasons. A few were historical, including the hit that won Game 7 and the 1997 World Series for Florida against Cleveland. But more reasons were in the present, including the way he offered advice. Renteria was never condescending, often unnoticed and always instructive. He never embarrassed anyone: His high regard for his teammates would never allow him to do that. But what would his body do? That was in question again in 2010. His speed was down. His defensive range was diminished. Renteria's noble work with youth baseball in his native Columbia could save him from neither aging nor further injury.

Even more ominously, third baseman Pablo Sandoval wasn't driving the ball as he had throughout the previous year, when he hit .330

with 25 home runs and 90 RBIs. Sandoval was expected to be at the core of the offense alongside Huff, and any decline from him would surely send writers scurrying for more vicious adjectives. Sandoval tried prescription goggles, hoping they would help him see pitches better. Goggles, however, would not help him lose weight, which was another alarming issue. Sandoval—a.k.a. the Kung Fu Panda—was already a beloved San Francisco figure, but at 23, he was already prone to excessive weight. Despite his own cheerful willingness to do every offseason exercise regimen the team asked of him, he had failed what the team called Camp Panda. Every pound he lost there in the fall he had regained over the Venezuelan winter. Being 5 feet 11 inches is not an issue of excess, but weighing 278 pounds at that height is (as Sandoval did by season's end). Discipline in many forms was a critical issue for Sandoval, and in that he mirrored the struggles of America at large. Very large.

All in all, it was not an infield that screamed "championship!" And the expected outfield was equally staffed by question marks.

Left field was supposed to be the home of Mark DeRosa, another offseason addition. Capable of handling almost every position, DeRosa displayed the same ease with people. His reputation as a leader quickly proved well-founded. "Getting him, we had more of a presence out there," Bochy said. The Giants had scored what seemed to be a coup in the free-agent market by signing him to a two-year, $12 million deal, beating out a dozen teams that had pursued him, convinced he would heal from wrist surgery in time to be an offensive force. The Giants dearly wanted a return on their investment, but DeRosa had only three extra-base hits in 55 at-bats in the spring, delivering the first sign that his wrist wasn't healing as anticipated. Like Sandoval, DeRosa remained mostly upbeat, although plainly searching fervently for solutions.

Over in center was Aaron Rowand, slated to bat leadoff despite not possessing the speed classically desired in that role. He'd previously had a little success in a nontypical way there, and his ferocious work ethic earned him admirers. Unfortunately, after a breakout year in Philadelphia had netted him a massive Giants contract, his first two years in the larger, colder stadium had apparently numbed his bat. No one worked harder, but for two years, the results had paled against his Phillies performances. Even more than with DeRosa, the Giants were in need of return on their Rowand investment. Sixty million dollars might be chump change on Wall Street, but if it's unproductive spending, it's enough to paralyze a baseball team's budget.

Meanwhile, over in right, the hopefuls weren't developing as hoped. John Bowker had shown powerful promise in the minors but hadn't been able to sustain it in the majors. Nate Schierholtz was already one of the most adept at defensively solving AT&T Park's right field conundrum, and his throwing arm was nearly peerless. But his bat was too frequently slumbering lumber, and on a team with offensive weaknesses already, that wouldn't be acceptable. Andres Torres had spent 11 years in the minor leagues, and 32-year-old outfielders with résumés like that almost never win jobs. Right field remained an open, unclaimed expanse.

Behind the plate was Bengie Molina, who carried himself as if he'd just stepped out of Mount Rushmore and moved only slightly more quickly. He was understandably tired of jokes about his being the slowest runner in the majors when his many better qualities were more vital. A surprise reacquisition by the Giants—who'd expected him to flee in free agency but instead signed him less than a month before camp opened—Molina was entering his fourth year as San Francisco's No. 1 catcher and unquestioned mentor for the team's skilled pitching staff. Tim Lincecum directly attributed his brilliant, unprecedented success to Molina's guidance. Bruce Bochy, recognizing Molina's hunger for positive reinforcement, cheerily addressed him as "Caballo"—Spanish for "horse," a fitting moniker for a man who never wanted a day off and had averaged catching a grueling 137 games per season. He was also called "Big Money" for his tendency to get hits when games were on the line. He was beloved in San Francisco both as a man and as a player. There was no indication yet that his season would take him on a uniquely strange path—and away from the Giants.

And on the bench . . . well, enough hopefuls to fill a Wal-Mart parking lot. Someone, somehow, would have to emerge from the chaos and get past the greeters if the Giants were to have a prayer of shedding the offensive dismissals.

Pitchers: Masters, Freaks and Tortured Artists?

By 2010, Tim Lincecum was recognized not only by stadium security guards and locally but nationally as well. He'd come to be known as "The Freak." There are not many contexts in which being called a freak is a term of endearment, but Tim "The Freak" Lincecum is an exception, as he is to most baseball guidelines.

Is "The Freak" an accurate nickname? It depends. In the Barnum and Bailey Circus sense, no, he is definitely not a freak, although more people pay to see him perform than the average dancing bear. He is an exceptionally well-trained, flexible and hardworking athlete. That is not terribly freaky. And in the 1960s sense of *faaaaaar out, man, let your groovy freak flag fly,* perhaps not so accurate either, although he's definitely an individual who fits the Bay Area's unique sensibilities well, and many Bay Area stoners spent 2010 trying to make him their poster child. But in terms of his gifts as a pitcher, his unique pitching motion devised by his father, his stature and his early career results, the freakiness cannot be denied. His pitching stride is somehow longer than his own body, which is rare to the point of ridiculous, even though his body is not long. He's officially 5 feet 11 inches, which is small on baseball's large scale—especially for a power pitcher—and much larger than when he entered high school at only 4 feet 11 inches, weighing 85 pounds. Not exactly major league material in the making. Yet in his first two full seasons in the majors, he won the Cy Young Award as the league's best pitcher, which no one in history had ever before done. And he did it while remaining capable of casually doing a back flip or joking with people just before pitching, whereas most pitchers retreat behind stony game faces.

How remarkable, to be so small of stature yet maintain such a commanding presence on the mound. In his first San Francisco seasons, Lincecum inspired hope, maybe more so than any San Francisco Giant ever had. In that sense, he's different from Willie Mays and Barry Bonds, the franchise's finest players. Mays was regal. He did things no one else could do, and fans of a previous generation idolized him for that. Meanwhile, Bonds was cold. He did great things, prompting thunderous ovations from the faithful home crowds. Bonds even acknowledged those crowds. Yet it never felt like you could wrap your arms around him. It's hard to imagine him moving legions of youth to admire him as Mays had.

Lincecum differed from both of them. He immediately made people want to believe anything was possible, even for an underdog. How could a little guy like that blow away so many hitters? How could he make a terrible team like the 2007–08 Giants look so good? When Timmy had his young game going, watching him work was pure joy. He was style and substance both. At his best, he was (and may still be) the best show in baseball.

Still, if Lincecum began 2010 as the team leader, he was a small leader. Not only was he physically dwarfed by some of his teammates, but he only pitched every fifth day, so he couldn't lead on the field in the same daily way as a hitter of overwhelming power can. It's just the nature of the game. Behind the scenes, Lincecum was merely one guy in the clubhouse.

Lincecum's extraordinary performance soon earned him another nickname: "The Franchise"—as in he's the player the entire Giants franchise is built around. His shaggy haircut and ski cap also earned him mixed fashion reviews. And his desire to wear the same baseball hat on the mound every game since being called up from the minors brought him questions about hygienic laundry habits. Yet he entered 2010 as The Franchise. Stardom may have affected him, but it hadn't ruined him.

In March 2010, though, there was a problem: The deceleration of Lincecum's fastball, which was noticeable as the 2009 season ended, had resumed. There was speculation that his lost velocity would never return. His complicated mechanics were off. His apparent invulnerability was suddenly very vulnerable. The many who had always doubted him had new reason to renew their lack of faith. They had only to point to his inflated 6.94 ERA in four spring Cactus League appearances.

Whether or not he would regain form, the pitching staff would need depth and balance. With so many possible weaknesses in the offense as well, it would take a veteran presence to balance The Freak. It would take the player who'd been on the team longer than anyone, who had maturity others looked up to, who had another historical perspective. It would take a player as steady and unspectacularly solid as Lincecum was colorful to achieve that balance. It would take . . . Matt Cain?

Matt Cain fits all of those descriptions, yet he's younger than Lincecum. Entering 2010, he had only 44 total major league wins, in part due to being as persecuted as Christ when it came to run support. Despite being only 25, he had already been in the majors for five years. He reminded many of a young Tom Seaver in the grace of his solid, traditional pitching mechanics. He had already learned to go from being a power pitcher trying to strike everyone out to learning the economy and efficiency of pitching to contact, trusting his defense and minimizing his pitch count. He was the Harpo to Lincecum's Groucho. He was the Abbott to go with Costello. He was a large man, but he, too, was only a small leader among many.

Third on the starting rotation depth chart was Barry Zito, equal parts ballplayer and renaissance man, who felt at home reveling in the oft-ribald humor of the clubhouse or conversing about deeper subjects.

"All artists are tortured," Zito said, indicating he considered himself part of this category. This might have had more to do with baseball than art (or his music, yoga and meditation), and it was more reasonable than the average fan might give him credit for. Zito's staggering $126 million, seven-year contract had thus far resulted in three years of relative mediocrity and the enormous pressure of failing to be the Messiah. Zito's public title was "$126 Million," like some people are stuck with "convicted felon." He was acknowledged as giving, hardworking, honest, talented and other qualities that left the win column unaffected when he couldn't command the strike zone with his magnificent curveball or the velocity of his fastball dropped dangerously close to batting practice level. If it doesn't come with results, $126 million can buy a lot of boos, which Zito had done over the course of three Giants years, despite his earnest efforts. That is enough to torture an artistic soul.

Rounding out the starting five were Puerto Rican fireballer Jonathan Sanchez—whose enormous potential had yet produced only erratic results—and by . . . somebody. Who? Help! Figuring out conundrums like that is what spring training is supposed to be for. Heir apparent was young phenom Madison Bumgarner—but he was only 20 years old, and Lincecum on a bad day looked better than Bumgarner on a good one. Bumgarner compiled an awful 6.43 ERA in spring and failed to record a single strikeout in three Cactus League outings. He clearly wasn't ready. So the Giants gave minor leaguer Kevin Pucetas a long look—and despite his hot spring, sent him back down. They considered Joe Martinez . . . and sent him down, too, before trading him to Pittsburgh. They probably also considered looking for a new line of work, something easier than assembling a pitching staff, like fixing the health care system or explaining to the Taliban why we should all just get along. In the end, the Giants signed Todd Wellemeyer off of the St. Louis scrap heap. He pitched well in spring, and he won the job, partially by default.

Despite its weakness at the back end, the sum total of the starting rotation was projected as one of the league's best. What greater curse is there than expectation? Ask Zito about that one.

The relievers were equally talented, engaging and occasionally enigmatic. Brian Wilson talked like he pitched—coming directly at you with hard stuff, free of artifice or deception. Yet what went on behind his first levels of directness? By season's end, it would be difficult for many to tell what was character and what was real—except for real results. He was a leader, too, a true and fierce one. A warrior, it was said. He was considered one of the elite closers of the game by some, though not in his own mind.

"I don't even know what that means," Wilson said in late March. "An elite closer is a closer who's part of a World Series win. If you get that final out in the final win of the season, then you can consider yourself elite."

In the progression of a game, Wilson frequently would follow Sergio Romo, a Mexican-American who loves baseball like a parent loves a child. Romo took pleasure in the mere act of changing into his uniform. For 2010, he volunteered to catch every night's ceremonial first pitch in home games, netting him hugs from famous and beautiful female singers who couldn't throw, handshakes from other celebrities who couldn't pitch and all sorts of other odd experiences. His slider was largely unhittable—except when it was misdirected and then hittable indeed. He didn't have overpowering speed like Wilson. He wasn't fearsome, just effective—or not, on rare and unpredictable occasions.

Also down in the bullpen was left-hander Jeremy Affeldt, coming off his best year in eight major league seasons. He was a subtle yet skilled comedian, despite also being seriously and admirably involved in offseason efforts against human trafficking. He'd rave about how manager Bochy (a former catcher) had been his favorite player, sounding neither disrespectful nor as if he was kissing ass. Affeldt was like the guy in high school who annoyed the hell out of you, yet you couldn't help but like him. As a quality left-handed reliever, he was vital to the team. Too bad he, too, wouldn't be able to stay healthy, although it would have an effect on the roster that turned out strangely positive.

The masters, the eccentric, the artistic, the quiet and the steady: These together are only a part of the flawed and brilliant cast. Named or nameless, the Giants would have to make do. They would have to win within their weaknesses. They would have to make their weaknesses into their strengths. They would have to take lesser players and make a greater team from them. Collective spirit was the only thing that would stay consistent throughout those 126 lineups and 162 games.

Sweet Sweat in the Baseball Jungle

No matter what transpires in the season and in the clubhouse, you have to get ready. You almost have to *start* ready. Woe to any major league player who arrived at the 2010 spring training expecting to fundamentally get in shape there. With the game's physical edge honed to a degree that pushed the body's highest limits and with the monetary rewards and pressures having climbed to dizzying heights, any player appearing in camp out of shape might as well pack bags. No more offseason jobs like Richie Hebner of the Pirates had in the 1970s, digging graves. The only offseason grave there's time to dig now is your own.

Except for the glaring difficulty of Sandoval's weight, the 2010 Giants reported in excellent workout shape and came ready to intensify and refine their conditioning—with the assistance of head trainer Dave Groeschner and his henchmen. Even in the offseason, Brian Wilson, Aaron Rowand and Andres Torres had ferocious workout habits, and so did many others, including tortured artist Zito. Even Sandoval had worked hard—he just didn't have disciplined success.

Players had to start earlier as well as starting ready. "Spring training" had become a misnomer, its beginning pushed into mid-February by the expansion of season and playoffs. By the time of 2010's actual first day of spring, the baseball season's opener would be a mere 10 days away. Spring training would essentially be over.

In terms of wins and losses, teams' spring training records rarely mean much. The need to view prospects and ease veterans into refined shape means scant playing time for any team's projected starting lineup. In the second game of spring, however, Barry Zito established immediately that the Giants wouldn't be the butt of anyone's jokes. There was a score to settle.

Giants players still quietly seethed over the Milwaukee Brewers' antics of Sept. 6, 2009, when the Giants absorbed a galling 2-1 defeat. After ending the game with a 12th-inning home run, Prince Fielder pranced home to his waiting teammates, who keeled over as if they were bowling pins as Fielder reached home plate. It was a clearly choreographed display and extremely cute—unless you maintain the time-honored belief that you must never rub opponents' misfortunes in their faces. And unless you are a Giant. It was beyond the bounds of established ethics.

The human bowling pin spectacle closed the Brewers-Giants season finale, so the teams didn't meet again until March 4. Following time-honored baseball custom, the Giants were obliged to retaliate then.

Circumstances provided an expedient denouement. The Giants, with Zito on the mound, faced Milwaukee with Fielder in the lineup.

With Corey Hart on first base and two outs in the first inning, Zito drilled Fielder in the back with a first-pitch fastball. He followed baseball's unwritten code by throwing a pitch that would hit Fielder without intent to maim, but with the reminder to save his theatrics. Zito threw it immediately. He threw it accurately. Artistically, he might has well have written the message in calligraphy on the ball. It was as elegant as a somewhat violent act can be.

Fielder said nothing as he headed for first base, though he picked up the ball that struck him and underhanded it insouciantly in Zito's direction. Later, he wisely refrained from criticizing Zito or the Giants.

"They have to do what they have to do. Whatever," he said. "I didn't see anything coming, but they have to do what they have to do. It's not going to take it away. It's chronicled. . . . It is what it is. I hit the home run. Hit me. If that's what you've got to do, then that's what you've got to do."

It was the beginning of the Giants doing exactly what they needed to do all year.

By settling the Fielder issue, Zito obeyed the laws of the baseball jungle as effectively as Don Drysdale, Bob Gibson or any renowned mound enforcer. By personally risking the massive Fielder's ire to serve the team, Zito was adhering to a higher code of service. Had the Brewers overreacted to Zito's purpose pitch, he could have found himself and his $126 million arm in a dangerous brawl. At his own peril, Zito chose what was right for the Giants—an attitude he gracefully maintained through the end of the season, under far more difficult circumstances to come.

The auspicious plunking of Fielder is not the kind of sign psychics look for in tea leaves, tarot cards or the alignment of the stars. There is little in feng shui about arranging sluggers' bruises. But it was the first of many competitive moments and symbols that, in retrospect, lent an aura of inevitability to a thoroughly unlikely path.

Watching Gerald Demp "Buster" Posey play also lent a feeling of inevitability in another sense. It conjured the vision that the future of the Giants was nearly at hand—a future in which the multitalented, dynamic rookie catcher would command a game from home plate, whether he was standing alongside it in the right-handed batter's box or squatting behind it receiving pitches.

Posey simply made people lean forward for a better look, including longtime baseball men. As those men will tell you, left-handed batters seem to have inexplicably cornered the market on elegant-looking swings. Will Clark and George Brett come to mind, among a select few. Posey is that rare right-handed batter who takes an equally breathtaking cut, sometimes "finishing high" with only his left hand clutching the bat for dramatic effect, as if he were a master fencer finishing off yet another inferior opponent. It isn't showy— it's merely uncommonly fluid.

Posey's swing is more than just aesthetically pleasing. His aptitude for driving pitches up the middle or to right field instead of simply yanking them to left reflects his ability to wait on a pitch and use the whole field. Any hitter will tell you that the longer he can wait on a pitch, the better off he is. "If you can let the ball travel, then you're less susceptible to off-speed stuff," Posey said. "It's a matter of trusting your hands and letting the ball get deep." Trusting and getting deep: Posey was already doing that in more ways than one.

Having previously been an infielder and a pitcher, Posey was entering only his fourth year of being a full-time catcher and was still learning the subtleties of his new position. Watching Bengie Molina, a master at catching's technical and mental aspects, furthered Posey's education. Later, during the regular season, bullpen catcher Bill Hayes would show Posey videos of four-time Gold Glove Award winner Mike Matheny, whose skill at blocking pitches in the dirt was virtually unmatched.

Like Madison Bumgarner on the mound, Posey was not quite ready for prime time. Nevertheless, he displayed startling aptitude defensively. He'd make throws that seemed to travel like the Warner Bros.' Road Runner, who'd stick out his tongue derisively before accelerating into another gear. Listed as 6 feet 1 inch and 219 pounds in the Giants media guide, he was more than sturdy enough to handle the physical rigors of catching. And he somehow seemed to have gained a rapport with and knowledge of the Giants pitchers, despite his relative inexperience at working with them. "You could tell that he worked," right-hander Sergio Romo said. "Not that he was lacking before. But you just saw this different character. He was a full-fledged big leaguer to me in spring training already."

Make no mistake: The Giants felt glad to have Molina back. Bochy described himself as "thrilled" during a Jan. 22 conference call that heralded the official announcement of Molina's return. "Obviously, he's one of the best guys you could have," left-hander Jeremy Affeldt said, referring to Molina's leadership skills, expertise with San Francisco's pitchers, offensive prowess and knowledge of the league.

But the Giants had seen the future, and its name was Buster Posey. Though Posey would begin the season at Triple-A Fresno—

skeptics charged that club management did this to limit his service time and delay his eligibility for salary arbitration—the sense that the future would descend upon the Giants sooner rather than later was palpable.

That future was already coalescing, the alchemy of unity already transpiring. Instead of harboring grudges over the teasing about his $6.2 million bonus—which he listened to during his first spring with the Giants in 2009—Posey maintained his genuine eagerness throughout camp, ready to participate in any drill or catch any pitcher, knowing full well he was likely to be sent to the minors at camp's end anyway. Instead of going their separate ways after a spring workout ended, Aaron Rowand and Aubrey Huff lounged in front of their lockers and bonded through rambling conversation, imagining themselves as college coaches in their next careers. Instead of sulking in the trainer's room after fracturing his left foot for the second time in less than eight months, infielder Emmanuel Burriss welcomed questions from minor leaguers such as Brandon Crawford, Darren Ford and Thomas Neal, each wondering how to act in their first big-league camp.

However meaningless win-loss records are in spring, the Giants thrived by that minor measure as well. In the end, their 21-10 Cactus League mark and 23-12 overall exhibition record—their best since finishing 25-8 in 1964—seemed a legitimate extension of their 88-74 finish in 2009, which broke a spell of four consecutive losing seasons. Within the meaningless, there was deep meaning indeed. As the Buddhist saying goes, form is emptiness, and emptiness is form.

The Paradox of Service over Self-Interest

Being trained, conditioned and disciplined is an essential aspect of the Orange and Black Ops team strategy, and Giants managing general partner Bill Neukom spoke in spring of the team's increased investment in training throughout the team's entire major and minor system. What the Giants weigh is a key part of "The Giants Way."

"The Giants Way," an overall view of the team's philosophy and action plan, was named as such by Neukom in a detailed memo. Its aims and philosophies were beyond reproach, yet such policy papers are risky. They may be as mocked as corporate motivation posters introduced into contexts where applying them is unrealistic. Although company culture does begin at the top, what would the Giants Way *really* be in 2010? That would be up to the players in the end.

It would also be up to Bruce Bochy to guide the players, and he had his own management frame for this Giants Way. "We touched on it," he said after the season. In meetings with the players, "I mentioned in the spring: It gets back to service over self-interest." And then he added a paradox: "You have to set aside your own self-interests sometimes if you want to get what you want." But isn't getting what you want your own self-interests? Perhaps. There are subtle levels of self-interests, often juxtaposed, and to merge with a team towards a common goal serves the self more deeply than to pursue individual short-term gain. Giving selflessly always returns more than any other pursued method of gain. The paradox is an elegant joke, really. If you listen closely, you can hear the earth itself laughing at the whole damn thing.

To be a true team as a complete organization—from front office staff to World Series champions to transient minor league wannabes—that is one aspect of the Good Book of the Giants. The Giants Way, yes. But what is it to be part of a team in unstable times? What does it mean to be selfless, to be in community, to release ego in search of contribution to the greater good, when the greater good is so restlessly mobile and no longer offers solid ground? Like lovers in wartime, you have to let go of the long term—there might not be one—for the eternal now. Yet again, that's paradoxically how the long term is best served. It's tough to live that way, but it also gives gratitude; it gives intensity to every precious, transient moment. It gives total presence in the moment, a spiritual ideal. It's enlightenment and trouble at the same time.

Given the eternal transient now, if you're on a winning team in any form, you'd better appreciate every instant of it—and give every bit of effort you can. Your teammates might suddenly scatter due to free agency or tough budget realities, retirement or injury—or a sudden urge to open fast-food restaurants in the Midwest.

There is instability everywhere, but that is no excuse to devalue loyalty. You can choose money over loyalty more easily, perhaps, yet that doesn't diminish loyalty's rewards or money's pitfalls. There is no less truth to Krukow's Good Book victory speech than ever. You do have to be loyal. You do have to love your team—even if, or especially if, your team cannot stay as one for as long. Loyalty and selfless community still have power that sheer talent cannot bridge. True teams can still outmaneuver more talented groups of more selfish individuals. Togetherness can create miracles. It doesn't matter what the context is. Baseball just happens to be one of them.

You have to know your role, too, if "team" is to deserve the word. You have to not fall prey to the illusion that your teammates are your competitors, even if you're both desiring the same job. They're still your teammates. You have to accede to the demands of the greater good, whatever dirty selfish thoughts may be coursing through your mind. In other words, pull your head out of your ass there, buddy, and stop whining about getting to hit only once a week. If that's your role, do it damn well. Only then will it maybe become twice a week, three times, every day. Or maybe that one at bat will be in the World Series and come out in a way that will be memorable for decades. Maybe your one tiny contribution will be so vital that all involved will look back and know that none of it could have ever happened without you—just because of that one tiny moment, that little contribution, for which you were supremely prepared and patient. That, too, is the Giants Way, and it was applied in 2010 rather than mocked.

The Orange and Black Ops team directing the Giants would have never guessed what other bizarre truths would become part of the Giants Way that year. If a modern mystic had announced the team's first baseman would have legitimate reason to offer his underwear to the Hall of Fame, disbelief would've been their only rational response. If it was mentioned that "torture" would be adopted as a positive mantra in the age of Guantanamo Bay, not only disbelief but outrage might have ensued. If it was suggested that false beard color would become an enduring and endearing trend of victory, who'd have believed? Even in San Francisco, would the popular leather-clad presence of The Machine have been fathomable? Not likely. Expectations of a Giants victory were still deemed unreasonable by the game's best minds at spring's end. Even within their own division of five teams, most "experts" placed the Giants to finish third at best. No sane human picked them to finish as champions of all the majors' 30. But predictions are unpredictable, whether of baseball or technology, relationships or politics. There are no experts on tomorrow. That's the beauty and the difficulty of it all, the sweetness of the sweat. Mystery is romance. Uncertainty is the essence of love and life and baseball. At the close of spring training, that essence was beautifully alive for the Giants.

On opening day, Giants third-base coach, professional musician and avid surfer Tim Flannery looked down the line of players, profoundly moved by their professionalism and attitude. "When the players were being introduced, I said, 'Wow—look at all these pros.' Good team that is here. Good times ahead. I love the way they take the field—and the way they approach it. Old school." Old school yet new breed. Traditional yet wild. And though he was right about good times ahead, there would be many times to question it. And though he was right about all the pros next to him, many would come and go during the course of the season. Leaders were yet to arrive. Some expected leaders would fall. There was no straight line the champion Giants ever walked. That is apparently the Giants Way, too.

To create the Giants Way in an unfathomable fashion, along a path that can't be followed: that will be the 2010 team's legacy. Yes, they defined it, but no one will ever be able to recreate it. They would become a team full of unlikely moments, irreproducible people. And that was why they'd be world champions while higher paid and more talented teams—with better batting averages and endorsement contracts—were stuck sitting on their sofas watching the Giants celebrate in inimitable fashion. That is why writer Tom Verducci would nominate the entire Giants team as one for the typically individual Sportsman of the Year award given by *Sports Illustrated* magazine. That is why they'll remain relevant for decades.

The Giants players weren't played by management according to their salaries, and they didn't perform according to their egos. And they had a damn good time together. You want to talk enlightenment? There it is. Enlightenment has laughter in it. *Shared* laughter. It has dominoes and strange bullpen conversations and time to go get weird without apology. That ain't so damn weird compared to some of the rituals in traditional religions. And those rituals get mixed in, anyway, when belief and baseball merge in a man, and when you really need the assistance of the proper saints to get one lousy, cheap Texas League base hit. You need to get back to the fundamentals, and nothing is more fundamental than letting yourself melt into the spirit of a team. It's way more transcendent than an acid trip. And if you can get a good team trip started, it can last far longer than psychedelics. This particular trip lasted from February until a perfectly beautiful San Francisco day on the first of November, when a fan in the gathered million could look at the guy next to him, wearing the popular T-shirt of Jerry Garcia with a Giants cap on, and say with a truthful, blissful smile what a long strange trip it's been.

Chapter 2

The Honeymoon Suite

Houston, We Have No Problem Yet

The 2010 Giants season started out easy to love. The honeymoon period was brief—and few want to honeymoon in Houston—but it was sweet.

Opening night featured a pitching matchup between Tim Lincecum and Houston Astros ace Roy Oswalt, two undersized right-handers with similar, long-striding deliveries who thrive as power pitchers. Lincecum has occasionally been compared to Oswalt, and it's one of the few reasonable comparisons for Lincecum. From the time Oswalt reached the majors in 2001, he had amassed 150 victories through 2010—more than any pitcher during that decade. Meanwhile, Lincecum was establishing unprecedented dominance of his own, from the day he was called up to the majors on Willie Mays' birthday, May 6, 2007. The match was potentially classic.

To the hardcore faithful, such pitchers' duels are the essence of baseball, if also the essence of boredom to the casual observer who prefers high scores. Such is the nature of the world: What you look at may seem uninteresting until you become still enough to really observe it.

Lincecum and Oswalt are apparently fated to duel: Despite an era of three divisions per league and imbalanced schedules, the two would face off no fewer than six times from their first 2007 match through the end of 2010. Their initial convergence was only 11 days after Lincecum reached the majors. That night, Lincecum yielded only one unearned run and two hits while striking out 10, marking the first time he reached double digits as a big leaguer. Oswalt blanked the Giants on four hits. Each pitched seven innings but received no decision in the Giants' eventual 2-1 triumph in 12 innings. It was a classic beginning and a harbinger of even better to come.

Entering 2010, Lincecum had yet to lose to Oswalt. Though Oswalt has always performed capably against Lincecum, his younger, flashier counterpart has consistently responded as Lincecum himself typically does when challenged—with persistent, unparalleled brilliance.

Still, Lincecum had just finished off his alarming spring. Lincecum and the Giants professed to be less worried about this than many observers. Of course, Mark DeRosa was also professing not to be worried about his wrist, and Wall Street and mortgage brokers had just spent years professing to be unworried about any potential financial and housing crises.

2010's first Oswalt/Lincecum showdown did not disappoint, as Lincecum's sluggish spring metamorphosed into an irrelevant mirage. He limited Houston to four singles in seven shutout innings while walking none and striking out seven. The slider that would sustain Lincecum through key portions of the season helped him bamboozle the Astros, some of whom mistook that pitch for his more familiar changeup.

"They're right around the same speed," Lincecum explained, sounding like an apologist for the Astros hitters. Lincecum's fastball still did not have the edge it had previously displayed, but would that matter if batters couldn't even tell which pitch he was throwing? Not on this night.

Aubrey Huff came away suitably impressed after watching Lincecum perform in a regular season game for the first time. "Just seeing some of the swings guys were taking—it's like, man, that's gotta be doing some stuff. Guys just didn't look comfortable," said Huff, who would never again joke about Lincecum resembling a batboy. "Just watching him tonight, I really get an idea what it's all about. He has an ability to step it up." Truth spoken.

San Francisco's offense matched Lincecum's efficiency. The Giants won 5-2, with five different Giants driving in a run apiece. Nobody suspected at the time that three of those five players would finish the season sidelined by injury or with other organizations. And nobody could have guessed that among the Giants in the Opening Day lineup, only Huff and Renteria would start at their same positions in Game One of the World Series—and even for them, there would be shifts in between.

Opening night always basks in the glow of history, and this one was no exception. With every matchup, every duel, there's a context stretching back into ages before the current players were born—especially on a team such as the Giants, whose tapestry of history weaves back to a time before automobiles were more than a distant curiosity.

The Houston Astros' history is not as deep, although it does include a few early years when they were known as the Colt .45s, before the space program of the 1960s inspired an image change from Wild West weaponry to astronautics. As with Lincecum and Oswalt, the Giants and Astros had an opening day history in which the Giants showed dominance.

The 2010 game followed the pattern of the Giants' three previous season openers in Houston. They thumped the Astros 8-3 in 1986, when Will Clark homered in his first major league at-bat off Nolan Ryan at the Astrodome. In 1998, coming off their first NL West title in eight seasons, the Giants shattered a 4-4 tie with five runs in the 13th inning to prevail. In 2000, the Astros moved out of the tragic Astrodome—once billed as "The Eighth Wonder of the World," although the only remaining wonder is why it was built—and back to fresh air and real grass in Minute Maid Park (née Enron Field). But the Giants maintained their opening day edge to christen the 2004 campaign. Barry Bonds' three-run, eighth-inning homer erased a 4-1 deficit as San Francisco claimed a 5-4 triumph.

Dramatic classics, all. But going back to Houston's major league beginnings in 1962, the Giants' most dramatic victory in the Bayou City had nothing to do with opening day. It defined the grace and frustration of the Giants. Temporarily strengthening their grip on first place—which soon would falter, leaving them to begin a painful annual pattern of finishing second—they outlasted Houston 7-5 in 10 innings on Sept. 14, 1965, after Willie Mays belted a two-run, ninth-inning homer that tied the score. Through Mays' at-bat, during which he fouled off four pitches, it became obvious he was trying to clobber a home run—which, as any ballplayer will tell you, is absolutely the wrong way to hit one. But baseball's logic frequently didn't apply to Mays, whose matchless performances that year earned him his second Most Valuable Player award. Even Russ Hodges, the Giants' famed broadcaster—who had witnessed most of Mays' stirring feats—struggled to put this one in perspective. "The man is unbelievable," Hodges blurted into the microphone.

Nearly half a century later, the same could be said of Lincecum. Yet the Giants still hadn't won a championship since moving to San Francisco.

Unfortunately for the Giants, Lincecum can pitch only every fifth day—although he might have pitched every fourth day in the Mays era, when there were different philosophies about the limits of pitchers' bodies.

The opening Houston series demonstrated that the 2010 pitching staff was not merely Lincecum and Some Other Guys, though. After Barry Zito followed Lincecum by yielding a mere three hits in six shutout innings, Matt Cain extended the starters' scoreless-innings streak to 16 before surrendering an unearned run in the fourth inning of the series finale.

Cain welcomed the challenge of trying to match the zeroes of his predecessors. "It puts a competitive pressure on you," he said. "You don't want to be the guy in the rotation that has a bad start." In Houston, no Giants pitcher had a bad start. There was no bad outcome as the team swept all three games to begin the year, breaking out offensively in the finale with a 10-4 win.

Omens

Despite three wins in Houston, there were ominous omens. For one, hitting into double plays at a prodigious rate is not the mark of a World Series champion. A double play is as mood-chilling as a beer fart at a romantic moment. And while the Giants were busy establishing they could beat a master like Roy Oswalt, they were also busy establishing they could and would hit into double plays in colossal numbers at unfortunate times. The metaphorical beer farts were violating the don't gas, don't smell policy widely being discussed in society at that point. Despite sweeping Houston under the carpet, the Giants managed to hit into seven double plays in three games—a very bad trend to establish and one that did not appear to be a fluke.

"You'll take the double plays," Bochy said diplomatically, "as long as you get the [scoring] opportunities."

One reason this bad trend did not seem a fluke—and an additional reason for concern—was the Giants had also established in the previous season that (with a few exceptions) they were primarily undisciplined hitters, frequently hacking at ugly pitches thrown only vaguely in the vicinity of the strike zone. Former hitting coach Carney Lansford was unable to shift this pattern and had to take the fall for his hitters' bad habits.

This was nominally a different year, with respected new hitting coach Hensley "Bam Bam" Meulens to guide them to repentance. There was some hope of redemption. But if so, it wasn't evident in Houston or during the first home series to come. The Giants were hacking away as quickly and unwisely as ever. There was only one key difference:

They were getting away with it. They were scoring runs, getting hits, living a charmed life. Ah, honeymoons—ya gotta love 'em.

Omens come in small cruel ways as well, and mistakes of inattention often befall those who are not primary in the team spotlight. In the parlance of the era, a player's expression for having to own a bad performance was, "You have to wear it." And it was literally so in Houston for Giants utility player Eugenio Velez, though it was not his own bad performance that left him standing in Houston with the misspelled "San Francicso" stitched across his chest, his road uniform scrambled like Scrabble letters. No matter how it was spelled, the uniform still said "big leagues" in code. It said Velez succeeded after risking the dream just to get there, though he never transcended utility status. What nicer compliment could a misspelling pay? It was an excellent omen of the improbable season.

The Necessity of Immediacy

The Giants' sweep of the three-game series at Houston appeared to place them on course for the fast start they coveted. Of course, the team in any major North American professional sport that *didn't* want a fast start hadn't yet been formed. So the Giants' goal was hardly a unique one, but they had particular reasons for wanting to break from the gate quickly.

Although discussions of baseball's elite divisions never involved the NL West, pundits had to admit it ranked among the game's most balanced groups. The West's five teams combined for a .519 winning percentage in 2009, best among the league's three divisions. Some would claim it was parity in mediocrity, since no division team matched the strength of the Yankees, Red Sox or other perennial major league contenders. The parity in the West often prolonged the Giants' postseason dreams, though. Witness 2008, when the Giants were 39-49 on July 5, yet stood only four games out of first place before eventually fading from the race.

"We're realists," general manager Brian Sabean said. "We have to get over at least two teams—the Dodgers and the Rockies for sure, and the rest of the division is going to be tough. I think Arizona's improved, and San Diego's quietly putting together a team that's going to be pitching-oriented, but they have some nice young players who are going to give you fits."

Added Bochy, "It's going to be a tight race that won't be decided until late. Every team has its strengths." Bochy proceeded to cite them: The two-time defending division champion Dodgers possessed a talented offensive core of Andre Ethier, Matt Kemp and James Loney as well as what he considered to be an underrated pitching staff. Colorado was coming off an impressive late-season surge that culminated in its winning the NL Wild Card. Arizona not only had improved, in Bochy's estimation, but it would benefit from regaining ace right-hander Brandon Webb, who seemed to be overcoming shoulder problems. San Diego, Bochy pointed out, finished strong in 2009 with a 37-25 record.

"It's not going to be easy," Bochy summarized. "We know that."

That it wouldn't be easy is about the only thing anyone could know, except that it would have a measure of heartache as well as success. Relating to a new baseball season is like beginning a relationship with a new lover: No matter how much optimism and passion with which you enter, the relationship will inevitably disappoint you. That's true not only if it doesn't work out but also if it does—for no matter what you think it will be, it will inevitably be something else. The only hope for having the excitement and satisfaction outweigh the disappointment is in finding the positive within the unexpected, the real traits within the events that are unimaginable and beautiful, funny and deliciously bizarre.

Coming out of Houston and coming home, this is the enduring relationship with 2010 the Giants had hoped for: A fast start had apparently begun. Dreams about the honeymoon's deepening were plausible.

Temple of Hopes and Memories

The undefeated Giants came home—and what a home it is. If societies are judged by the majesty of their temples, San Francisco should fare well when alien archaeologists someday land and peer back into the ruins of AT&T Park.

It offers exceptional contrast to the wicked winds of the team's former home of Candlestick Park, where the haunted old stadium's distant foggy bleachers sat near the bitter ghettos of Hunters Point. 2010 celebrated a decade in the new glittering stadium, pristine yet somehow infused with all the grace of history. AT&T Park felt exquisitely ancient the instant it opened—as if a century of baseball had already transpired there, as if all the old team heroes from Willie Mays to Orlando Cepeda, Gaylord Perry to Juan Marichal, back all the way to Christy Mathewson, Mel Ott and John McGraw, had already played and managed there and imbued it with the spirit of tradition.

The stadium was brilliantly designed, with the field itself as quirky as the city. The seven archways in right field leave only a fence between the field and free bystanders, creating the first new knot-hole gang in decades. The odd angles of the bricks still give shivers to visiting outfielders and unpredictability to every drive to right. The staggered dimensions create a unique field that swallows flies which would be home runs in any other park, while compensating by leaving wide green spaces for hitters' balls to roll for triples when they fall. And where else can people paddle kayaks so close to right field they have a legitimate chance of catching a home run? (Baseballs float, and so do most kayakers who dive in after baseballs.)

A stadium is a living being more than it is a building. Sure, it's bricks and concrete and corporate sponsorship. (The whims of stadium naming rights were another thing that had changed during the Murphological Age. Over 10 years, the Giants stadium had already been Pacific Bell Park, SBC Park and AT&T Park, while Houston's stadium had been rechristened Minute Maid Park when Enron Field became unpalatable.) But never mind the name, whatever it may be by the time you read this: The Giants' stadium is the primary temple in which their Good Book is worshipped. It inspires reverence among visitors, especially if they're nine years old and Dad is taking them there for the first time. It's a masterpiece of baseball design, with symmetry and beauty and LIFE in capital letters. It has history and modernity, personality of forms existent nowhere else, which translates to home-field advantage—and bizarre events that could happen nowhere else. That's exactly like San Francisco itself, which is perhaps why the temple has felt integral to the city since the day it opened.

It's not only the stadium itself that's such a masterpiece—it's also the setting, the revived neighborhood around it. Eastern monks remind us that lotus flowers grow out of muck; that AT&T Park grew out of a polluted shipyard is just as apt a metaphor. It's hard to imagine that shipyard now, even when disembarking from one of the ferries that come right up to the stadium's outfield porch—or when walking down along the Marina from downtown, past the sailboats, under the Bay Bridge, and alongside all the cafes, pubs, apartments and businesses that have sprung up in concert with baseball, like ferns on a tree trunk. It's a place that feels invigorating, even in the offseason. If you're still hungering for baseball in mid-December, take a stroll along the stadium's plaza side to see the team's Wall of Fame in the bricks, with key characters from the field immortalized on plaques.

For lo, Mathewson begat Ott—although not in the Biblical sense—and Marichal begat Will Clark, sort of, and on down the long line to Jimmy Davenport and Roger Craig, and a couple of guys named Bonds. Willie Mays himself stands in bronze in the plaza, forever frozen in his beautiful swing. Even in the winter, the stadium is alive with the memories of history and the promise of new ones yet to be revealed.

Nerves, Chants and Wins

All this might have weighed on Jonathan Sanchez's mind as he confronted Atlanta in the April 9 home opener. Moreover, Giants fans didn't seem seduced by the Houston sweep. The sellout crowd fell silent in the first inning as the first two Braves hitters reached base safely against Sanchez.

"Why is everybody so quiet?" one reporter in the press box asked.

"They're nervous," explained a colleague blessed with deeper understanding of the patrons' collective psyche. Their nerves were based on the wisdom of experience.

The audience exhaled in cheers as Sanchez collected a pair of strikeouts that helped him strand the runners. Although he would last just 4 1/3 innings, allowing three runs and seven hits, a home opener is a bigger, tougher stage than most. Teams don't observe the other 80 home dates by hanging bunting and arranging players on the foul lines for pregame introductions. Now tempered for other pressured contests, Sanchez would often respond admirably in critical situations.

The game extended into extra innings with the score tied 4-4. Atlanta threatened in the 13th, but Jeremy Affeldt stranded runners on the corners. Foiling such rallies tends to spur the surviving team to victory, and the Giants indeed capitalized. Juan Uribe walked and stole second base, advanced to third on catcher Brian McCann's accompanying throwing error and scored the winning run on Rowand's infield single. Not exactly a mighty show of offensive force, but exactly enough.

Right-hander Brandon Medders emphatically summarized the game's greater meaning. "This shows what this team's really made of—that we *will* fight, that we *will* come back, we *will* score runs late in the game," said Medders. "We're not going to give up and be defeated late in the game." Being defeated cannot always be controlled. Not giving up can be.

Uribe didn't steal another base all year. Yet he handled the task with his typical confidence. "When they give you the sign, you never think you can't do it," he said, at once referring to the order to steal and mastering the double negative. English is not Uribe's native language, but he brings an expressive creativity to it.

Recording his lone theft when it counted reflected Uribe's reputation as a winner. Uribe was an experienced winner, too: He was the everyday shortstop for the 2005 Chicago White Sox team that had captured the World Series, which he punctuated by making three slick defensive plays in the eighth and ninth innings to preserve a 1-0 victory over Houston in the Game Four Series clincher. Then, in 2008, as the White Sox surged to the AL Central title, he'd assure teammates, "On Uribe's back," meaning that he felt capable of carrying the ballclub. Upon joining the Giants the following year, he'd tell anybody who'd listen, "Uribe's never down," to articulate the undying confidence he exuded.

Uribe's reputation for bringing an uplifting presence grew naturally from his on-field deeds. He didn't walk through the clubhouse: He strutted, thrusting his chest outward while occasionally glancing sideways to see who might be checking him out. Playing cards there, he'd taunt the other participants by attaching the winning card to his forehead when he collected it first, light perspiration functioning as a natural adherent. Had Uribe been hitting .210 and been stuck on the end of the bench, his act would have worn thin—if he ever attempted it in the first place. More likely, he'd refrain from such behavior. But as the Giants' "super utility" infielder began the season by capably replacing injured Freddy Sanchez at second base, Uribe was free to release his inner showman.

Uribe was adored by the Giants fans, not only because of his performance and his attitude—a love that would deepen until a November sense of betrayal—but also because of history and his name. He was a relative of Jose Uribe, a beloved former Giant shortstop who had passed away far too young. As with the elder Jose, the Giants faithful had fallen in love with turning "Uribe" into a two-part chant. The first fans would shout "Ooooooo!!!" and wait to receive the equally enthusiastic "Rrrriiiiiiibaaaayyyy!!!" in return. It was fun, in a similar way to how other names with "oooo" in them had inspired chants for other players in other towns. The "oooo" sound is apparently the baseball fan's version of "Om," the mantra said to contain all sounds. It became a rallying cry of the faithful. Fans loved to chant it for Uribe, Uribe loved to hear it and it inspired him to even greater performance. That too, was an omen of the year.

Calling the Shots

The Giants family being as continuous and welcoming as it is, Rich Aurilia was more than welcome to drop by before the home opener. (The retired Aurilia's locker had been commandeered by Barry Zito, who'd previously been next to another Barry. Zito gave credit to Aurilia's team presence when claiming his locker while also mentioning it was closer to the kitchen.) No, Aurilia didn't come by to play the infield. Apparently, his role on this April day was primarily as a psychic, because before the game, he predicted to Edgar Renteria that Renteria would hit a home run—and Renteria proceeded to do just that, along with getting two other hits as he continued his personal hot start. After generally making a mockery of the Astros' pitching skills, Renteria had come home hitting a cartoonish .727, which sounds more like a Boeing product than a batting average.

Predicted home runs are the kind of events only remembered when they're correct. Who immortalizes days when someone predicts you'll hit a home run, and instead you strike out three times and only break the string by hitting into a double play? Strike that from the record, judge. Objection sustained.

Even correctly predicted home runs rarely make it into legend alongside Babe Ruth reputedly calling his shot off of Charlie Root in the 1932 World Series. This Aurilia prediction may not make it into history either, with the minor exception of whatever place this book finds on dusty shelves. But before the year was over, another called Renteria shot—one he called himself—would find its way indelibly etched into wider history.

If only the history between that call and this one would be smooth for Renteria. When it comes to .727s, few planes may crash, but all batting averages do. All battered bodies do as well. It wouldn't last. It couldn't.

Sideshow

Rain fell before Sunday's finale of the Braves series, enabling reporters who would otherwise invent ways to kill time during the delay to focus on the home stand's biggest sideshow: Barry Bonds.

The all-time home run king—whose link to performance-enhancing drug use made him the most controversial baseball figure of the early 21st century—was back at AT&T Park as part of a celebration of the 2000 Giants squad that won the NL West in the ballpark's first year of existence. After reporters flocked to spots throughout the park where it was believed Bonds might appear, he agreed to address the media briefly. During Bonds' mostly unremarkable chat—with his perjury case still pending, he couldn't respond to questions about legal issues—he mentioned he had dispensed batting tips to Ryan Howard, the Philadelphia Phillies first baseman who'd sought his advice during the offseason. This gave Bonds the platform to hint that he might like to coach someday. "I was given a gift with the things that I know and I can do in this game," he said. "Sooner or later, I will be able to pass that along. Whoever wants it, I just talk to them about it."

As the supreme hitter of his era, regardless of how he achieved it, Bonds must have succeeded in helping Howard, the 2006 NL MVP who hit a whopping 198 home runs from 2006 to 2009. That could be dangerous for the Giants. But a little more than six months later, Howard would look anything but Bondsian as he faced them with the season on the line.

Homers of the Mind

Pennsylvania was on the Giants' minds in ways far more direct than Ryan Howard, after continuing to roll by and taking two of three from the Braves. But it was the Pirates, not the Phillies, who were the state's ambassadors to San Francisco at that moment.

As noted, San Francisco is a much better place to honeymoon than Houston, by most accounts, and definitely better than Pittsburgh. So it was nice of the Pittsburgh Pirates to visit the Giants' beautiful temple as the 2010 honeymoon continued with the Giants again claiming two out of three.

The honeymoon home stand was also the first one for Aubrey Huff in a Giants uniform, and Huff was bound to quickly find out the hard way about the beauty and horror of the hidden corners of AT&T Park. It giveth, it taketh away, and more of the latter if you're a hitter. On the third and last day of the Pittsburgh series, Huff Daddy saw the light. One ball he crushed carried to the deepest recesses of right center field, and from his trot between home and first, his expectation was obvious that the ball would clear the fence. Home run for sure, right? Right. But wrong. It died not far from the 421-foot marker, which warns of vast pastures where even sheep dare not dwell. It hit the edge of one of the archways, just as Huff figured out he'd damn well better speed up since it wasn't going out. But the ball hit the edge of the bricks on the archway, taking a carom as random as politics and backing away from the right fielder into the place of green where no one was left standing. Triples Alley, the locals call right center. A bit short of truth, in this case, for third was easy. The ball was still rolling as Huff rounded it, waved on by Tim Flannery, nominally in the third-base coaching box but actually half-way to home and chasing Huff there. It would've been a stand-up inside-the-park home run but for prankster Mark DeRosa, himself flat on the grass near the plate and frantically signaling for Huff to slide—presumably for style points—although the ball was still too far away for even a throw.

"I was already gassed," Huff said later. "So I didn't need that. . . . [But] I didn't even know where I was at that point. If he told me to slide, I'm sliding."

There was laughter in the dugout. There was Pablo Sandoval waving a towel in Huff's face, cooling him off from the heated run with a smile. There was the bizarre truth that the first home run Huff had hit in a Giants uniform did not clear the fence—the first of his 203 big league home runs not to do so. It was new life in a new place. It was weird, and it was good, and sometimes there is no difference.

"That's right, Mr. Huff," said announcer Mike Krukow on the air. "You hit home runs here, you gotta earn 'em."

Overall, Huff nearly earned three homers that day in a 6-0 shutout (led by the tempered pitching of Jonathan Sanchez), but the park held the others in play, too. One shot became another double that nearly took the same path as his home run, but Huff stopped at second.

"I don't think he could have made it around again," joked Giants manager Bochy.

"I've never had a three-home run game," Huff declared. "I'm going to go ahead and chalk up today as a three-home run game in my mind."

Primed to Achieve

Homers of the mind don't count in the standings, but wins do, and after vanquishing Atlanta and Pittsburgh, the honeymoon home stand was complete.

No matter that the runs and home runs were coming in unexpected forms: These Giants were not power-laden like the clubs Bonds led or the 1960s teams of Mays and McCovey. Bochy had emphasized that to thrive, his club would need contributions from every spot in the lineup. The Giants indeed displayed enviable balance while winning eight of their first 11 games to occupy first place in the NL West. They averaged six runs per game while eight different players amassed at least five RBIs.

Through this stretch, Aubrey Huff recorded a .417 on-base percentage, reflecting his overall polish at the plate. He also scored a team-high 11 runs. Bengie Molina hit a robust .448 with a .621 slugging percentage and eight RBIs in eight games. Uribe posted a .333 average and led the team with nine RBIs. Displaying no hints of trouble yet, Pablo Sandoval built a .326 average, a .587 slugging percentage and a .380 on-base percentage. At the top of the order—bent on rebounding from the disappointing .261 average he had compiled in 2009—Aaron Rowand went 0-for-10 in the season's first two games before hitting .412 during a seven-game hitting streak. Though he wasn't spectacular in the leadoff spot, he certainly looked competent. And when Edgar Renteria went 3-for-5 with a homer in the AT&T Park opener two days after his 5-for-5 performance in Houston, his batting average actually dropped from .727 to .688.

The Giants looked primed to achieve that fast start they wanted. And Rowand, who had accepted the leadoff role because none of the other regulars were suited for it, seemed destined to spearhead this effort.

So the Giants were in first place, heading down to the hostile climate of Los Angeles. And then, with one fastball to the face as devastating as divorce papers, the honeymoon was over.

Chapter 3

Ugly Reality

The Shattering

For a rivalry to endure, there must be some competitive balance. Over the course of more than a century—including the teams' coordinated move to the West Coast—the intensity of the Giants-Dodgers rivalry has been fueled by the greatness of each organization. In 2010, the Dodgers were no longer dodging trolley cars in Brooklyn (the supposed origin of their odd name). They were instead dodging their own recent decades. Since the O'Malley family had sold the team in the 1980s, the team's fortunes had declined. They hadn't won a World Series since their underdog team managed to off the 1988 Oakland A's in classic style. Still, they'd recently climbed the heap again to win the NL West in 2008 and 2009, and as the Giants headed to Los Angeles in April, the Dodgers seemed a key team to beat.

April 16, the first night of the Dodgers-Giants series, happened to be baseball's annual salute to Hall of Famer Jackie Robinson, the man whose 1947 ascent to the majors had led the way for future African-American players. Breaking the baseball color line was one of the Dodgers' most noble legacies, and they had chosen Robinson for his prodigious talent, yet with the careful demeanor of a man who could withstand the expected small-minded abuse. Without Jackie Robinson, there would be no Willie Mays, no Ryan Howard, no Bob Gibson, no Reggie Jackson nor a countless list of other greats.

Recently, baseball had decided to recognize Jackie Robinson in a touching but potentially confusing way: For one night each year, players on every team wear "42" on their uniforms. This is not because "42" is the Ultimate Answer to the Ultimate Question About Life, the Universe and Everything in *The Hitchhiker's Guide to the Galaxy* books by Douglas Adams—although that is also true. It's because "42" was Robinson's uniform number and remains the ultimate answer to the ultimate question about who would finally break down baseball's abhorrent racial barrier.

An upbeat Aaron Rowand expressed how privileged he felt to wear Jackie Robinson's No. 42. "Regardless of ethnicity, race or whatever color you are, I think everybody owes a huge debt to [Robinson]," said Rowand, ever respectful of the ballplayer giants who had preceded him. "I'm proud to wear his number."

Robinson probably would have reciprocated Rowand's appreciation. Like Robinson, Rowand plays aggressively. He pursues flyballs without regard for his skeletal structure, as he demonstrated in 2006 when he broke his nose and the bones around his left eye while colliding with the center-field wall at Philadelphia to make a catch. In a sense, he even pursues the ball while hitting, leaning towards home plate as each pitch approaches.

This trait left Rowand particularly vulnerable in the fifth inning that night, just a few hours after he had lauded Robinson. He was hitting against Dodgers right-hander Vicente Padilla, who had a reputation for headhunting—cemented in 2009 when he plunked New York Yankees slugger Mark Teixeira twice in one game while pitching for the Texas Rangers. Placed on waivers the day after he hit Kurt Suzuki of the A's, Padilla and his bad reputation were soon claimed by the Dodgers.

Padilla's first-pitch fastball darted high and inside, striking Rowand squarely on his batting helmet—a protective device, but not protective enough. Rowand fell to the ground, face in hands, motionless for too long. Rowand is one of the toughest to walk the field, with a pain tolerance far beyond most, but he couldn't play through shattered cheekbones and a concussion. He eventually walked off the field under his own power but was soon placed on the disabled list.

Some observers were quick to accuse Padilla of trying to hit Rowand, although Padilla denied any intent. The question came up not only because of Padilla's reputation, but also because Giants starter Todd Wellemeyer had earlier thrown high and tight to Dodgers star Matt Kemp, and retaliation was a possibility. Retaliation was especially plausible in the context of the fierce Dodgers-Giants rivalry, which contained such explosive moments as the 1965 incident when Juan Marichal attacked Dodgers' catcher Johnny Roseboro with his bat. Many fights are still etched in the rivalry's memory, and every new incident brings question.

There was no fight this time. Giants manager Bruce Bochy chose his words carefully after the game. "You're always going to wonder what the intent was," he said. "[But] in that situation, that's not a time when a pitcher is going to hit somebody [intentionally]." Entering the inning with a 7-0 lead, Padilla had already allowed runners to score. Hitting Rowand only inflamed the Giants rally, giving them a chance to get back into the game—not a wise time to hit a batter.

True to his nature, Rowand was anything but depressed. "I'm lucky it's not worse," he said. But when the subject of Padilla and his possible intent was raised, Rowand declined to comment. "I'm not in the business of stirring up the pot." His reluctance to elaborate spoke clearly enough.

In the end, the pitch wasn't intentional—or it was. The answer isn't "42," and intent made no difference to Rowand's cheekbones. It was a devastating blow, more than the ugly 10-8 loss of which it was part—a game not nearly as close as the final score would indicate. Rowand was central to the Giants, and now he was felled.

The Shattering Deepens

The pitch from Padilla that fractured Rowand's face also shattered the Giants' fragile facade of invincibility—and with it Bruce Bochy's lineup plans for the foreseeable future. Rowand's misfortune hurled the Giants into a miserable stretch, although the KO Rowand absorbed didn't immediately send the Giants to a neutral corner. In the second game against the Dodgers, they were blessed to face little-known knuckleballer Charlie Haeger, who had a total of two major league wins to his name.

Knuckleballs are a dying art, like being a blacksmith or knowing how to whistle. It's a difficult pitch to master, but if mastered, even more difficult to hit. And catch.

"You have to make sure you let it travel and don't commit too early," Bochy said. "Then you swing and hope."

The Giants did more than hope. They routed Charlie Haeger and Los Angeles, 9-0. Lincecum used his changeup a lot, mixed his deliveries and got away with diminished velocity as he breezed through six innings on the mound. At the plate, he also did a pretty fair Tony Gwynn imitation, singling in each of his first three at-bats and driving in three runs.

More significantly—or so it seemed—Eugenio Velez went 3-for-5, scored a run and drove in another. The Giants' decision-makers had begun to realize Velez might never thrive as an everyday player, but he remained more than capable of performing adequately for brief stretches. In 2008, he hit .310 and stroked three game-winning hits after the All-Star break. Down the stretch in 2009, Velez started 58 of the season's final 64 games, mostly in left field. And the chance still lingered that Velez would seize this opportunity and force the Giants to keep him in the lineup—not necessarily at Rowand's expense. In that 9-0 win, left fielder Mark DeRosa lasted only three innings before leaving with a strained right hamstring. Suddenly, the Giants needed outfielders, especially since they had traded outfielder Fred Lewis to Toronto two days previous. Velez might do. He might have to.

But he didn't. Beginning with the final plate appearance of that three-hit game, he went hitless in his next nine at-bats, commencing a 1-for-25 skid. Bochy decided to platoon Andres Torres and Velez for the final seven games of Rowand's absence, which would last until early May. The Giants ultimately found reinforcements, but Velez wasn't among them.

In the final game, Barry Zito continued his resurgent brilliance by pitching seven shutout innings, leaving the game with a slim 1-0 lead as the Giants' offense suddenly vanished. Sergio Romo entered the game in the eighth. With the Giants five outs from winning the game and series, pinch hitter Manny Ramirez—the most controversial and reviled of the current Dodgers, partially because he was also the best—drilled a two-run homer off Romo, which left the Giants with a heartbreaking 2-1 loss.

The Ramirez home run was a hard blow to the Giants, sending them off to San Diego to be greeted with more indignities. There would be more than one hazard, more than one poor game to follow. The pitching that ultimately would sustain them hadn't yet jelled. Suspect from the start, the ballclub's hitting became worse than sporadic. The Giants couldn't beat the team they needed to beat—the San Diego Padres, the surprise NL West leaders. And, as Rowand's fate portended, injuries would prove to be an issue.

Death Traps (Apparent)

"Those who cannot remember the past are condemned to repeat it." So goes George Santayana's famous quotation, often misquoted by those who cannot remember it and therefore are condemned to being unable to properly repeat it. Ol' Santee—as he would've been called, had he been involved in baseball—surely possessed a brilliant mind, but he obviously lacked a crystal ball with visions of the Giants in it. Acutely aware of the three-game sweep the Padres had handed them in April 2009, the Giants were still condemned to repeat it during a somber trip south from Los Angeles.

For some reason, stretching back over more than a full season, the Giants' weaknesses seemed most evident when they faced the Padres. Against San Diego, their penchant for wasting solid pitching with ineffectual offense was most pronounced. Meanwhile, San Diego out-Gianted the Giants by relying on airtight pitching. While the Giants' starters primarily accounted for the staff's reputation, the Padres established themselves with a formidable bullpen, led by closer Heath Bell. Like the Giants, San Diego generated just enough offense to prevail, their offense led by tremendously skilled first baseman Adrian Gonzalez. The Padres were predicted by most to be in the division's lower echelon, but they led the pack as the Giants faltered.

In the series opener, it was parallel heartbreak to the previous game against the Dodgers. David Eckstein, a pest who's impossible not to respect, homered off Jeremy Affeldt to open San Diego's half of the 10th inning and break a 2-2 deadlock. It would be Eckstein's lone homer in 492 plate appearances in 2010, and it nullified Juan Uribe's one-out homer in the top of the ninth that had tied the score. Eckstein's teammates did not fall like bowling pins as he reached the plate, but there's still something galling about losing on a walk-off homer by a guy who is not expected to homer at all.

The next night was worse. The Giants again wasted stellar pitching as Jonathan Sanchez pitched a one-hitter in combination with Sergio Romo . . . and lost, 1-0. It marked the Giants' first defeat in 24 one-hit efforts since the franchise moved West in 1958. The Giants went 0-for-9 with runners in scoring position against Padres starter Mat Latos and two relievers to run their three-game total in those situations to 1-for-25. It was the third consecutive one-run loss, all of them potentially emotionally crushing.

The only Padres hit was in the fourth, a clean single from Chase Headley. Later that inning, Kyle Blanks lifted a foul flyball on which Aubrey Huff made a stellar defensive play—continuing to positively rewrite his defensive reputation. Huff tumbled headfirst into a deep camera well as he did so, hitting head and shoulders on metal camera supports on the way down. He hung onto the ball as Chase Headley tagged up and moved from second to third, now in position to score what would be the only run of the painful game.

"That's definitely a death trap right there," Huff said later. He was referring to the photographer's well, but he could have been referring to the game or even to San Diego itself. Every small vista contains microscopic versions of the large: An atom resembles a solar system, an ant colony resembles New York City. San Diego began to resemble hell.

That death-trap feeling after the 1-0 loss inspired broadcaster Duane Kuiper—if inspiration is the correct term—to coin a phrase that would resonate all too well. As he described during the offseason, "We get on the pregame show [the next day], and I think we were talking to Gary Radnich and F.P. Santangelo. They asked me a question about the game, and at the end, I said, 'You know what this is? This is Giants baseball—torture!' They laughed." It stuck. It became the iconic, enduring description of the season—the only championship season ever described that way.

Back in the clubhouse, Aubrey Huff theorized that although Manny Ramirez doesn't pitch, his game- and series-winning homer for the Dodgers on the previous Sunday had put the Giants in their offensive funk.

"It seems like that took the wind out of a lot of the boys," Huff said. "You can definitely feel it's not as much fun the last three days in the dugout. Have a good time and play baseball. Our guys are squeezing the bat too hard in those situations with [runners on] third base and less than two outs." The team was pressing, stressing, holding tight death grips on their choking bats. They were torturing themselves emotionally.

That didn't change after Huff's observation. The Padres completed the sweep with a 5-2 decision in which the Giants went 0-for-5 with runners in scoring position, bringing their total for their four-game losing streak to 1-for-30. They also grounded into two double plays to hike their major league–high total to 20. They only scored five runs in four days, beginning with the last game of the Dodgers series. They left town no longer in first, no longer deserving to be.

Death Traps (Real)

San Diego might feel like a death trap for the Giants, but like Huff and the photographer's well, they would escape it essentially unscathed in the end. As for people familiar with *real* death traps, *real* torture— such as those in Iraq and Afghanistan? During the Padres series, the San Diego City Council honored Barry Zito for his service to them, despite his role as a baseball opponent. San Diego is a military town, and Barry Zito's efforts have transcended any baseball rivalry. (Later in the spring, the Giants would also honor Zito's efforts at home.)

In 2005, Zito founded his Strikeouts for Troops nonprofit organization, dedicated to assisting wounded veterans through donations based on performance—not only his own performance but also those of other participating major league stars. As of 2010, at least 65 major league baseball players were participating—as well as one football player, somehow—and a few players either retired or were back in the minors. Zito and his civic-minded friends had managed to raise $2 million for the cause so far. Among other things, Strikeouts for Troops has made it possible for loved ones to be close to the wounded during their time of healing, purchased assistive equipment for those moving on from hospitals to home recuperation, provided necessities for the hospitalized, supported morale-building events and given holiday gifts and meals to military children. It is the kind of service that must be measured as part of Zito's contractual return, for would he have been able to give so much without his position of influence and affluence?

"To have a small window into their world, their experience, is something that has affected me in a major way," Zito said in San Diego.

The effect has been mutual. In recognition of Zito's impact on his life, retired Marine Staff Sgt. Christopher Hill drove several hours from Las Vegas to be at Zito's honoring ceremony in San Diego. Wounded in Fallujah after four tours in Iraq and suffering a combination of spinal cord injuries and post-traumatic stress disorder, Hill was so traumatized that he'd spent nearly a year without leaving his room—until shortly before being brought to spring training as part of Zito's annual Arizona gathering for wounded troops. Now Hill was able to drive the hours himself and speak the message.

"For him to extend his hand in friendship the way he did really made a significant change in my life," Hill said, referring to Zito. He turned to Zito and added, "It's not *what* you gave that made you my brother, it's *that* you gave."

Zito's continued giving has made him a brother to many. His curveball has taken him there along its beautiful arc. Strange and wondrous, how the path of life travels. Service over self-interest, Bochy says. That is the Giants Way, even when the offense disappears or the curveball begins to wander.

In Full Color

In the natural world, things bloom in spring. But when the Giants came home after their disastrous road trip to Los Angeles and San Diego, they were doing anything but blooming. The closest the Giants came to blooming on that trip was that their results smelled like fertilizer.

There are also no bright orange jerseys in the natural world. However, with the Giants centered in a city willing to take off-center risks—witness their Crazy Crab mascot of a previous era—they decided to sport a little flash beyond the staid edges of traditional orange and black. On Friday home games in 2010, the team donned bright orange jerseys, unveiling them against St. Louis on April 23. Ready to get in the spirit of things, Todd Wellemeyer claimed he had eaten equally bright orange Cheetos in their honor and had tried on one of the wearable orange blankets the team was giving to fans as a promotion that night. The year was already beginning to turn orange.

No Broom Service

The first bright orange evening began a Giants home stand that brought quality teams from across the country. First the Cardinals, widely expected to win the Central Division crown. Then the Philadelphia Phillies, the 2008 world champions and 2009 National League champions. Finally the Colorado Rockies, reigning National League Wild Card champions. Fierce opponents, all.

A different team in their own park, apparently, the Giants responded to challenges aggressively. Facing top pitchers didn't faze the Giants, and in the first two games against St. Louis, the undefeated Lincecum outdueled Jaime Garcia (who would go on to become a serious Rookie of the Year candidate) before the also-undefeated Barry Zito outdueled Cardinals ace Adam Wainwright. But in the third game, the continually hard-luck Matt Cain lost to former Giant (and Dodger) pitcher Brad Penny in a 2-0 shutout as the Giants' offense once again went the Hoffa way. Fans who had brought brooms to celebrate a series sweep took the unused brooms home and put them back in the closet.

On April 26, in the first game against Philadelphia, the Giants distinguished themselves by defeating Philadelphia's Roy Halladay 5-1. One of the game's true masters, Halladay entered the game 4-0 with an 0.82 ERA and an opponents' batting average of .087 (2-for-23) with runners in scoring position. That boded poorly for the Giants, who had gone 5-for-54 in those situations in their previous seven games. San Francisco rendered those numbers meaningless by going 3-for-7 in RISP situations against Halladay. Mark DeRosa lashed a two-out, two-run single in the first inning; reserve catcher Eli Whiteside drove in two runs with a double and a homer; and Huff contributed an RBI single as Jonathan Sanchez patrolled the mound. "It's a big win for us, just showing we can beat guys like that," Whiteside said. The Giants would continue to show all year long that the Giants

Way is to beat the best, at their best—whatever other troubles might befall them in between.

After Todd Wellemeyer finally notched his first Giants win by beating the ageless Jamie Moyer of the Phillies the next night—a mere 46 years old and still tough—the Giants were again poised to sweep, with Lincecum on the mound for the finale. The brooms returned. And with a dominant Lincecum staked to a 4-1 lead entering the ninth, a sweep looked all but certain. After a tiring Lincecum walked Shane Victorino on four pitches with one out, though, Bochy brought in fresh closer Brian Wilson, who proceeded in torturous fashion to load the bases with one out, before Jayson Werth hit a pop-fly double that scored all three runs to tie the game. The Phillies scored again in the 10th—only to have the Giants tie it again. Then the Phillies scored two more in the 11th—and the Giants came back with one, but only one, losing another heartbreaker, 7-6. Fans probably wanted to eat their brooms in frustration.

Again, the Giants had a chance to sweep against Colorado. Barry Zito beat Aaron Cook of the Rockies, and Matt Cain finally got run support and won his first game at last—but this time, it was Jonathan Sanchez who was on the losing end in the final game as the brooms came and went one more time. Three series, all victorious, yet all frustrating in that they ended with a loss instead of a sweep. Do nothing easily: That was definitely proving a key aspect of the Giants Way.

April was now over, and with a 13-9 mark for the month, the Giants completed Step One of their goal—that proverbial "fast start," defined by posting a winning record in each of their first two months. They displayed enviable balance in April, batting an NL-best .280 and ranking second with a 2.75 ERA. Opponents hit only .214 off San Francisco, lowest in the NL. They were in second place as the home stand ended within easy striking range of first. So why did it already feel so frustrating?

No time to think about that. Off to the next airplane, the next hotels in Florida and New York, before coming home to face the cursed Padres again. That started out fine, but as May deepened, it became apparent the Giants wouldn't maintain their high statistical standards.

Chapter 4
Struggle Becomes Normal

Broom Service at Last

The Florida series started with a win that gave hints as to why the season already felt grueling. Lincecum ended up striking out 13 batters in his seven innings of work, but he gave up a three-run homer on an ill-placed pitch to Hanley Ramirez, tying the game. Juan Uribe—who was evolving from the expected super-utility role to a centerpiece of the offense, when it existed—momentarily put the Giants ahead in the eighth with a two-run bomb of his own. That was immediately negated when Sergio Romo gave up a three-run homer to Dan Uggla in the bottom of the inning, the ugly Uggla blast nearly sealing the Giants' fate. They were losing with two outs and no one on base in the ninth. But Aaron Rowand—back from the disabled list and performing as if he'd never been away—tied the game again with a last-gasp home run of his own. The game dragged on until Aubrey Huff's two-run single finally helped propel the Giants to a 9-6 victory in the 12th inning. Brian Wilson closed it out perfectly, completing a night in which the Giants pitchers had struck out 20 batters—and only narrowly came away with a win. Grueling, yes. Torturous, some might say.

The next night was no less stressful. Barry Zito was again brilliant, walking away with his record still perfect at 5-0—but not before Sergio Romo bailed him out of a bases-loaded, no-out jam. Romo calmly struck out Hanley Ramirez—one of the league's best hitters—and induced a double play from cleanup batter Jorge Cantu. The Giants held on for a 3-2 win.

The third and final game was the only one with any hint of ease, as Matt Cain took a no-hitter into the sixth inning before settling for an eventual 6-3 win. Taking the pressure off of Cain, the Giants scored a few runs, led by Aaron Rowand—who continued a hot series—and Mark DeRosa and Nate Schierholtz—all of whom would fade to offensive footnotes too quickly.

A sweep is a sweep, however stressful. The Giants finally had reason for their fans back home to dance with their brooms.

Unfortunately, they then proceeded to lose the next two games to the Mets, in even more stressful style. The Giants lost the first one on a two-run homer by Rod Barajas in the bottom of the ninth, moments after John Bowker had tied the game for the Giants with a ninth-inning homer of his own—and after the Giants had left the winning runs on base as a badly slumping Pablo Sandoval fouled out. The second game took even longer before becoming another disastrous heartbreak. This time, it was Henry Blanco whose home run in the bottom of the 11th ended the contest.

Despite the boost Aaron Rowand's return gave the team, other injuries began to pile up. Edgar Renteria, for one, was hampered by a strained right groin and went on the disabled list on May 7. "Nobody wants to go there," a sullen Renteria said. He would soon have more company in his misery.

It's times like those that make a player want to call home. "Mom??!" The next day was Mother's Day. Maybe that would help.

Thinking in Pink

Pink is never a color for a major league uniform—except on Mother's Day. As a tribute to mothers and as part of an effort to raise money for breast cancer research, Major League Baseball teamed with the nonprofit organization Susan G. Komen for the Cure to sport pink paraphernalia for one day, much as teams had worn "42" for Jackie Robinson. Suddenly, for a moment, pink was noble, hip and beautiful in the world of baseball.

Quite a number of Giants participated by ordering pink bats and wearing pink wristbands and batting gloves. In the case of Pablo Sandoval, the Kung Fu Panda suddenly had a pink fielder's mitt. This being the Giants with their ever-changing lineup, Sandoval found himself playing first instead of the expected third, leaving his pink mitt on the bench until a late-inning switch allowed him to move to third and use it after all. Meanwhile, Juan Uribe's pink bats rarely strayed from his shoulder as he walked four times and was hit by a pitch. Aubrey Huff came in late and went 0-for-2 with pink lumber, while Eli Whiteside and Pablo Sandoval went a collective 0-for-9 with their pink bats. A few other Giants with pink bats didn't get to play. Perhaps there were good reasons pink was generally shunned in the majors.

There were other plausible explanations for struggle than pink, as conditions were hardly any more normal than the pink gear. The wind was blowing 40 mph, bringing back memories of games in the Giants' old haunted house of Candlestick Park, where pitcher Stu Miller was once famously blown off the mound and the wind regularly plastered trash against the chain-link outfield fences.

Struggle simply seemed to be excruciatingly normal in the Giants Way. The Giants were often in their own way, and Mother's Day was no exception—to Mom's certain dismay. The Giants received more gifts than Mom did—getting two hit batsmen and 11 walks in one game—but they only managed to turn three of those walks into runs. The six hits they eked out were overshadowed by yet another failure to collect them with runners in scoring position, adding another weak 1-for-9 in those situations. On the mound, Tim Lincecum started out in control—and somehow, the Giants were ahead—but let the Mets back into the game in the sixth. The wind assisted as the Giants let their 4-0 lead slip into a 5-4 deficit by the seventh, fierce breezes turning Jason Bay's hit from a medium-deep flyball out into a two-run single that fell not far from the infield.

"The ball kept going in, in. It was amazing," said Andres Torres, the fastest runner on the team, who—even with the wind at his back—was unable to come back in fast enough to chase it down.

Somehow, though, one of the Giants slipped one through the wind in the eighth. With runner John Bowker on first after yet another walk, Aaron Rowand hit as hard as he could into the wind.

"That's all I've got," Rowand said. "That's as hard as I can hit a ball that way. And I honestly thought it was going to be caught."

But it wasn't. It had just enough to slip over the wall for a home run that gave the Giants a 6-5 lead, despite being outhit by the Mets 11-6. That brought a clean-shaven Brian Wilson in to attempt to save the day, with one out in the eighth and the right attitude as usual.

"The environment's out of my control," Wilson said. "The only thing I can do is try to do everything in my power to throw strikes and get outs. It's not part of my job description to be concerned with wind or garbage." He did not throw garbage. He threw strikes. And strikeouts, with the one exception of another Jason Bay flyball in the ninth that went "backwards," according to Aaron Rowand, as it fell for a double. Throwing nearly nothing but fierce fastballs, Wilson struck out every batter he faced but Bay, finishing with a career-high five that left the tying run stranded on second. He did not throw pink baseballs.

Even if the pink gear wasn't used for the win, the players still cherished their new equipment.

"I'm going to send one of each to my mom," Andres Torres said, looking fondly at the pair of pink bats and the sets of pink wristbands and batting gloves in his locker. "And I'll give the other to my wife."

Pablo Sandoval echoed the sentiments of Torres, thinking of his own mother, Amelia, who was then living dangerously close to an old natural gas pipeline in San Bruno.

"She means everything to me," Sandoval said. "Without her, I wouldn't be here. She supported me every day when I was little. She took me to the field for practice every day. To put what she means in one word, I can't imagine."

Catcher Eli Whiteside echoed Sandoval's gratitude. "She's always been there for me," Whiteside said of his mother, Cindy. "She always took me to T-ball games and Little League games and has been a big supporter of what I've tried to do throughout my career. I owe a lot to her for helping me get started and for helping me get to practice and games when I was growing up."

All in all, for one brief but vital moment, pink was a Giants baseball color. Be it color of skin or uniform, bat or batting gloves, beauty is all a matter of perception. Unless you're the Giants playing San Diego, in which case there is simply no beauty.

Zito Before the Fall

Barry Zito approached the Padres series from a place of calm rather than anxiety. Given a 5-0 start, he finally had that luxury, having pitched in the way the Giants had not only hoped but expected when they collared him with the immense weight of a seven-year, $126 million contract. Over the course of his career, he'd had a consistent pattern of being excellent in the season's second half after struggling in the first. Having apparently overcome that, he was able to relax and sensitively discuss some of the challenges of excessive expectations and their capitalization—and the process of returning to center.

"It's been an etching away back to my old self," said Zito. "I can deal with failure in this game if I'm just being who I am completely. But if I'm trying to be more than I am, that's just a double whammy. It's a daunting situation. 'Here's $120 million, buddy. Just go be yourself.'

But I'm very well-equipped now to deal with things. I would have given it all back to be 5-0 last year or two years ago. But now I just want to be at peace, and I want to be myself. And I want to be comfortable in my own skin. That translates to out on the mound. When you do that, your talents come through. I still have talent, and I'm just allowing it to come through."

Zito's sincerity about giving it all back in exchange for better results was more plausible than the average impoverished observer might understand. Eloquent sympathy for Zito's plight came from across the tough borders of rivalry: Joe Torre, managing the Dodgers after a long tenure of managing overly-salaried players on the New York Yankees.

"[Zito] got signed for a lot of money," Torre observed. "And with that, you can say all you want. Sometimes we dehumanize people when they get so much money. You forget there's a heart in there and that there's a responsibility that weighs heavy on some of these players." Torre had seen it from the most moneyed of trenches.

"I feel things. I'm sensitive to things," Zito confirmed. And feeling the very public disappointment of the entire Bay Area was a load to bear.

Under those challenges, Zito felt a heightened need to practice what is not only another essential aspect of the Giants Way but also a model for how the rest of us can exist peacefully under our own individual challenges. More likely, our struggles are intensified by a lack of money rather than too much of it, by too little attention rather than too much. Still, equanimity is the place that remains the calm eye of all storms—that ability to maintain equilibrium in face of all situations and emotions.

"Uribe's never down," would represent that principle in the Giants' case, but "Uribe's never too far up" would be the equally important flip side of the same coin. Excessive mood swings do not serve—in baseball or other forms of daily practice. The seasons of baseball and life are too long, too fickle, to allow the excesses of either depression or gloating. The world has a way of humbling the successful, even as it resurrects those who continue to give persistent, positive effort without initial reward.

Zito had seen both sides. He would see them again. He would handle them with grace, as part of a team that coalesced around that equanimity at a level few achieve. The challenges do temper you if you embrace them. The inner payoff eventually moves outward and turns to measurable results.

The Death Trap Moves North

After escaping the howling winds of New York, the Giants came home to their temple of AT&T Park, ready for home and redemption. But it was the Padres visiting—and watching the Giants play the Padres, at this point at least, was like watching another gruesome wreck along the highway. Fascinating, bound to be riveting, yes. And yet in the end, nothing to see here folks, move along please, just move along.

But a bitter Mark DeRosa could not move along. Still pained by the left wrist that had required surgery the previous October, DeRosa displayed unusual candor on the first day of the Padres series by calling the surgery a "total failure."

After an examination and tests that day, he said the ligaments in his wrist were "flapping all over the place again." He also was suffering numbness in the ring and pinky fingers of his left hand, which prevented him from swinging the bat effectively. "When's the last time I crushed a ball?" DeRosa asked, and the answer wasn't obvious. His batting average was merely .194 with three doubles, one home run and 10 RBIs in 26 games. "The game's no fun hitting .190. That's not why I was brought in here."

No one could argue that. And no one could argue his work habits in trying to overcome it. Manager Bochy speculated that part of the issue might actually stem from DeRosa working too hard, taking too much batting practice while trying to overcome his struggles.

"He's a tough guy," Bochy said. "He's a football player. He was trying to play through this."

DeRosa couldn't play through it any longer, and he knew it. "I'm not going to stink all year," he said. "I'm doing myself and the team a disservice." Although extreme conditioning, fierce work habits and a failure to complain are all a part of the Giants Way as much as equanimity, owning up to reality and admitting injury have to be, too. Hidden injuries are deceit and do further damage to both player and team in the long run. By admitting his injury with exceptional honesty and joining Edgar Renteria on the disabled list when it was necessary, DeRosa manfully showed one of the harder aspects of living according to the Giants Good Book and its call for loyalty to the team.

Meanwhile, on the field, the change in venue failed to alter the results. The Padres won the opener 3-2, handing Barry Zito his first defeat after a 5-0 start. In that game, the Giants put 10 runners on base in 4 2/3 innings against Padres starter Wade LeBlanc, but they again squandered most of their opportunities. After a 5-2 Padres victory in the second game, the series ended as Mat Latos pitched a one-hitter for the Padres, again besting Jonathan Sanchez, 1-0—a terrible sequel to the Giants' one-hit loss in San Diego. Latos added insult to injury by singling to drive in the lone run after reserve second baseman Lance Zawadski, who played in only 20 games for the Padres and hit .200, doubled with two outs to prolong the fifth.

Furthermore, Mat Latos—with whom the Giants would have further quarrel—made one of history's worst attempts to throw a baseball into the stands. Showing the arm strength that was quickly launching his promising career, he managed the difficult feat of throwing the ball *over* the stands. And then he achieved the even more difficult (and random) feat of having the ball come down in the Giants players' parking lot, where it shattered the sunroof on the car belonging to broadcaster Dave Flemming. The Giants sent the Padres the bill.

Nope, nothing to see here folks, just move along please. Move along. Quickly.

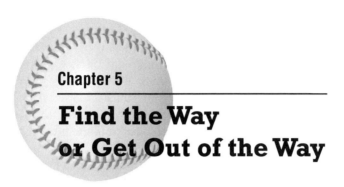

Chapter 5

Find the Way
or Get Out of the Way

Houston, We Have No Problem Again

Maybe there are advantages to Houston after all. Or at least to having the Houston baseball team visit AT&T Park when the Giants are in need of a major pick-me-up.

Immediately displaying equanimity, the Giants refused to act beaten after the Padres had brutally beaten them. The Giants offense returned from visits with Jimmy Hoffa long enough to pound the Astros in the opener, 8-2, as starter Todd Wellemeyer resumed his mysterious pattern of pitching well at home but being hammered on the road. Bochy had frequently called Wellemeyer "his own worst enemy," but Todd was a friend to himself that night in the win—another of the Orange Fridays that had previously caused him to eat celebratory Cheetos.

The next night was an even better rerun. For the second time of the season, ace Roy Oswalt fell prey to the You-Can't-Beat-Lincecum hex, losing a 2-1 decision despite five walks by Lincecum. That finally broke a hex of Lincecum's own—a stretch of three straight starts in which he left with a lead, only to watch the bullpen blow the lead each time. The offense was largely provided by Juan Uribe, who was not only never down but was also all over a pitch from Oswalt after a Bengie Molina single. His fourth home run of the year was all the team needed offensively.

But few of the witnesses at that game left AT&T Park talking about Lincecum or Uribe. They instead were buzzing about Brian Wilson, who drove everyone apoplectic with a memorable confrontation against Kaz Matsui—after first driving them halfway there by giving up two walks and a single in the ninth. With the bases loaded, two outs and the game riding on every pitch, one of the year's most intense duels ensued. Over the course of 15 pitches to Matsui—14 of them fastballs—Matsui slowly worked the count in his favor, fouling off four 2-2 pitches and then five 3-2 deliveries. One more ball at any point late in the sequence would've meant walking in the tying run—another devastatingly blown lead in a Lincecum game. But Wilson kept throwing strike after strike after strike, forcing Matsui to bite. Finally, on the 15th pitch, as "The Thinker" Bochy watched pensively in the dugout, Matsui hit a catchable flyball to left field. The game was over. The latest torture resolved in a happy fashion.

"Willie had the nerve to ask me if I was worried," Bochy said, using one of Wilson's nicknames. Bochy obviously had cause.

Wilson wouldn't admit to any worry of his own. He could afford to be glib afterward. "I couldn't pick a better time to have recess," he said.

And when Zito regained his place in the win column the next day, it was almost recess in comparison, even if it was only another extremely tight, one-run, 4-3 win. The fans with brooms could use them. The Giants had recovered from the Padres debacle by sweeping Houston again. They finished the brief home stand only half a game out of first, optimistic again before heading out on the road. They were rewarded with yet another two games in San Diego before heading off to Arizona and Oakland.

The Emergence of Andres Torres

As May settled in, outfielder Andres Torres began his unexpected emergence.

Torres regarded the ballpark as a classroom where he studied his craft diligently. A native of Aguada, Puerto Rico, where he grew up too poor to even own shoes at times, he was a runner who began approaching baseball seriously only after he reached Miami-Dade Community College. Torres went there on a baseball scholarship, which he received after being recommended by a recruiter who couldn't help but notice his remarkable speed as he shagged flies.

As Torres said, "I didn't know how to hit." So he spent most of 11 professional seasons in the minors, striving to learn his craft. Continuing his education in earnest with the Giants, Torres started scribbling entries in a notebook early in the 2010 season, recording snippets of advice he'd receive or fundamentals he learned. Torres figured keeping this baseball journal would help him absorb the knowledge he encountered. "I try to talk to everybody . . . every player and coach,"

Torres said. In 2010, advice from Willie McCovey and Hensley Meulens had helped him learn to keep his bat more still as a left-handed hitter, honing his increasingly valuable switch-hitting skills.

Several years earlier, Torres would have been too distracted to sustain this kind of project. He had been diagnosed in 2002 with Attention Deficit Disorder, but he didn't start taking suitable levels of medication to control the ailment until 2007. Not coincidentally, Torres thrived that year, batting .292 with 21 doubles, 20 triples and 10 homers for Detroit's Double- and Triple-A affiliates. The following season—at an age when most would've conceded the defeat of his major league dreams—he exceeded the .300 level for the first time as a pro, hitting .306 with the Chicago Cubs' Triple-A Iowa outpost.

Torres signed with the Giants as a minor league free agent before the 2009 season and made the opening day squad—despite being a non-roster invitee to spring training. Besides hitting a commendable .270 in 75 games with the Giants in 2009, Torres generated one of the year's most startling statistics by hitting eight triples in only 152 at-bats. Cherishing the opportunity he had seized, Torres freely expressed his gratitude. What may have seemed like gratuitous clichés from the mouths of others became wholly sincere when uttered by Torres. "I need to respect the organization for giving me this job," he said. "I want them to know I'm going to work hard, try to get better and help the team win." He backed up his words.

In return, the Giants welcomed Torres' unquenchable enthusiasm. "He never has a bad day," manager Bruce Bochy said. Torres was successfully practicing the Giants Way of positive equanimity alongside Uribe and others. He began to succeed beyond anyone's expectations, beyond what almost any have done after a long hard decade of bus rides in the minors.

While the Giants played uncertainly in May, Torres asserted himself. He hit .351 (13-for-37) in 10 games between May 12 and May 22, finally prompting Bochy to assign him the leadoff role for good on May 23. Playing mostly right field, Torres had remained patient and persistent while three other outfielders failed to hold jobs. John Bowker, the opening day right fielder, would start 18 games in both corner outfield spots. Nate Schierholtz, Bowker's initial replacement, hit for average but not for production and couldn't hold the job either, despite brilliant defensive work. Eugenio Velez, a fleet switch-hitter like Torres, endured his eight-game, 1-for-25 skid shortly after replacing the beaned Aaron Rowand. Now in May, center fielder Aaron Rowand himself began to struggle at the plate, and it became clear

Mark DeRosa would be lost for the season. The Giants desperately needed someone to emerge in the outfield, and Torres was the first.

"I always say, I'm ready no matter what," Torres said. "Even if I'm not playing, I have to be ready, because you never know."

Torres would go on to win the year's Willie Mac Award, the annual award in honor of the still-inspirational Willie McCovey. Voting their teammate most inspirational player was part of the vast payoff for Torres' incredible persistence, positivity, hard work and, finally, opportunity. Emergence couldn't have come at a better time, nor could it have happened to a better guy.

Nothing to See Here, Either

Oh, hell, back to San Diego, anyway. Another gruesome loss. If you must know, another lack of run support for the ever-excellent Matt Cain in a well-pitched loss. The Giants fell to 0-7 against the Padres for the year if you must know that, too. Just keep moving, folks. Nothing to see here. Nothing to see.

Something simply had to change, even if the players were outwardly keeping equanimity and a carefree attitude—to the point of deep laughter before stretching in San Diego. Bruce Bochy and general manager Brian Sabean were meeting behind closed doors to discuss possible personnel directions in seeking help. Baseball being as superstitious as it is, the Giants also tried other avenues of luck and change. Before the second game of the series, the injured Edgar Renteria took the lineup card to home plate instead of Bruce Bochy. And broadcaster Duane Kuiper, in his wisdom, turned to the legacy of Kirk Rueter's famously lucky ears for assistance.

From 1996 to 2005, Kirk Rueter was a left-handed pitcher for the Giants—one of those pitchers other teams always felt they should beat but rarely could. His speed wasn't blinding, his off-speed pitches tempting. Yet he had great command of those pitches, hit his spots beautifully, kept hitters off balance and ended up with a high winning percentage for seven straight years. He won more than 100 games for the Giants and was one of their most beloved players. Rueter always seemed to have good fortune, and he brought it to the team. Even after retirement, he continued to bring it by having the team over for a party when they passed through St. Louis each year. A Giant forever, he continued to follow the team closely.

Along with good fortune, Rueter also had large, protruding ears. It became the team custom to rub his ears for good luck when walking along the bench. It seemed to work. And if there was ever a time when the Giants needed his lucky ears, it was now. Since the physical Rueter wasn't available, Kuiper found a photo of Rueter and taped it up in the dugout before the second game of the series. That would have to do. Rueter's presence in spirit would surely break the Curse of the Padres.

But how? Who was listening to the wisdom of Torres and the Giants Way of always being ready?

Well, Matt Downs was, for one. Ryan Rohlinger, for another. And Eli Whiteside.

Who?

Downs was a career minor leaguer, up for his latest short stint with the Giants. Rohlinger, too, was trying to climb that last, hardest rung from the highest level of the minors to a reliable job in the majors. Eli Whiteside, meanwhile, had found a nice little role in the shadows with the Giants after a minor league career almost as long as Andres Torres'. A man from Mississippi with prematurely grey hair—it started turning in high school—Whiteside had carved out a niche as the backup catcher to Bengie Molina. His offensive contributions were limited, but the pitchers loved working with him, and after almost a decade in the minors, he'd learned a lot about the game the hard way. He'd already earned a few priceless memories, including catching Jonathan Sanchez's no-hitter in 2009.

The May 18 game against San Diego may be forgotten by many, but certainly not by Downs, Rohlinger or Whiteside. It would be as key to the pennant race as any other game, breaking the Curse of the Padres at last. Barely. As usual.

It took until the 12th inning before a two-run double by Downs scored Rohlinger and Whiteside. This put the Giants in the lead 6-4 and capped off a three-hit night by Downs.

"That, my friends, is a thing of beauty," the Reverend Mike Krukow said reverently on the air, watching the replay of Downs' double sailing into the left-field corner before waxing rhapsodic about his three-hit night. Eugenio Velez then made a key contribution of his own with an RBI single, extending the lead to 7-4.

Of course, even then, it wasn't over. No, this is the Giants Way, already famously beginning to be associated with torture. Brian Wilson once again came in to save the game, and the single by Velez became vital as Wilson allowed a two-run double and then put the possible winning run on base before striking out Chase Headley.

"He'll go by my gravesite and say, 'I helped put you there,'" Bochy joked of Wilson. But the Curse of the Padres was broken at last. The Giants could move on to Arizona and Oakland.

But again: Nothing to see here, folks. Just a tragic mess. Does anyone really need to view explicit carnage of the Giants allowing more than 10 runs per game in Arizona as they were swept in a short series? Do the bloody remains of the games in Oakland need attention as the Giants' offense vanished more completely than ever, scoring a total of one miserable run in three games? Only as a measure of larger concerns.

Concerns

Usually the Giants' greatest strength, pitching soon began to emerge as a concern. Five consecutive defeats dropped their record to 22-21. It reminded the Giants that teams with ordinary staffs only hope for a strong pitching outing as often as the Giants had come to expect one.

Having excelled at home and struggled on the road, Todd Wellemeyer followed this pattern as the losing streak began in a 13-1 shellacking at Arizona. The next night, Lincecum endured his first subpar appearance of the season after eight starts. It was easy to dismiss Lincecum's dud as an aberration, although his second five-walk total in a row should have caused consternation among veteran Lincecumologists.

Zito, who compiled a sparkling 1.49 ERA while going 5-0 in his first six starts, slowly continued his inexorable unraveling. The left-hander yielded all of Oakland's runs in a 6-1 loss. Zito insisted facing his former team was no longer a novelty, but Zito was now 0-4 with an 8.85 ERA in four starts against the A's.

Matt Cain's performance didn't arouse worry. He owned a fine 2.88 ERA, among the best of the league's starters—yet his record was 2-4 after his 1-0 loss to the A's, during which the Giants mustered only three singles.

Then there was Jonathan Sanchez, who had begun the season in such promising fashion. In his three outings following the home opener, he permitted two runs in 20 innings while striking out 27. Sanchez proceeded to go 0-3 in his next five starts, despite building a fair 3.86 ERA in that span. He also walked five batters three times in a six-start span that concluded with a 3-0 loss to the A's in the series finale.

Erratic pitching wasn't limited to the rotation. Through 40 games, left-hander Jeremy Affeldt had three losses, one more than he had compiled during the entire 2009 season. Pitching through increasing discomfort, right-hander Brandon Medders compiled a 7.20 ERA in 14 games before he went on the disabled list with left knee inflammation.

Right-hander Sergio Romo, who sported an 0.93 ERA after nine appearances, allowed six earned runs in his next five outings, absorbing the defeat in two of them. His ERA had climbed to 4.50—a common hazard for relievers, who pitch so few innings their statistics can be skewed by one poor game.

Then there was Wilson, getting it done at the end, but in a manner that threatened to send Bochy to his grave.

And as for the offense?

Rowand healed from the Padilla beaning without complications, but pretty soon his bat looked broken instead of his face. Like Sandoval, Rowand's batting average continued to plummet until May 12, when it finally sank below .300—and kept sinking. Good thing for the emergence of Andres Torres.

Catcher Bengie Molina looked sluggish at the plate, tumbling into a 4-for-50 slump that lasted 15 games between May 19 and June 6 and dropped his average from .330 to .248. He had one RBI and one double in that stretch.

This malaise infected the entire team. During their five consecutive losses from May 19 to 23, the Giants hit .184 and scored nine runs total—and seven of those runs came in one game. The Giants were shut out twice and scored one run twice in that stretch. Second baseman Freddy Sanchez's return from the disabled list on May 19 was a welcome development, but it wasn't enough to stop the collapse.

What would be enough? It wasn't evident. Nothing to see here, folks. Nothing behind that yellow "DO NOT CROSS" crime tape but another terrible five-game losing streak with which to come home across the Bay Bridge.

State of the Timmy Address

Tim Lincecum motivates himself at least partially by repeating the bromide, "It's not what you've done; it's what you're doing now." For a guy who owned an undefeated record, Lincecum didn't seem too thrilled with his personal here-and-now on the morning of May 23, a little less than two hours before the A's would begin completing their three-game sweep of the Giants.

Lincecum was in a slump, though few realized it. Even while surrendering one run and four hits in eight innings on May 15 to defeat

Roy Oswalt, he issued five walks and struggled to put away hitters. Then he was downright ineffective on May 20 at Arizona, recording that pitching line of unwanted consistency—five innings, five hits, five runs and five more walks.

On this particular day, a reporter was asking Lincecum to gauge the significance of his 100th career start, which he would make on May 31 against Colorado. That angle might have been a little bit of a stretch, since a starter's 100th outing has never been regarded as a milestone. Even if it were, the nationwide baseball buzz wouldn't have surrounded Lincecum, despite his 5-0 mark and 2.35 ERA. It was enveloping Colorado's Ubaldo Jimenez, who was 8-1 with an 0.99 ERA. And it just so happened that Lincecum and Jimenez would oppose each other in that Memorial Day game.

Being a good sport, Lincecum patiently answered each question. His responses amounted to a State of the Timmy address. If he were Muhammad Ali—the boxing legend who himself had visited the Giants' spring training camp to spark players' participation in a charity drive—Lincecum would have been fretting that his jab suddenly lacked sting. Since the subject was pitching, Lincecum spoke candidly about his diminished velocity.

"I'm not worried about it, but it's in the back of my mind," he said. "I'm aware of the fact that my fastball isn't 95 [mph] anymore. I'm not saying I don't feel like it's going to end up to the point where I can't get there, but it just isn't that way right now."

In a different conversation, Lincecum actually referred to himself as a "thumber"—short for "cunny thumber," baseball lingo for a weak-armed pitcher who survives by throwing curveballs.

Tim Lincecum a *thumber*? Surely he jests.

Here, however, was a clear view into Lincecum's self-image. He had built his identity around being "The Freak," the undersized power pitcher who defied the odds as he dazzled hitters. To be sure, he'd throw off-speed deliveries, but he'd use them to offset the fastball. Nothing surprising there; that's just Pitching 101. Already, Lincecum's changeup—which often sank like a split-fingered fastball or veered towards the right-handed batter's box like a screwball—had become his most devastating pitch. But without the fastball to anchor his repertoire, Lincecum knew he would have to adjust.

As he spoke in the middle of the visitors' clubhouse at the Oakland Coliseum, Lincecum perched in a chair with his legs jackknifed in, arms hugging his knees as if to comfort himself, displaying his remarkable flexibility even in repose.

"I'm becoming more of an all-around pitcher," he said. "There are days when my fastball's going to be a little better and some days when my fastball's not going to be that great, and I'm going to have to work around that. I'm trying to be prepared for any event or situation I run into. You know how people say, 'I wish I would have known now what I did later?' Well, I'm trying to know now."

This really was the essence of Lincecum the ballplayer. Not the long hair. Not the marijuana-related run-in with the law during the previous offseason. Not the nicknames or even the two Cy Young Awards. This is a guy who's serious about his game—just study his facial expression on a telecast anytime he pitches. The same guy Matt Cain dubbed "the human jukebox" for his encyclopedic musical knowledge was capable of sounding like an exercise physiologist, using terms like "pronate" and "torque" when discussing his pitching technique. He had set a higher standard for himself, and he'd be damned if he'd slip from it.

"I think it's my natural competitiveness that makes it that way, a 'Find the way or get out of the way' kind of thing," he said.

Find the way or get out of the way: That was more than the Giants Way. It was the constant, relentless reality of Major League Baseball. There were always a hundred hungrier than you, just waiting to take your place.

In Full Color, Continued

When the Giants came home from their disastrous trip to Arizona and Oakland, the Giants announced they would retire the number of Monte Irvin, the first black player on the Giants, following Jackie Robinson's courageous major league entry by two years. Irvin had mentored Mays when the latter was a rookie. He had led the league in runs batted in during the classic 1951 season that culminated in Bobby Thomson's legendary pennant-winning home run. And he'd helped the Giants get to their last World Championship in 1954. Although not as lauded as Robinson, Irvin earned his own berth in the Hall of Fame, despite that as many of his playing years had been spent in the Negro Leagues as in the majors. He never played in San Francisco, but—still alive and well at 91 in 2010—he was embraced there as one of the city's own for the magnitude of his contribution to Giants history. His No. 20 jersey would be retired at season's end—or when John Bowker was traded to Pittsburgh, whichever came first. (The latter possibility was not yet a known condition.)

The odd tides of race in baseball were continuing to shift in 2010. The explicit barriers had fallen, and few thought anything of the presence of players of any color in the majors by this point—progress, indeed. Not only were African-American players welcomed, but players from as far away as Japan, Australia and Curacao had found major league success—most significantly, a number of players with roots in the Dominican Republic, Venezuela and other Spanish-speaking lands. Yet the percentage of African-American players was falling precipitously again, despite the shifted climate. The only African-American on the 2010 Giants was Emmanuel Burriss, and after breaking his foot (again) in spring training, his entire major league season would consist of five at-bats.

Economic and social disadvantage was still an African-American reality, and baseball was losing out as a result. Few baseball fields grace the tough inner city; basketball is much easier to play there. Basketball and football have traditionally attracted more black athletes, although baseball still drew more than, say, polo or yachting. Emmanuel Burriss himself was seeking to revive inner-city baseball, not only as the Giants' only African-American but also as the first to reach the majors from Washington, D.C., in more than three decades. The sandlots of the Dominican Republic were a better breeding ground for American major leaguers than the country's own urban areas. The All-American baseball dream was turning around on itself, reinventing itself in ways that Jackie Robinson and Monte Irvin never could've imagined when they risked their lives and careers for the greater betterment.

The new realities of baseball often divided teams into two camps based around language: English and Spanish. The 2010 Giants were no exception, with players from the Dominican Republic, Puerto Rico, Venezuela, Colombia and more. As a bilingual Mexican-American, Sergio Romo helped bridge the gaps. Puerto Rican Andres Torres could also bridge the cultural gap, especially with his natural friendliness. Mark DeRosa could bridge it via sheer personality—and his constant respect for the difficulties Latino players face.

"I have a lot of respect for the Latin players," DeRosa said. "I know how difficult it must be for them to come over here as teenagers." His understanding of the challenges these players faced in assimilating into the odd American culture was heightened by his own reverse experience early in his career, playing winter ball in Venezuela. DeRosa always made a point to reach out, regardless of origin.

"I try to get to know every one of my teammates, not just [say],

'Hey, way to swing it,' or something like that," DeRosa said. "What their upbringing was like, where they're from, what they're about, what their tastes are. If you get a common ground and build some type of relationship, they can trust you."

That kind of deeper relationship, that trust: Therein lies another key to the Giants Way and its 2010 success, just as much as in any on-field statistics. When Bruce Bochy mentioned in spring that the team had a different presence with DeRosa on it, this aspect was a key part—and a part no wrist injury could ruin. Teamwork is about that trust—developing it across lines of culture, language, personality and style is essential to creating oneness. In the end, whether the team is in baseball or business (or both), its players are human beings before they are players, workers, statistical machines. It does not matter what color their skin is. Differences may be as strong between players with a conservative Mississippi background and a liberal Seattle one as between a Venezuelan and a San Franciscan. To be a true teammate, you need to know if a player's going through a mid-season divorce in his twenties, if he's best motivated by gentle reinforcement or challenge, if he needs to be left alone before he pitches, if having a beer together after the game is a good or a bad idea. You need to know not only how he plays this game, but why. For what reason and reward? This kind of knowledge is essential to developing the oneness that makes it possible to flow cohesively through the challenges of a season. As much as the visible game may take place only between the foul lines, the truth of its players extends deep into the invisible realm of living. It reaches into sleepless bedrooms; onto tough streets; into family issues, discipline and addiction; and every aspect of being human on a long, tough road. Know your teammates, yes. DeRosa has been a spirit master in saying that and living it, and that is why his former Cubs teammates were still singing his praises long after his own unpredictable road led him to San Francisco.

A Change Is Gonna Come

Regardless of skin color or cultural difference, the Giants needed new blood at the moment they were announcing Irvin's number retirement. At 91, Irvin was too old to help. The team needed to escape the ugly reality of their non-blooming spring.

The soundtrack in the background might've been from near Irvin's era. It might've been the late, great Sam Cooke singing, "A

Change Is Gonna Come." Mr. Cooke was singing from a place of faith, rather than a place of reason. But the Giants had both faith and reason awaiting them in the Good Book's chapters yet to be written. A hardened veteran and a hard-nosed rookie would soon arrive, stimulating the team through summer and into autumn. One would be rescued from off of his own jobless couch, while the other would fulfill his vast promise. Men for all seasons, Pat Burrell and Buster Posey would accelerate the pace of the march towards October.

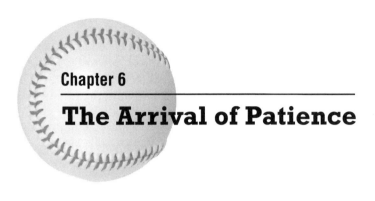

Chapter 6

The Arrival of Patience

Unlikely Places

"You get something started in the most unlikely places. That's how you get out of a rut," said Aubrey Huff after the Giants beat the Washington Nationals on May 25. The teams were locked in a scoreless duel, with the Giants batting, no one on base, two outs and a two-strike count to pitcher Todd Wellemeyer, who was hitting a fearsome .071 for the season. In the first of five consecutive two-out hits from the Giants, Wellemeyer somehow managed to hit a fastball from Livan Hernandez into left field for a single, leading them to a badly needed rally and a 4-2 win. The team was vacillating between third and fourth place in the division, although never more than four-and-a-half games out of first.

Unfortunately, Edgar Renteria got hurt again in the game, returning to the disabled list only three days after coming off of it. It was another depressing blow to a team still struggling with injuries and finding it nearly impossible to keep a stable offensive lineup.

"You're trying to get some consistency. That's what's frustrating," Bochy said after Renteria's latest injury made consistency impossible. (At least Freddy Sanchez had returned to patrol second base, and he was beginning to contribute like the defensive ace and former batting champion he is.)

There was challenge on the pitching staff, too, as Jeremy Affeldt and Brandon Medders were still out with injuries, and Bochy felt it necessary to tell the slumping Lincecum to relax after he gave up five more walks and four stolen bases against the Nationals in a 7-3 loss the next night. Championship teams are not supposed to struggle to beat the worst, and the Nationals were the worst team in the league. The Giants were not looking like a championship team.

It's an easy temptation with any situation in dire need of change to throw money or people at the problem. Without careful design, doing so can increase the cost of the current disaster without fixing it. It's hard to notice you're still digging when you're already in a hole. Near the end of May, however, the Giants certainly noticed the looming hole, and something simply had to be done. And sometimes more people or more spending—if it's the right people and the right money spent—really can change the direction of things. It can get things started in the strangest of places. It might even be a more reliable strategy than rubbing Kirk Rueter's ears.

The Giants were indeed getting something started, in a place as unlikely as a Todd Wellemeyer at-bat—namely, on a couch in Arizona. They were also getting something started in a more inevitable place: on a field in Fresno.

Inevitable Arrival

The inevitable occurred on May 29, when Buster Posey was recalled from Triple-A Fresno. The Giants were ranked 14th of 16 teams in the National League in runs scored and were feeling uncertain about the health status of injured veterans Mark DeRosa and Edgar Renteria. The team figured Posey could bolster the offense. Posey's performance at Triple-A Fresno, which included a .349 average in 47 games and six home runs, 32 RBIs, a .442 on-base percentage and a .552 slugging percentage, prompted the Giants to act.

Skeptics charged the Giants left Posey at Triple-A to start the season so he wouldn't accumulate enough service time to qualify for salary arbitration before the 2012 campaign. Given their vast financial commitment to Barry Zito through 2013 and the potential of also paying eight-figure salaries to Tim Lincecum, Matt Cain, Jonathan Sanchez and Brian Wilson, the Giants might have deemed limiting Posey's service time a necessity. Club management insisted Posey needed more polish defensively, which was a plausible explanation, particularly since he hadn't begun catching full-time until his sophomore season at Florida State.

Then again, Posey had moved behind the plate from shortstop with consummate smoothness. "The first day he walked toward us with the catching gear on, it seemed like he had worn those shin guards for years," Florida State coach Mike Martin said.

Posey's arrival in San Francisco created other issues. Bengie Molina remained the No. 1 catcher, forcing Posey to play first base (where he was even less experienced than at shortstop) and moving

Aubrey Huff to one of the outfield corners. That forced right fielder Nate Schierholtz to the bench, since Aaron Rowand remained in center field and Andres Torres would occupy whichever corner out-field spot Huff didn't. Even then, the lineup changes wouldn't end, as another arrival would occur within a week, shifting the human chess pieces again. Bochy "The Thinker" would have to think some more, despite his desire to find a stable lineup.

Since being drafted in the first round in 2008, Posey represented a potential threat to Molina, despite the veteran's esteemed status. From 2007 to 2009, Molina was a primary offensive force for the Giants, batting .278 while averaging 18 homers, 85 RBIs and 137 games per season. Those statistics led some veteran Giants observ-ers to theorize Molina was the best catcher in the franchise's San Francisco history, eclipsing the likes of Tom Haller, Ed Bailey, Dick Dietz, Dave Rader, Kirt Manwaring and Benito Santiago (with apolo-gies to anyone who might have been inadvertently omitted).

Molina spent a large part of his Giants tenure batting cleanup, largely because manager Bruce Bochy had nobody else remotely ca-pable of filling that role. Molina's response to this challenge helped him command his teammates' respect, which resulted in his winning back-to-back "Willie Mac" awards in 2007 and 2008.

Baseball can be a cold business, however, where past performance guarantees no role in the present, let alone in the future. Molina was acutely aware the Giants wanted to replace him with Posey as soon as they saw fit. That's why it was stunning when Molina re-signed for one year and $4.5 million on Jan. 19. Barely a month earlier, general manager Brian Sabean had all but dismissed chances that Molina would return. "That ship has sailed," Sabean said, not anticipating that Molina would remain anchored to San Francisco by a lack of multiyear offers and the Giants' lingering desire to sign a veteran backstop to handle the position while Posey progressed.

In retrospect, some of Bochy's pregame comments on May 29 bordered on hilarious, offering no more future assurances to Posey than to Molina. Bochy wouldn't guarantee Posey would stick with the club if DeRosa and Renteria returned healthy and effective. "This is not long-term, but it's going to make sense for us until we get all our guys back and we'll see where we're at," said Bochy.

In deference to Molina, Posey played first base against the Arizona Diamondbacks in his May 29 season debut, the first of 30 games he would start at that spot. Bochy felt compelled to offer assurances that Posey would still receive chances to catch. "We'll make sure he gets enough catching this year, believe me," Bochy said. "Maybe not this week or the next couple of weeks, but he'll get back behind the plate." In San Francisco—or in Fresno? The question might arise given Bochy's pregame comments, but if he hit successfully in the majors, it was hard to imagine Posey being sent back down.

Without meaning any disrespect towards Molina, Posey displayed his preternatural confidence when asked about playing first. "Personally, I view it as a short-term thing," said Posey, who played first at times in spring training and at Fresno. "You never know, I guess."

Fans cared more about how Posey hit than about where he played. Batting sixth, he made an immediate impact.

After Posey rapped a first-inning RBI single in his first game, first-base coach Roberto Kelly whispered something in the rookie's ear. Posey laughed. He later recalled, "He was just joking, 'It's that easy, huh?'"

That night, Posey ended up going 3-for-4 with three RBIs in a 12-1 crushing of the Diamondbacks—a season-high run total for the team—as they won their third consecutive game. The RBIs were the first in the majors for Posey, who didn't drive in a run while going 2-for-17 in a September 2009 call-up. In the heart of the order above him, Pablo Sandoval, Aubrey Huff and Juan Uribe combined to go 8-for-11 with a homer, four RBIs and eight runs scored. On the mound, Jonathan Sanchez was wildly effective for five innings, only allowing two hits and one run while striking out seven, but in typical Sanchez fashion throwing a mammoth 103 pitches in the process. At his limit early, he was lifted. The trio of Sergio Romo, Dan Runzler and Denny Bautista stepped into the void, combining to no-hit the Diamondbacks the rest of the way.

Posey made hitting look so simple Huff felt compelled to call him "Jesus Christ" in the clubhouse after the game, capturing his immediate impact and the nearly messianic expectations heaped upon him. Turning serious, Huff conveyed the sense that Posey had joined San Francisco to stay. "You know he can hit," Huff said. "I saw him in spring training, and he's a good kid, has a quiet demeanor about him, does his work and just takes good approaches up there." Suddenly, the free-swinging Giants had a hitter whose patience would enable him to work deep counts. Soon, they'd have two.

Posey's quiet demeanor showed as immediately as his hitting. "I felt pretty relaxed," he said, despite the ovations and expectations. It was his turn for confidence and ease upon arrival, just as it had previously been Tim Lincecum's. The tides had turned, although Posey's presence and performance would soon help to relax everyone—except perhaps Bengie Molina.

The Wisdom of Burrell's Law

On the same day Buster Posey arrived, the Giants signed left fielder Pat Burrell to a minor league contract. A formidable presence with Philadelphia from 2000 to 2008, Burrell mistakenly thought he could thrive as a designated hitter, the role he'd assumed after signing a two-year, $16 million contract with the Tampa Bay Rays as a free agent. The Rays released him on May 15 after he had endured a miserable season-and-a-fraction with them. Burrell's final numbers in 146 games with Tampa: a .218 batting average, 16 home runs, 77 RBIs and a shockingly low .672 OPS (on-base plus slugging percentage).

As Burrell would repeat later, he retired to his couch at his Scottsdale, Ariz., home. But he reclined in uncertainty, not comfort. Athletes can feel miserable in multiple ways. They experience frustration, confusion or even anger when they're performing poorly. But they can work their way out of that. They might feel helpless when an ailment sidelines them, but unless it's a catastrophic or career-ending injury, the body heals.

It's quite a different feeling when you're not wanted. Or at least when you're wondering whether any team wants you. That strips away the layers of confidence an athlete wraps himself in over the years, even decades, to warm himself against failure's inevitable chill.

Four days into Burrell's limbo, on May 19, the Giants opened their two-game series at Arizona, which the Diamondbacks would sweep. Seeking solace and fellowship, Burrell had lunch with two former teammates: Aaron Rowand, with whom he had patrolled the outfield in Philadelphia, and Aubrey Huff, a University of Miami contemporary. Huff had already lobbied the Giants to sign Burrell, although Rowand joked, "I'm not privileged to divulge that information."

Burrell's record was his most significant endorsement. He hit 251 homers in nine years with Philadelphia, reaching or exceeding 30 in four separate seasons. He struck out a lot (through 2010, his prorated 162-game average stood at 157 whiffs annually), but he also knew how to patiently draw a walk, accounting for his respectable .367 on-base percentage as a Phillie. His pedestrian .254 batting average in that span confounded a handful of Phillies coaches, who simply couldn't understand why Burrell wasn't a better hitter.

In the current day, some said Burrell was over the hill. Others said his plodding defense was too much of a liability for him to return to a National League outfield. But people are too quick to write off anyone who has had a bad year: It's a natural but short-sighted human tendency to project recent events into the future as an unchanging trend. Call it Burrell's Law. It was the same law that allowed the Giants to cost-effectively sign Burrell's friend Aubrey Huff.

Regardless of Burrell's Law, "Pat the Bat" was the latest castoff without a job. And if the Giants were interested, Bruce Bochy was not publicly willing to say it, no matter Huff's lobbying—even the day before Burrell was signed. "Right now, we have our guys," Bochy said. "I can't be concerned about another guy right now." Bochy wasn't personally in discussion with Burrell, anyway. But Burrell was inked to a minor league deal the day after Bochy made those comments.

Burrell headed for Triple-A Fresno, bent on proving he still possessed sufficient bat speed and remained in decent physical shape. Five games in the minors was all it took to convince the Giants to bring him to the bigs. He joined the club in Pittsburgh on June 4, doubled in his first at-bat as a Giant the next night and delivered a pinch-hit sacrifice fly to help the Giants win the series finale in 10 innings. Immediately, it was plain to see he belonged, in more ways than one.

Mark DeRosa, who reported to Fresno for an injury rehabilitation stint in one final attempt to determine whether he could cope with the pain in his left wrist, engaged in serious conversation with Burrell on June 3, the latter's final day in Triple-A before joining the Giants. While DeRosa had been advised he'd eventually need another surgery, Burrell recalled being advised to skip surgery after sustaining a wrist injury in 2004. Burrell's discomfort indeed passed, and he hit six home runs in September.

Perhaps encouraged by Burrell's reminiscing, DeRosa went 3-for-4 with an RBI. "I think sometimes the body has a way of adapting," Burrell said. DeRosa's didn't; he would still needed surgery. But the message was clear: Burrell was more than willing to help a teammate, whether he was yelling encouragement from the dugout or quietly imparting wisdom. Another misfit had found a niche.

Burrell's background made him seem even more at home. He'd grown up in the Santa Cruz mountains, a few Dave Kingman home runs south of San Francisco. He attended Bellarmine College Prep in San Jose and grew up following the Giants, although he didn't bleed orange and black like Nate Schierholtz or former infielder Kevin Frandsen, other locals who just happened to be drafted, developed and brought to the majors by the team they'd loved throughout boyhood.

Nevertheless, during those days on his couch in Scottsdale, Burrell pictured himself wearing a Giants uniform. He liked the image. "I hoped the Giants would call," he said. They wisely followed Burrell's Law and did.

Chapter 7

Spring Surge

The Pressure of Time (Part One)

The spring surge that resulted from the addition of Posey and Burrell also placed the pressure of time on Bengie Molina. Everyone (including Molina) knew Posey was considered the catcher of the future, and that future might start any day—particularly if Molina's recent hitting woes continued.

Molina was still invaluable to the Giants, however, especially to Lincecum, who frequently gave credit for his massive success to Molina. Guidance from Bengie was particularly needed at the moment, for in his recent slump, Lincecum often appeared unfocused and was having difficulty holding runners on base—as evidenced when the Nationals stole four bases against him. The word was getting out around the league: You can run on Lincecum. And his velocity is still down.

Molina said of Lincecum, "I know he's probably a little worried about his velocity and stuff like that, but he should learn quickly to pitch with what he has that certain day." Working with what you have, rather than with what you used to have, what you wish to have or what your ego is sure you have despite evidence to the contrary—therein lies wisdom and another necessary element of the Giants Way.

Molina also spoke then of the increasing challenges Lincecum's previous success would bring him. "The hitters are going to have tougher and tougher and tougher at-bats against him. It's not going to stop. A lot of hitters take it as a challenge when they face a type of pitcher like him. They think, 'Hey, man, this is a two-time Cy Young Award winner, this is The Freak, this is the guy who they talk so much about. I want to get a hit off him. I want to do some damage.'" Success always paints a target on your back.

According to Molina, an unyielding attitude would help Lincecum counter his rivals.

"Confidence has to tell you what to do," Molina said. "Confidence means that I don't have to throw my changeup to get you out. I don't have to throw you my fastball all the time to get you out. I have to have my confidence to throw any pitch at any time. I think that's what's going to make the difference."

Confidence is an elusive beast: The times it deserts you are the times you need it most. And when your manager tells you to relax, he is most likely telling you because you've been unable to. As Lincecum reached the point of his 100th start in the majors, he was also reaching his highest point of difficulty so far.

Molina was also invaluable to pitchers enjoying both confidence and success, as illustrated in early June. Matt Cain was exquisite in the second game of a series against the Reds, throwing a complete-game shutout against one of the league's best-hitting teams in their hitter-friendly home stadium on June 8. Bengie Molina was back behind the plate, and Cain was the latest to give credit to Molina for his recent success.

"He's definitely opened up a lot of pitches for me," Cain said. "He's confident with [calling] different pitches on different counts and really, really accepted my stuff."

As noted, Molina was mired in a terrible hitting slump, although it was he and Cain who drove in two of the Giants' three runs that night. Cain spoke to that issue too, defending Molina's offensive struggles.

"He's a great hitter, but I think he's kind of getting overlooked for what he can do behind the plate, calling games," Cain said. "It's not easy for a [catcher] to go back there and hit. He gets beat up, getting foul balls off his chest, off his fingers. It's a tough situation for him. I think he's handled it great. He's done a great job of keeping the pitchers locked in and throwing well." No one questioned Molina as a team leader, even if the fans were growing restless with his falling batting average. Behind the plate, Molina was the still the man, and Posey was still at first. It was, as Cain said, a tough situation.

A Passing of the Torch?

This season, the Giants would play dozens of games their fans would later want to savor.

Their May 31 date against the Colorado Rockies at AT&T Park was not among them.

This game pitted Tim Lincecum, winner of the two previous NL Cy Young Awards, against Colorado ace Ubaldo Jimenez, who seemed poised to claim that prize this year. Although the Memorial Day matinee was billed as a sublime pitching matchup, Jimenez plainly appeared to be the superior pitcher at this juncture. He was 9-1 with an 0.88 ERA, entering the game with a streak of 17 consecutive scoreless innings. By comparison, Lincecum was a respectable 5-1 but had walked five batters in each of his previous three starts, a red flag that could be spotted on Google Earth. In two starts since defeating Houston's Roy Oswalt on May 15, Lincecum had yielded 11 runs in 9 2/3 innings, and he was coming off both his worst performance and first loss of the year, the 4 2/3-inning, six-run clunker against Washington that had included his inability to hold runners.

For the most passionate Giants fans, this game represented not only Lincecum's opportunity to reclaim his status as the NL's most formidable pitcher—it was also a matter of defending the Giants' historical honor. Since ERA became an official statistic in the early 1910s, Jimenez had been the fourth pitcher to own a sub-1.00 figure after 10 outings. The last man to accomplish this was the Giants' finest pitcher since they moved West: Juan Marichal, who posted an 0.59 in his first 10 starts of 1966. Yes, Jimenez was good. No, superb. Maybe even a budding superstar. Plus, he had a fine first name and was respected as an intelligent, polite human being. But the Giants couldn't let him perpetuate the notion that he was better than the great Marichal.

Those who saw Marichal pitch will remember him forever—how he reached for Candlestick Park's soaring light towers with his impossible leg kick, how he muted the league's most formidable lineups, how he dominated the hated Dodgers (career record against Los Angeles: 37-16), how he'd freeze hitters with an occasional sidearm delivery and how he *never* lost command of the strike zone. Marichal combined the skills of Greg Maddux, Pedro Martinez and Roger Clemens. Control, verve, power. For the earliest generation of San Francisco Giants fans, there never was, never has been and never will be any pitcher as magnificent as him.

None, that is, with the possible exception of Lincecum—who, when photographed at the apex of his delivery, looked identical to Marichal in similar depictions.

Lincecum seemed in tune with himself before the game as he danced in front of his locker while mouthing the lyrics to Billy Ocean's "When the Going Gets Tough (The Tough Get Going)."

Facing the Rockies, the going quickly got tough again. Lincecum faltered after throwing a perfect first inning. He walked two batters to open the second inning in extremely un-Marichal-like fashion, which set up a two-run single by Clint Barmes—who had been hitless in 11 career at-bats against Lincecum. After escaping a bases-loaded jam in the fourth inning by retiring Jimenez, Lincecum surrendered an RBI double to Todd Helton, which would have been excusable in the recent past. But this was an older, more vulnerable Helton, who logged only his ninth extra-base hit and finished the game with a lowly .329 slugging percentage. Lincecum, who was also charged with a sixth-inning unearned run, lasted 5 2/3 innings and again walked five, which made him the only starter in the club's San Francisco history to issue that many free passes in four consecutive starts—not the kind of record any pitcher would desire to hold.

The sellout crowd still saw plenty of pitching excellence, all belonging to Jimenez. He posted his second shutout of the season—his first being an April 17 no-hitter at Atlanta—and permitted four hits, three by Pablo Sandoval. The 4-0 score seemed tremendously lopsided. After the game, Jimenez stood at 10-1 with an ERA of 0.78—an impossible standard to match.

With a 162-game schedule looming over them, major leaguers avoid thinking in symbolic terms. Basic reality poses enough of a challenge. But those who cared to ponder this game's larger meaning couldn't have liked what it meant for the Giants. Colorado's best, who rendered them helpless at the plate, beat their best, who continued to look uncomfortable on the mound. "I feel kind of out of sync," Lincecum said, predictably enough. The somber tone of Memorial Day for the Giants seemed less for the country's fallen soldiers than for Tim Lincecum's deceased dominance.

Lincecum also sounded nearly political. "I'm not necessarily saying something's wrong," he said of his pitching. "But you have to fix it." If nothing was wrong, what would there be to fix? He wasn't necessarily saying everything was right, either. His performance was judged by Bochy and others to be better than in his last few starts, but something did indeed need fixing—even if the truth of Burrell's Law held, that projecting recent performance onto the future is a terrible idea.

Pass the Torch Right Back

Fortunately for the Giants, they had Matt Cain to bolster them.

No starting rotation, however imposing it might seem, will benefit from each member pitching at his peak for very long. That's a product of natural ebb and flow, not just of the season but also personal performance. It's why a ballplayer who didn't excel frequently acknowledges a teammate who did by saying, "He picked me up." Successful teams thrive on an excess of such reciprocal efforts.

So now it was Cain's turn to pick up the Giants as well as Lincecum.

Beginning with a typically luckless 1-0 loss at Oakland on May 22—when he yielded an unearned run in eight innings yet fell to 2-4—Cain allowed merely two earned runs in a 41-inning stretch spanning five games. On May 28, he recorded his second career one-hit shutout in a 5-0 triumph over Arizona—then the league's highest-scoring team—launching a personal four-game winning streak.

On that Orange Friday, Cain faced only two batters over the minimum and retired the last 14 batters in a row. He stayed in perfect rhythm with Molina, letting the catcher artfully select the pitches, only shaking off one or two pitch selections the entire game. He dominated, while Freddy Sanchez again sparkled on defense.

"He just fires up everybody," Cain said of Sanchez. "When guys start making good plays early, it rubs off on everybody." The 5-0 win was a needed boost—as was every game during Cain's run of supreme dominance.

Cain's 0.44 ERA during this stretch appeared ridiculous—as ridiculous as the numbers of Ubaldo Jimenez—but the actual sight of him dominating opponents was nothing unusual. Numbers had never defined Cain, particularly when his run support had been so abysmal over the years. Since he'd reached the majors in August 2005, Cain had impressed others with his mere presence—quiet, mature, always in control. That summarized his demeanor both on and off the mound. "He acts like he's 30," Lincecum once said of Cain in amazement, as if attaining that age represented the height of wisdom.

The Giants dropped a 2-1, 11-inning decision the day after Jimenez topped Lincecum to fall to fourth place, but Cain put them back in third by working eight innings in a 4-1 triumph over the Rockies on June 2. He continued to accelerate the Giants' momentum. His fourth career shutout, a 3-0 win at Cincinnati on June 8, left San Francisco two games behind the division-leading Dodgers. His seven-inning, one-run effort against the A's on June 13 led the Giants to a 6-2 victory that left them one-and-a-half games out of first. Cain was proving himself as good as anyone anywhere, and developing the depth of composure under tight, tough circumstances is the best training available for pitching in the playoffs. Again, the Giants were getting something started, whether or not the places were unlikely.

The odd truth of the team's tight, tough circumstances is that it was tempering them perfectly for the pressures of championship play. Their challenges in eking out wins were giving them constant readiness and toughness out of necessity. Had they been more physically dominant, they might not have become as mentally honed. The pressures were fusing deeper bonds and preparing to give greater rewards. Through the late May and June stretch when they went 15-7, they were plenty able despite ragged edges. There were signs of life—signs of readiness for anything. If only there wasn't the truth of Burrell's Law yet to contend with.

Readiness and Relief

It isn't just bench players who have to always be ready in case of unexpected need for their services. The same mindset applies to relief pitchers, who don't have the luxury of starters' set schedule. It helps to have a generally defined situational role; as a former catcher, Bruce Bochy understood that and practiced developing clear roles for relievers. It had helped him build a reliable relief corps when managing the San Diego Padres, and now he was repeating that success in San Francisco. Despite injuries, the Giants relief corps was solidifying, and knowing their roles was one reason why.

The Giants relief pitchers steadily established themselves during the spring surge. Right-hander Santiago Casilla replaced the injured Brandon Medders and allowed one run in his first 15 appearances while striking out 20 batters. After yielding five runs in his first three May appearances, Sergio Romo went unscored upon in 15 of his next 16 outings. Brian Wilson was pitching like an All-Star, blanking opponents in 25 of his first 29 appearances and recording a 2.05 ERA.

Even knowing your role and performing it well doesn't prevent unexpected situations from arising, though. No one's role in the bullpen was more defined than that of Brian Wilson, who was fully installed as the closer and could therefore expect to pitch almost exclusively in the ninth inning when the Giants had a lead.

With this team, though, it might not be clear until the end when that would occur. With excellent pitching but little offense, the Giants were rarely far ahead or far behind. The game could change at any moment, which is one reason the games were so torturous to watch—and also so compelling, win or lose.

Thus Wilson, too, had to be prepared for the unexpected on a daily basis. "The one thing you can't do as a reliever is not be prepared to pitch," he said. "You can never do that with this team. It's always a close game no matter what."

He spoke this on the occasion of his 100th major league save on June 4, after the Giants came from behind against Pittsburgh, turning an early 4-0 deficit into a 6-4 victory. It was a milestone game for the Giants, but not so much because of Wilson's personal save number. (Said Wilson about his save total, "It's nice to harbor on for about five or 10 minutes, then it's back to work tomorrow.") It was critical because the Giants—then ranked 13th in home runs out of 16 National League teams—hit three of them. Their bats were beginning to awaken. Uribe and Huff hit classically long blasts, but the most important home run was the least dominant: Eli Whiteside got the comeback going with one in the fifth, on the 12th pitch of the at-bat off of Zach Duke, fouling off six consecutive 2-2 pitches before connecting. It was focused, persistent, clutch.

Two days later, the Giants again drew upon their bullpen depth—even when their best faltered. Still in Pittsburgh on June 6, Wilson failed to hold a 5-3 lead when Delwyn Young homered on a full-count pitch with two outs in the ninth. That followed a single by Ronny Cedeno, who had been hitless in his previous 20 at-bats. But the Giants inched ahead 6-5 in the 10th, before Wilson allowed a bloop single and walked the next hitter with one out. In came Casilla to record the next two outs and earn the save. You could almost hear Wilson say of Casilla, "He picked me up."

Contrast that with the Pirates, whose relievers allowed the Giants to break ties in each of the final two innings. Pittsburgh's trouble began when a left-hander named Javier Lopez mishandled Pablo Sandoval's grounder to open the ninth—not the last contribution Lopez would make to the Giants' cause. Readiness and relief would still keep coming from the strangest places.

Sacrifice and Bittersweet Returns

In the win over Pittsburgh, the Giants didn't help their own cause when they left 14 runners on base and went 2-for-13 with runners in scoring position, prompting Bochy to flash his dry wit afterward. "Did we win?" he asked.

They did, their winning run provided by Freddy Sanchez, who scored Andres Torres on the team's fourth sacrifice fly of the night, tying a team record.

In using sacrifice flies as the primary offensive weapon, the Giants won according to the principle of service over self-interest that Bochy preached. It fit with the Bochy Paradox that had been laid out at the beginning of the year. ("You have to set aside your own self-interests sometimes if you want to get what you want.") Again, the Giants were succeeding in doing that. They were finding a way, even if it was a Giants Way that Bill Neukom would never think to put in a memo.

For Freddy Sanchez, who drove in the winning run with the final sacrifice fly that night, playing against Pittsburgh surely brought forth mixed emotions. Sanchez had played for the Pirates, thrived there and wanted to stay with the team until retirement—a rare sentiment on a franchise mired in an 18-year run of losing teams. But the increased freedom of the free-agency era had a double edge: Where it had once been impossible to leave a team, now it might sometimes be impossible to stay. It wasn't just players who had more freedom, in that sense—teams did as well, when contracts ended, agents demanded exorbitant money or situations otherwise changed. They could find other help. For whatever reasons, it didn't work out for Sanchez to return to the Pirates; he had to sacrifice his initial vision and move on to the Giants. Now he was back in Pittsburgh, and with smaller sacrifice, gifting his former teammates with a loss. Bittersweet, most likely.

That bittersweet feeling was one Bengie Molina would come to know before the World Series was over.

Effective, Not Excessive

Despite the offensive lapses that caused Bochy to inquire if they had indeed won, the Giants' offense made an impact during the surge. It was effective without being excessive. Starting with Cain's June 2 victory, San Francisco scored at least four runs in nine of 13 games, hardly a record-setting volume or pace. But the Giants won eight of those games, reflecting general manager Brian Sabean's belief that four runs often would suffice for the pitching-rich Giants.

Burrell helped fuel the surge by proving he still could hit. He finished June with a .338 average in 22 games, garnished by five homers and 11 RBIs. Moreover, Burrell wasn't proving a defensive liability in left field, particularly because Bochy usually replaced him around the seventh inning of games the Giants led. In would come Schierholtz to play right field. Huff, who played mostly right field while Posey manned first base, moved to left. "The Thinker" kept thinking effectively.

Huff, Burrell's buddy, generated ample offense by driving in 19 runs and scoring 16 in June, both team highs. Huff never hid his frustration at losing extra-base hits and home runs at AT&T Park, where drives smashed by pull-hitting left-handed batters such as him were rendered meaningless by the dimensions in right and right-center field, along with the 25-foot–high wall in right. But by year's end, Huff would have 12 home runs at home, only two fewer than he hit on the road. He supplied two of his AT&T Park long balls on June 13 as the Giants completed a three-game sweep of the A's, avenging Oakland's sweep the previous month.

Posey helped give the Giants that dramatically different look. He batted .429 while hitting safely in 12 of his first 13 games. Also, he handled first base in smooth and occasionally spectacular style, maintaining his coexistence with Molina nicely.

"He looks more and more comfortable over there," Bochy said of Posey. "He's only going to get better with playing time there. It's not easy when you haven't played first base a lot, but he's athletic and he's shown that in the plays he has made."

Also, Juan Uribe maintained his knack for getting the maximum from the minimum. Uribe hit only .242 in June but ranked second on the team, with 17 RBIs for the month. Bochy stated that Uribe "without question" merited All-Star consideration. "To me, he *is* an All-Star," Bochy said. "You look at his numbers and the way he has played shortstop. He's a very strong candidate."

Juan Uribe was a true center of both the offense and the confidence. He was on pace to reach 100 RBIs—although pace is a useless number, a projection subject to the failings of Burrell's Law.

Aubrey Huff called Uribe the team's MVP to that point in the season. "He's just been tremendous," Huff said. "You can't write it up better. He's been pretty much a platoon guy his whole life and comes in and gets a chance to play every day, and he's taking advantage of it. He's going up there and driving in a lot of big runs in clutch situations." Uribe had returned to the Giants for a second one-year contract after few, if any, other teams had shown interest in his services. He was another castoff, another who was a misfit no longer.

No matter the opinions of Bochy, Huff and the rest of the Giants, Uribe was not even on the All-Star ballot since no one had predicted his success at that level—or even his regular place in the lineup. And, just as in wider politics, a successful write-in campaign was highly unlikely. Uribe's success would have to be appreciated in the San Francisco shadows. The cheers in the stands would have to do. "Ooooooo!!!" would keep being answered with "Rrrriiiibayyyy!!!" That spoke loudly enough.

The annual All-Star balloting process makes the country's political balloting look positively upstanding in comparison. In 2010, each fan was allowed to vote 25 times—something that only happens in, say, occasional mayoral races in Chicago. Fans can vote for the starting eight, which often means a hometown popularity contest as much as it does merit. The All-Star manager (whose team was last year's league champion) has control of most of the bench players and pitching staff, which helps to correct any voting inequity. Then there's a fan vote-off for the "final player," the last roster spot left to be determined after the dust of the voting and appointing has cleared. That, too, can involve multiple if not massive chances to vote and more hometown scrambling. Democracy is a very strange, multiheaded beast.

By being effective but not excessive, the Giants were not within striking range of getting any starting players onto the All-Star team in July. Aubrey Huff was having a fine year at first base and in the outfield, but there was no chance of him besting Ryan Howard of the Phillies in the voting process—whether or not Barry Bonds kept giving Howard advice. Not many other Giants were even in the running. Bruce Bochy had been named as a coach by manager Charlie Manuel, so he would provide representation there—and the rule that each team had to have at least one player on the All-Star squad would necessitate requesting the presence of one of the Giants. In the end, both Tim Lincecum and Brian Wilson would be selected, despite Lincecum's struggles. From the Giants' perspective, it was an All-Star game that would primarily be remembered for shoes. But the game was still a few weeks away, and the best part of the All-Star break for the majority of players is that it would be three days off in the middle of a grueling season. The Giants were more focused on team goals, and the primary goal was to reach the playoffs.

Uribe now rated the Giants as very strong candidates to advance into the postseason. His tenure with the Chicago White Sox, the 2005 World Series champions, indicated to him that the Giants had the same mettle.

Said Uribe, "I'm not thinking *maybe* we're going to the playoffs. I think this team *is* going to the playoffs. I believe in this team."

Walking Tall

After the Giants moved on from Pittsburgh, a series-opening victory at Cincinnati on June 7 strengthened Uribe's conviction. The surprising Reds were leading the National League Central Division, with former Giants manager Dusty Baker at the helm. The four-game series was a major test for the Giants—and for Buster Posey, who would get his first start at catcher to open the series, with Zito on the mound.

The opener was one of those beautifully balanced games in which everyone contributed. Uribe's four RBIs—a personal season-high to that point—paced the team's 6-5 win, but each Giant in the starting lineup collected at least one hit. That included Barry Zito, who served a two-run single into left field with two outs in the second inning.

Zito later praised Posey's presence behind the plate; the two had a rhythm right away. Zito had good stuff but left a few breaking balls hanging in inadvisable places, coming out losing after giving up five runs in 5 2/3 innings. The Giants managed to get him off the hook with two quick answering runs in the seventh and four relievers—Sergio Romo, Santiago Casilla, Guillermo Mota and Brian Wilson—who, in another superb hitless effort for the next 3 1/3 innings, combined to close it out. Romo initiated that hitless stretch by fanning Orlando Cabrera to strand a pair of Reds base runners in the sixth.

That stretch remained hitless only because of the defensive wizardry of Andres Torres, who was establishing himself as one of the finest fielders in the league. His speed gave him extreme range and an ability to make spectacular catches, even if his routes to the ball were sometimes a little unusual. The first batter Wilson faced in the ninth, Ramon Hernandez, crushed one to left that first looked like a game-tying homer or a sure double, only to find Torres making a leaping, twisting catch at full speed just in front of the fence.

Torres had reason to walk tall—as did the bullpen, as did Posey, as did the whole Giants team as they beat the Reds in the first two games of the series.

Catching for Profit

When Buster Posey hit his first major league home run off Aaron Harang of the Reds on June 9, he was unable to walk across enough water or change enough water into wine to keep the Giants from losing to the Reds 6-3. The only "Jesus Christ" anyone might have uttered was as an epithet under the breath as Jonathan Sanchez's control unraveled—and the Giants' along with it. (Bochy did his best to stay positive but only found faint praise for Sanchez. "Really, it was a pretty good effort, despite his not having his stuff and command," he said. Molina's comments about Lincecum learning to pitch with what he had also applied to Sanchez.)

Posey was expected by some to have insufficient power to hit many home runs in the majors, but his first one traveling 439 feet into the second deck was a strong statement that doubters were wrong. Even in a hitters' park, few hit them there.

As is the case with firsts (and with large round numbers), Posey sought and got the ball back as a souvenir. Generously, the fan who'd caught it only asked for an autographed ball from Posey in return.

"Most of the time, they want the keys to your car," said a grateful Posey.

The next day, the Giants lost a second consecutive time to the Reds, playing the four-game series to a draw. It was time to go home, keys in hand, to avenge previous losses to the Oakland A's.

Different Now

By the time the Oakland A's were taking their turn to cross the Bay Bridge and visit the Giants in their home, a great deal had shifted since the A's had swept them in May.

"We're a totally different team," opined Aubrey Huff.

The first game featured Lincecum's return to Cy Young form (had he continued his decline, Lincecum might have had to rename his French bulldog, Cy). After suffering through a stretch of winless starts with a 6.85 ERA—his only consistency being five walks per game—Lincecum regained his mojo. Or his stuff. Or both.

He had rebounded from the dispiriting Memorial Day loss to Colorado with a capable outing in the June 6 game at Pittsburgh (seven innings, three runs, six hits, six strikeouts). Then came three wins in a row, beginning with this 6-2 victory on June 11 against the A's.

Lincecum started slowly by throwing two wild pitches in the first inning—and then settling down to retire 16 of the next 17 batters, only walking one and striking out seven. In eight assertive innings, Lincecum didn't hesitate to use his fastball, velocity (or lack of it) be damned. "I just felt like I was hitting my spots when I needed to," he said. "If I got behind a guy 2-0, I wasn't scared to throw a fastball in the zone. I just relaxed, remembered I could do it and quit doubting myself."

In his first home game as a Giant, Pat Burrell returned to the region of his youth with a booming home run—his first for the team—and Bengie Molina broke out with one of his own.

"We're not trying to [make] these series the key to the season, but we remember what happened over there [in Oakland]," Molina said. "We were all pumped to face those guys. Hopefully tomorrow we bring the same intensity."

They did. Barry Zito finally beat his former team at last, for the first time in his career, giving up two solo home runs but turning in a solid seven innings. After other relievers faltered to begin the eighth, Brian Wilson came in to escape a bases-loaded, one-out situation without damage—and then created a mess of his own in the ninth before extricating himself from it once more, sending observers into familiar paroxysms before emerging victorious.

"I don't even think about the failure option," Wilson said. Others did.

This time, Bruce Bochy did not mention his grave or Wilson's role in putting him there early. He merely singled him out for a job extremely well-done in a tough circumstance. That had become the essence of Wilson's bottom line.

The Giants finished off the A's the next day with both power and pitching as Aubrey Huff homered twice, Jose Uribe once, and Matt Cain continued his mound dominance in a 6-2 win. With the fans dancing with their brooms, the Giants brought themselves within one-and-a-half games of the first-place Padres—the closest they'd been in weeks. Close to first place, yet far away from it, still. The toughest goals are often the ones just out of reach.

Out of Reach, out of Character

Meanwhile in Fresno, the major leagues were still just out of reach for Giants phenom Madison Bumgarner. He was regaining results after his disastrous springtime with the Giants, and his performance with the Fresno Grizzlies was promising—but just then, he had a blowup that quickly hit YouTube and the other buzz networks. After arguing a call on a pickoff attempt at second base, Bumgarner was ejected from the game and had to be held back from the umpires by his teammates. As he was escorted from the field, still angry, he turned and threw the ball into the outfield. He was fined by the Pacific Coast League and suspended for three days.

It wasn't a graceful moment, but the event's significance was downplayed by the Giants, who respected his intensity. However, when Todd Wellemeyer sustained an injury while running, it was Joe Martinez rather than Bumgarner the Giants called up to start against Baltimore. Many wondered whether the Giants would press Bumgarner into major league service before his 21st birthday.

Halloween in June

After Oakland, Baltimore came to town as interleague play continued. Many traditionalists still considered interleague play a somewhat blasphemous concept, a violation of history, statistics and The Way Things Ought to Be. In part, the idea was intended to fuel cross-town rivalries: A's-Giants, Cubs–White Sox, Yankees-Mets, Angels-Dodgers. In those cases, it made sense, and the games were often well-attended by boisterous crowds.

However, scheduling necessities made for some interleague matchups that drew only yawns. The Baltimore Orioles vs. the San Francisco Giants? There was no rivalry there whatsoever. They played in opposite leagues on opposite coasts and shared almost no history. They hadn't played each other in six years. Furthermore, Baltimore was suffering through the worst half of one of their worst years ever, coming to town with a pitiful record. (They would leave town 18-48.) What excitement could there possibly be?

Their primary connection was they both featured orange and black uniforms. So the Giants decided the first game of the series would be Halloween in June, with the team breaking out their Orange Friday jerseys on a Monday, and fans were encouraged to come in Halloween costumes to be judged before the game. If the Orioles kept losing, their uniform would presumably be considered a costume soon enough.

The horror in the Fright Night was all on the Orioles as the Giants crushed them 10-2 behind a solid outing from Jonathan Sanchez, another home run from Pat Burrell, quite a lot of other offense and four consecutive ugly walks in the eighth from a Baltimore pitcher, who (for his own protection) shall remain anonymous. Winning for the 14th time in their past 20 games and improving to 6-0 while wearing their orange jerseys, the Giants drew within half a game of the Padres at the top, tying the Dodgers for second. A race was developing.

Although the Giants would drop the next game, with Joe Martinez on the mound, the Giants decisively won the series with another crushing win in the third game, behind back-to-back home runs from Huff and Uribe—their second such feat in a week—and another resurgent performance from Tim Lincecum.

The lowly Orioles nagged Lincecum, collecting eight hits and four walks against him. But he yielded only two runs and struck out 10. He also impressed Hall of Fame right-hander Jim Palmer, the Baltimore broadcaster who praised Lincecum's ability to use multiple pitches. "People think that when you win Cy Young Awards, you have to be perfect," said Palmer, an eight-time 20-game winner. "It's not about the radar gun. At the end of the day, if you lose velocity, it's not like you have to jump overboard. You want to know how the batters are reacting to you, and if you still have three or four pitches, it can be pretty comfortable."

The final out Lincecum recorded was anything but comfortable, however. It brought Fright Night back, as Miguel Tejada screamed a line drive up the middle and off of a diving Lincecum's pitching shoulder. The ball caromed to Freddy Sanchez at second, who threw to first for the out while Lincecum lay flat on the pitcher's mound.

"I was more kind of shocked than anything," Lincecum said. "I knew it hit me and I didn't know what to do, so I kind of just laid there." He was unhurt, and the Bay Area breathed a collective sigh of relief. Halloween in June was over.

A Different Dedication

Matt Cain did not pitch against Baltimore, but he still had an important team duty during the series, which was as much a part of the Giants Way as anything.

As part of an ongoing community effort, the Giants Community Fund organizes the Junior Giants, a youth baseball league for at-risk boys and girls that offers alternatives to such disreputable behavior as drugs, gangs and rooting for the Dodgers.

The Junior Giants now comprise more than 17,000 players in California, Nevada and Oregon. Across those three states, boys and girls ages five to 18 play in 85 noncompetitive leagues for free. Instead of competition, the Junior Giants focus on character development in four areas: confidence, integrity, leadership and teamwork—all, incidentally, competitive keys to winning.

The Giants Community Fund has built fields where possible for the Junior Giants. The Peter A. Magowan Fields for Kids program—named after the former Giants president and managing general partner—has made it possible to fully refurbish over twenty youth baseball fields. Many of the fields were partly sponsored by and named for Giants stars in the process. In the midst of the Baltimore series, Matt Cain took time to dedicate the latest field, the Matt Cain Junior Giants Field in Sacramento. It was an emotional ceremony, with all of the players remembering their first fields and the central role those fields had played in making their major league dreams come true.

Even if there is no direct path to the majors for the Junior Giants playing there, it's still a path to exercise, healthy release of energy and fun. For any who call sports a frivolity, they only need look at the alternatives for at-risk kids to reconsider. The Junior Giants program does not need to produce a single professional baseball player to succeed—the very act of engaging these kids in a productive, confidence-building activity is a success.

As of 2010, more than 6,000 Junior Giants did not have fielding gloves, and most come from families who cannot afford them. Every year, the Giants sponsor a Glove Drive, in which fans donate gloves (or money to buy them) to assist with the effort. Fans bring gloves to AT&T Park as a donation, and in 2010, fans donated nearly 1,000 gloves and $37,000 at the Giants/Red Sox interleague game on June 25th.

This was subtly risky scheduling, for another of the last remaining knuckleballers was scheduled to pitch that day, the 44-year-old Tim Wakefield. Presumably, no one would tell the kids receiving gloves that using them to attempt to catch a knuckleball would be somewhere between frustrating and useless. "The best way to catch a knuckleball is to wait until the ball stops rolling and pick it up," former catcher Bob Uecker famously said. No, best to leave the little tykes to someday find out for themselves. Reality would be along to hit them with a high inside fastball soon enough. Then again, it already had. That's why the Junior Giants leagues had been so vital to them in the first place.

The Baseball Gods Control It

After Baltimore left town, the Giants did, too. It was on to Toronto, where in backwards fashion, the Giants won only the game they played poorly, while losing two tightly played pitchers' duels. So it goes in the strange game of baseball, and enough said.

Then came a return to Houston, and—what else?—a defeat of Roy Oswalt by Tim Lincecum, his third of the year in as many starts against the Houston ace. Just one unearned run impeded Lincecum during his eight-inning stroll at Minute Maid Park, meaning that in three 2010 games against Oswalt, Lincecum allowed just one earned run total in 23 innings—an ERA of 0.39.

Similar as their styles and skills were, the two pitchers' records in their six career head-to-head meetings now diverged sharply:

Lincecum: 4-0, 0.85 ERA.

Oswalt: 1-4, 3.07 ERA.

Lincecum didn't try to explain his success against Oswalt. "The baseball gods control it," he said.

Allowing seven hits tempered Lincecum's satisfaction. "It seems to be a battle every time out there," he said. "I kind of want it to be a little more simple and give up less hits." If only increasing simplicity was really that simple.

Nonetheless, this 3-1 victory on June 22 improved the Giants' record to 39-30, matching their season-best above-.500 total. A compelling race—Brian Wilson would say "delicious"—was developing in the NL West. San Diego led the Giants by one-and-a-half games, followed by Los Angeles and Colorado, three and four games back, respectively.

The Giants were 7-0 against the Astros, with two games left in the series. With Zito (7-3) and Cain (6-5) scheduled to pitch, it was easy to envision that the Giants would win at least once more before returning to San Francisco for what promised to be a rousing home stand—three interleague games against the Boston Red Sox, followed by three games against the Dodgers. With a 24-12 record thus far at AT&T Park, the Giants had maintained the knack for winning at home they'd revived during the previous season. (They were 52-29 at home in 2009, after finishing below .500 by the Bay in three of the previous four seasons.)

Surely, the Giants were in excellent position to advance their cause. But the baseball gods control it. And Oswalt would find a way to face the Giants again.

Wounded, Yet Fine

During the spring surge, injuries disrupted the Giants' momentum only minimally. On June 16, shortstop Edgar Renteria returned from his second stint on the disabled list and went 8-for-18 in his first five games, lifting his batting average from .326 to .346. Assuming Renteria stayed healthy and productive, Bochy would be forced daily to bench somebody worthy of starting: Posey (if Sandoval played first base and Uribe played third), Freddy Sanchez (if Uribe played second base), Sandoval (if Posey played first and Uribe manned third), Uribe (if Bochy found no room for the super-utility man) or Renteria himself (if Bochy wanted to rest him).

An injury announcement that had been anticipated for weeks became official on June 22, when the Giants announced that Mark DeRosa would undergo season-ending surgery on his left wrist.

DeRosa's wrist had never healed properly after having surgery last October for an injury he suffered in mid-season 2009. The Giants had coped without their opening day left fielder, who hit .194 in 26 games and hadn't played since May 8. But their uneven offensive production left them wondering whether they could have avoided such fluctuations had DeRosa stayed healthy.

Also, after right-hander Todd Wellemeyer, the No. 5 starter, strained his right quadriceps in Cincinnati on June 10, further shifts would be necessitated. He wouldn't pitch again until Aug. 8. By then, the Giants had changed to a rotation that would become permanent.

With all of the continued changes, "The Thinker" would probably need aspirin to keep his mind from suffering an injury of its own.

Father's Day

There was a moment for a different kind of reflection as the June calendar brought Father's Day around. Although there was no Father's Day field ceremony as obvious as on pink Mother's Day, Giants reliever Dan Runzler took time to speak about the influence his father Terry had on his development into a baseball player whose mental approach was as refined and balanced as his physical one.

Terry was not a coach for his son and did not push him to be a major leaguer. He stayed away from the overbearing intensity that infects too many Little League fathers, whose intensity can backfire and turn into a son's suffering and rebellion.

"That was something that kept me motivated to play, because he never burned it out," Dan said. "He wanted me to play the game right, but he wanted to make sure I was having fun."

By playing the game right, he meant always respecting the game and his teammates as well as keeping enjoyment alongside discipline. In that, Terry Runzler perfectly if unintentionally mimicked the approach Bochy later brought to the Giants. Dan Runzler already had known and practiced that approach since childhood.

Dan recalled being chided by his father after not running hard to first after hitting a ground ball, back in sixth grade. "[If] you disrespect the game, you disrespect your teammates," his dad told him. The lesson stuck: Giving every effort at all times is the only way to honor your teammates—and the integrity of the game.

Terry Runzler also impressed upon his son the need to stay in the moment—the same principle Buddhism teaches as a key to mindfulness in all aspects of living. Dan now recalled that as a key element of his influence. "I feel like he was a big part of my mental game," Dan reflected. "Not how to throw or hit, but how to battle. Realizing you can't carry every at-bat, every appearance, everything with you, every time you'd go out there. Because I'd get upset at a young age if I didn't get a hit. He'd say, 'Well, you have a lot of at-bats coming.' We talked about mentally flushing the last appearance or the last at-bat that I had, whatever it was, even if it was good. You can't sit there and hold onto it, which is what I try to carry over into the game right now."

His father also taught him the necessity of equanimity in demeanor. As the younger Runzler put it, "When people look at you, they shouldn't be able to know the score of the game. If you're getting your teeth kicked in, you should still look like you're winning 4-0, pitching with confidence."

"He's a huge part of where I am today. Not even as a player, but as a man," Dan continued, summarizing his father's deep influence. "I learned a lot from him. He's just a caring, solid, good guy. I want to carry that on for our family, so I do really respect him. He's one of my closest friends. I'm very fortunate to have him and my mom, [Debbie], in my life."

There is no overstating how important a solid family background can be to becoming a good player, a good teammate, a good person. And Runzler had become a very good player indeed. He was at the opposite end of the spectrum from Andres Torres and Eli Whiteside when it came to the climb through the minors. Whereas their ascent had been glacial, his was meteoric. In 2009, the left-handed pitcher started out near the lowest level of the Giants farm system, with the low Class A team in Augusta, Georgia. When he was overly dominant there, he was moved up to the higher Class A league—the San Jose farm team in California. Thriving there, too, he was quickly bumped up to Double A and shipped off to Connecticut. That also proved too low, so he was suddenly back in California, on the Fresno Grizzlies in Triple A, the highest level of the minors. Even then, his success was beyond the league's capacity. In total, Runzler's minor league numbers for 2009 were astounding: His combined ERA was 0.76, and he struck out 83 batters in only 59 innings, losing just one game in four leagues. So he next found himself in the big leagues with the Giants, where he appeared in 11 games and held a beautiful 1.04 ERA at season's end. Five levels of pro baseball, from bottom to top, all in one year—the first Giant on record to ever do that. All stints were successful to the point of amazement. As a hard-throwing, left-handed reliever with strength and size—6 feet 4 inches and 230 pounds—Runzler was a rare commodity, and the Giants welcomed his presence. He was another unexpected arrival, on no one's radar at the beginning of 2009. Now he was vital in 2010.

But solid family background and pitching success don't necessarily make a man a good hitter in any given at-bat. In the only at-bat Dan Runzler would take all year, the results would be devastating—yet would have side effects that brought good fortune to the Giants. Good news, bad news: one is rarely completely devoid of the other.

The Pressure of Time (Part Two)

The end of June and the end of the spring surge also saw the realization of the Giants' commitment to honor Hall of Famer Monte Irvin, the first African-American Giant. At 91 years old, Irvin was not only a father figure to the Giants, but a grandfather figure, a living legend. Yet as the celebration approached, Irvin, too, credited his own father as a reason why he (like Jackie Robinson) was selected as a man whose character could withstand racist abuse.

"My father always said to treat people the way you want to be treated," Irvin said, adding, "I live by the Golden Rule and do everything in moderation. I've been lucky enough so far."

At his honoring ceremony before an interleague game against the Red Sox on June 26, Irvin was wheeled onto the field in a vintage turquoise-and-white convertible (complete with fuzzy dice hanging from the mirror). Of sound mind but fragile body, he was assisted to the center of the diamond, where other equal legends awaited him: Willie Mays, Willie McCovey, Juan Marichal, Gaylord Perry and Orlando Cepeda.

Irvin's mentoring of Mays has frequently been mentioned among his contributions that transcended statistics—especially as Mays proved to be another one who kept his grace under pressure. It was a long Giants tradition that Irvin was a part of, an aspect of the Giants Way long before that term had been coined.

"The man knew how to rise to the occasion," said Jon Miller, citing Irvin's .394 lifetime World Series batting average as he introduced the legend to the Giants crowd.

Irvin was still able to rise to this occasion, the Hall of Famers surrounding him as orange-and-black balloons were released to the sky. He mentioned that one of his few disappointments was not being able to play in San Francisco, saying what a pleasure it was to be there now. "At my age," he joked, "it's a pleasure to be anywhere."

The ceremony was beautiful and complete, and so was Irvin's career, his No. 20 forever retired. Still, Irvin had one remaining base-ball-related ambition, which he had shared a couple of days earlier.

"I'd like to live long enough to see the Giants win another pennant and World Series," he said.

With Irvin in his fragile nineties, there was indeed the pressure of time—as the Giants' opponents that day knew too well. The Red Sox had to wait 86 years from winning one World Series to the next. For Irvin's sake, the Giants had no time to do the same. But again, seasons are like relationships: Just when you think you know it, it becomes something else again.

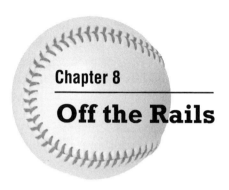

Chapter 8

Off the Rails

Magic Dissipates

After the third Lincecum-Oswalt duel of 2010 was over, so was the spring surge. Whatever express track the Giants appeared to be on suddenly became rusty rails that disappeared into the weeds.

One mystery of baseball is how suddenly magic dissipates, how success appears and disappears like apparitions in the fog. The night after Lincecum's magic dominated Oswalt, Barry Zito's vanished. In his shortest outing of the year, Zito gave up five runs in four innings—with four of the runs coming in rallies that started with two outs and no one on base. Two of them included key hits by Astros pitcher Brett Myers, who entered the game hitting a pathetic .038.

"A squirrel finds his nut every now and then," said Myers. "I guess I got lucky." Squirrels find their nuts considerably more often than .038 of the time. And the Giants needed to find their nuts in a hurry, so to speak.

Although the Giants made part of the early 5-0 deficit disappear, they continued to strand runners and left Minute Maid Park 6-3 losers in a game better forgotten.

The next night, Matt Cain's magic was the next to vanish. He was absolutely clobbered by the Astros and came out losing 7-0 in the bottom of the third, ending a beautiful six-start run with an 0.92 ERA. After his first bad day in a long, long time, his season ERA rose in one ugly evening from 2.16 to 2.72, knocking him out of the league's top five.

Every pitcher has such days on occasion, but you can't begin to anticipate them. As Cain pointed out, "You don't sit there and wait for a bad day to come," he said. "You keep going out there like you're going to pitch well or you're going to hit well."

The Giants didn't hit well enough to erase a seven-run deficit, though the promise was there. They managed to get not only the leadoff batter on base in each of the fourth through seventh innings, but the first *two* batters—only to hit into double plays three times in a row within that four-inning span.

"Nobody's trying to hit into them," Bochy said, stating the obvious.

Double plays were such a problem that it could turn into a mental issue as well as a physical one. Cain's thoughts about not waiting for a bad day also applied to this, as Bochy elaborated. "I don't want them to get in their minds where they're thinking *not* to hit into one. That's going to compound the problem." The problem was bad enough as it was.

Little by little in that game, the Giants scratched back anyway, beginning with another Pat Burrell home run (his sixth already) in the fourth. They eventually climbed back to within two, while a parade of five relievers combined in beautiful style to only allow the Astros two hits over the final 5 1/3 innings after Cain departed. Still, the ending 7-5 score was a loss, and the Giants left town having dropped a series to a team with one of the poorer records in the league.

At least the Giants found a believer in Astros star Lance Berkman, who saw through the vanishing of their magic. "This is a tough team," he said. "I expect they're going to be in contention the whole year."

It was time for the Giants to go home and face Boston, one of the American League's perpetually strongest teams.

Transition and Transformation

Magic didn't exactly begin the series against the Red Sox and Tim Wakefield's maddening knuckleball, but all's well that ends well, especially for the Junior Giants, who received plenty of donations during the Glove Drive that day and did not have to catch Wakefield's knuckleball themselves.

A wild Jonathan Sanchez needed 37 pitches to survive the top of the first inning alone, by which time the Giants were already in a 3-0 hole after a three-run homer by Kevin Youkilis. But the Giants—skilled and fortunate in their Orange Friday jerseys once more—clawed back to tie the score, beginning with an RBI single from Buster Posey, later followed by an RBI bunt single by Jonathan Sanchez himself that Jon Miller called "the best bunt of his career."

Sanchez and his high pitch count only made it until the top of the sixth, by which point the Giants were clinging to a 4-3 lead. Things only got more torturous from there. Sergio Romo came in to successfully leave the bases loaded with Red Sox that inning. Santiago Casilla then managed in the seventh to pull off the difficult feat of walking three batters and throwing three wild pitches in the same inning—without allowing a run. A clean-shaven Brian Wilson came on during the eighth and stranded two more. With the Giants then leading 5-3 going into the ninth—thanks to a very necessary clutch home run by Juan Uribe—Wilson gave up a triple, two walks and a single, so the lead was only 5-4 and the bases once again loaded with two outs in the ninth. Torture, sheer torture. But with the game on the line, Darnell McDonald grounded out to Uribe at short to end it. Despite walking 10 batters and throwing four wild pitches, the Giants were in the win column. It wasn't pretty, but it was successful. Style isn't an official statistic in baseball.

Before the next game, the Giants sent pitcher Joe Martinez back to Triple-A Fresno; he'd lasted exactly one outing as the fifth starter. The Giants admired Martinez, who showed toughness after being struck in the head by a Mike Cameron line drive in the 2009 season's third game. (Martinez sustained a concussion and three hairline fractures but healed in time to appear in seven late-season outings.) But in 2010, his usage after his spot start in Baltimore was limited and did not align well with the starting schedule. He had only been called up to fill in for the injured Todd Wellemeyer, who proved a conundrum even when healthy. (As the No. 5 starter, Wellemeyer would finish the season with a 3-1 record and a 2.97 ERA at home, compared with 0-4, 10.07 on the road.)

Neither Martinez nor Wellemeyer could match the skill and potential of the Giants' top pitching prospect—Madison Bumgarner, who was called up to replace Martinez in the team's next key moment of transition and transformation.

When the Giants brought up Bumgarner, he was still well short of his 21st birthday and only weeks removed from his angry outburst in Fresno. Having experienced the hubbub of getting married in the offseason and the heartache of his half-sister's death during spring training, Bumgarner had weathered the distractions. He had been ineffective in spring training, striking out none of the 35 batters he faced in three Cactus League exhibitions. But he steadily righted himself and regained his rhythm through the routine of the regular season. He also improved his command of his slider and a "cut" fastball, superb complements for any pitcher. At the time he was summoned to San Francisco, Bumgarner's record was a very respectable 7-1 with a 3.16 ERA in 14 starts for Fresno.

Bringing up Madison Bumgarner—inescapably saddled with "Mad Bum" as a nickname—completed the presumed battery of the future, with Bumgarner on the mound and Buster Posey behind the plate for the second game against the Red Sox.

Bumgarner was nervous. At 20, who wouldn't be?

In the first inning, Darnell McDonald (who had ended the previous game in failure) planted a pitch from Bumgarner in the bleachers. Mike Cameron followed in the second with his first home run of the year, a three-run shot, and the Giants and Bumgarner were once again in a shutout hole early: 4-0 after two. Bumgarner and his admitted nerves then settled down beautifully, retiring 16 of the next 17 Red Sox. Still, it was too late for this day. The Giants could only muster six hits off of eight Red Sox pitchers—nearly the whole staff, after starter Clay Buchholz hyperextended his left knee and left after one inning. It was a quiet 4-2 loss, no matter how much it heralded a better future. The baseball gods were teasing the Giants.

Boston's pitcher of record over Bumgarner and the Giants was Scott Atchison, who hadn't pitched in the majors since 2007, when he made 22 appearances for—you guessed it—the Giants. After that, Atchison proceeded to Japan's Central League and a two-year stint with the Hanshin Tigers.

The unassuming Atchison wasn't vengefully trying to splinter the Giants' bats. He did admit, however, "It's fun to face your former team. It gets you excited a little bit. I think it'd be like that for anybody."

Still, the Giants sensed that Bumgarner setting down 16 of 17 was no fluke. They hoped he was ready to advance towards the destiny envisioned for him when they drafted him in the first round in 2007.

"It would be ideal if he's our guy," Bochy said of Bumgarner. The kid himself said it would be "awesome" if that happened but wasn't willing to take anything but the moment for granted.

Like a Robot out There

Taking nothing for granted the next day was an even better idea as the teams closed the series. This was the marquee matchup—a Sunday showdown between Tim Lincecum, fresh off his latest masterful defeat of Roy Oswalt, and Red Sox ace Jon Lester. Often the best way to prevent something is to predict it, and that includes pitching duels. The Red Sox were developing a nasty habit of thrashing Cy Young winners, too. In their six previous 2010 games against pitchers with Cy to their credit, not one Cy pitcher had come away with a win.

Add one more. Lincecum had nothing from the start. Not velocity: His fastball was only in the high 80s by the time he was gone after three innings. Not control: He walked three in that short span. Not mechanics: He was off. He even fell behind pitcher Jon Lester—who had a total of 14 career at-bats—before Lester hit a 3-1 pitch with the bases loaded to the warning track for what was dangerously close to a grand slam. That it was "only" a sacrifice fly was small consolation.

Bochy pulled Lincecum after only three innings. "In my mind that was plenty, that was enough, he was done. His stuff just wasn't there." Bochy added, "He was fatigued. ... You could see him laboring, and at that point, it's not worth trying to get some more innings out of him." Bochy did not express any long-term concern about fatigue or other issues, simply calling it an "off day." They happen, even to the best.

Despite five Giants relievers putting in quality innings and largely shutting the Red Sox down, there was no closeness—no positive torture. The Giants could only find five hits against Lester, who pitched a solid complete game. The T-shirts in Boston could read *Let Lester Smoke Tim!* The Red Sox now left town with another Cy Young winner in their pocket, the Cy winners holding a collective 6.81 era against them.

Heading for the clubhouses after Boston's 5-1 victory, one underwhelmed Boston writer coldly declared that Lincecum should immediately undergo "Tommy John" elbow surgery, since that procedure conceivably could help him throw hard again.

Lincecum didn't sound as if he would resort to such measures, but he echoed the same incredulous questions observers were asking: "What's up with Timmy?"

Said Lincecum, "You don't think I go home saying the same thing to myself? At the same time, you go through these outings and—you don't accept it. You just get through it and try to bounce back."

Lincecum depends heavily on finding the right rhythm for his pitching motion. Lacking the right pace often dooms him to a poor performance. "I felt like I was a robot working out there," he said. "Things weren't moving smoothly, the way I wanted."

Things weren't moving smoothly for the whole Giants team, and then on came the Dodgers and Rockies.

"This is an important stretch," said Bochy. Fortunately, he was wrong.

Only Poetic Justice

The strange thing about rivalries—even such intense and long-standing ones as between the Giants and Dodgers—is that many times, the intensity of the rivalry is centered in the stands rather than on the field. Especially in the era of ever more mobile players—some would say "mercenaries"—it's the fans more than the players who have a long history with the rivalry. On the Giants, the longest-tenured player was still Matt Cain, in his sixth year with the team and yet a little short of his 26th birthday. There were many, many Giants fans who had been rooting passionately for the San Francisco team (and against the Los Angeles one) for far longer than Cain had even been alive. So even though a new player may instantly sense the rivalry and psych up for it, the intensity might not have had time to build inside.

In one sense, Bruce Bochy wasn't wrong that playing the Dodgers (and the Rockies to follow) was an important stretch. Playing division rivals—especially the Dodgers—is always important. There is extra intensity and significance in the standings, especially when the teams are in such a tight, delicious race. It's just that Bochy was wrong about the results of this particular series being vital to the outcome of the season. In fact, the outcome of the series could hardly have been worse—and the outcome of the season couldn't have been better.

The quirks of the unbalanced 2010 schedule meant the Giants had not faced the Dodgers since the early April series in which Vicente Padilla had beaned Aaron Rowand and Manny Ramirez had ended the match with a devastating home run. The Giants had a few scores to settle—and a chance to do it in their home park.

Unfortunately, what the Giants couldn't settle was their ability to score. They spent the next three games against the Dodgers with frustrating consistency, scoring exactly two runs per game—not enough, despite some fine pitching.

In the first game, an excellent effort by Barry Zito on the mound was wasted when the Giants hit into five double plays, eventually losing when Casey Blake hit a tie-breaking home run off of Santiago Casilla to seal the 4-2 loss. The Giants made a couple of key mistakes as well and ended up beating themselves as much as being beaten. To add further injury and insult, this loss allowed the Dodgers to take over second place from the Giants—and in the Giants' own temple, no less. Blasphemy!

Curses following the next night would be at least as blasphemous to sensitive ears. Matt Cain struggled in the first and fifth, and although he was close to a good outing, he wasn't quite there. Cain fell to a lifetime 0-8 against the Dodgers, a terrible record tempered by equally terrible run support over the years. The record books noted the second consecutive 4-2 Giants loss, both of which featured an egregious baserunning mistake by an overly aggressive Pablo Sandoval. It was a quiet crowd leaving AT&T Park, where the "Beat LA" chant began to seem more like a desperate prayer than a statement of likely outcome.

The third game of the series had the most heat around it, not only because the Giants needed to salvage something but also because it featured the rematch of Vicente Padilla and Aaron Rowand. There was the potential for conflict, with the unsettled score of Rowand's beaning still fresh in mind.

Unfortunately, Padilla shut down the Giants early, while the Dodgers built a 5-0 lead off of Jonathan Sanchez. That unsettling score included assistance from the Giants again as Pat Burrell's error in left turned a single into two key runs.

During the sixth, however, at least one score was settled properly. It's always best to settle with actions rather than words—particularly actions within the context of the game itself. Rowand came up against Padilla, and poetic justice was served when Rowand hit a fastball from Padilla over the fence to dead center field for a home run. That hit spoke eloquently for itself. It was on an excellent pitch—good velocity, low and outside, on the corner. Rowand beat Padilla at his best. He said nothing to Padilla as he rounded the bases and didn't even look at him. He didn't need to. He'd spoken the correct way.

"I gotta believe that felt real good for him," said Mike Krukow on the air. "Take the guy deep that broke your face."

Just to make sure the point was completely made, Santiago Casilla threw a wicked fastball behind Padilla when the Dodgers' pitcher came up to hit in the seventh. Message again silently delivered. As with Prince Fielder's previous antics, the Giants would not tolerate any damage done beyond baseball's unwritten code of ethics.

Poetic justice was only minor, though, when the Dodgers answered Rowand's home run with effective silence of their own, adding three runs in the seventh on the way to a lopsided 8-2 victory. The Giants were swept at home by their most-loathed rivals, and it wasn't even close. The Giants had to wear it and climb on the plane to Colorado, where the high-altitude atmosphere tends to treat visiting teams unkindly.

Homage to Bengie

The Giants bridged June and July with a season-high seven-game losing streak, increasing the necessity for a personnel change or two.

"We had issues with the club," one anonymous insider said. "I
don't think any of us felt like we were going to take off with the club
we had."

Initially, Bochy and general manager Brian Sabean indicated the
transition wouldn't be drastic. But a transition was indeed imminent.
On June 24, Bochy announced that Posey, the catcher of the future
who had started exactly once behind the plate since his recall from
Triple-A nearly one month earlier, would begin catching at least once
a week, if not once through the rotation.

Five days later, Sabean reiterated the Posey plan. At that time, Pablo Sandoval was spending some time at first base, meaning Posey
would have to catch in order to crack the lineup. "Which he will,"
Sabean said.

Less than 24 hours after Sabean made that remark, word leaked
that the Giants had traded Bengie Molina.

Whenever a favorite player is traded, a sense of betrayal always
ripples through the stands, for it's akin to selling off a family member. (Would you trade your own mother to Cleveland?) That sadness
and sense of betrayal remains even if that player is no longer the
central figure he once was—such as when the Giants traded Willie
Mays to the Mets at the close of his brilliant career.

In San Francisco, it felt that way again on June 30, when Molina
was traded to the Texas Rangers for reliever Chris Ray and a player
to be named later. Everyone knew the future was named Buster Posey, in that place behind the plate, but Bengie had been a true center
of the team since his arrival, whether as the catcher responsible for
the rise of Lincecum and Cain, as the cleanup hitter who could do
it when no one else could or as the consummate teammate on and
off the field. Bengie was revered for good reason. And one day, suddenly—without his own consent—he was gone.

Trade was always a possibility, but it still seemed to surprise and
wound the sensitive Molina. He did not return to San Francisco expecting to be traded. He was deeply invested in his teammates. He had
thrived in the city. He was deeply loyal in his life. He was the epitome
of the Giants Way. He was one of the disciples of their Good Book.

Shortly after being traded, Molina said, "When I was with the Giants, I became a brother. I became a father, sometimes. I became a
guy who took aside a lot of the young kids and talked to them about

not only baseball but life itself. And how difficult it is out there. I don't think I do it to show off, it just comes out natural for me. That's the person I am."

He had pursued that path even with his own potential rival. In January, after his surprise return to the Giants, Molina felt compelled to send a sympathetic text message to Posey, who might have been expecting to start.

"I told him I'm not here to take his spot," Molina said.

Posey appreciated Molina's professionalism and friendship. "He helped me a lot," Posey said. "It was a relationship I felt like from the get-go was pretty comfortable."

Molina's most important constituents, the pitchers, paid him the homage he deserved.

"He helped me mature and succeed. I've said time and time again that he deserves half of those awards that I've gotten," Tim Lincecum said.

"The things he's done for me—for calling a game, to give me confidence throwing different pitches in different counts—really, really, really benefited me," Matt Cain said.

Both, however, stopped short of expressing fears that the staff would unravel without Molina to bind everything and everybody.

"This is a game where you have to evolve and adapt. Constantly, actually," Lincecum said. He was currently a man with much adaptation to do—and he would be the starter needing the most adaptation to Posey's style.

"It essentially comes down to us, as the pitchers, making sure that we have the right pitch we want to throw," Cain said. "If he [the catcher] puts something down, and we throw it and we didn't want to throw it, it's our fault. It's not his fault. The game's in our hands." Take responsibility for your own situation, in other words. Amen.

All things equal, the Giants probably would have preferred to keep Molina. But Molina wasn't equaling his offensive production from his previous years in San Francisco. His .332 slugging percentage reflected his inability to drive the ball. By contrast, Molina slugged .440 from 2007 to 2009 with the Giants.

When Molina was dealt, Posey happened to own a pedestrian .381 slugging percentage himself, but that changed dramatically within weeks.

Defensively, Posey had been sharpening his catching skills almost daily in pregame drills, but now he would have to undergo on-the-job training.

Posey probably could find a way to downplay winning a Super-Lotto—and given his $6.2 million signing bonus, he essentially had some practice at that. He avoided making a fuss over succeeding Molina.

"It's still baseball," Posey said. "I'm going to play the game, work hard and give it everything I've got." Simple, boring wisdom.

More had occurred than Posey's inevitable promotion to a regular job behind the plate. The Giants had jettisoned a man—emphasis on *man*—who amplified the pitching staff's skills as if he were Leonard Bernstein conducting the Boston Pops. Moreover, Molina handled psyches more adroitly than split-finger fastballs in the dirt.

At least Molina was going to a first-place team. Perhaps leaving the Giants of 2010 would be his own path to the World Series.

Not out of Focus

Given how the pitchers were throwing, it didn't matter whether Molina, Posey or Kirt Manwaring was behind the plate. In eight games from June 23 to June 30, Giants starters recorded a 7.82 ERA.

Matt Cain dismissed the suggested notion that the Giants suddenly lacked focus.

"We're trying to get things done, and sometimes that gets the best of you," he said. "It happens with us on the mound—you get excited in certain situations and you leave a pitch up or you don't get things done—and that's usually how ballgames are won."

Focused or not, the Giants weren't winning many games lately.

And Still No Panic

Something was still missing throughout this sorry stage of the Giants' season: Panic.

The Giants had every reason to worry, if they were so inclined, while losing 10 of 12 games. Their ace pitcher was enduring his second slump of the first half. They scored five or more runs only three times during this spell. Yet they won two of those games, hinting at what they could accomplish if they mounted any offense at all.

But double plays continued to be a concern for the team. "It's gotten contagious. It's become an epidemic, really," manager Bruce Bochy said. "I wish there was an easy cure for this. ... It just so happens we're in a little funk right now, even [hitting into] unusual ones—fly-ball double plays—and it's something I hope we get through soon."

Almost five months into the season, they hadn't gotten through it yet.

The composition of the club helped the Giants stay calm. A mostly veteran group, they knew better than to jump to conclusions about themselves. And they certainly didn't point fingers at each other while assigning fault.

Bottom line: Big leaguers don't panic in June.

"They know what's at stake," general manager Brian Sabean said. "They know the sense of urgency. Having said that, I don't see them, at least in the clubhouse, uptight or not understanding it's a long season."

The long season fostered the belief that Lincecum would regain his effectiveness. He had scaled his obstacles once already this year; doing it again certainly seemed attainable.

Jim Bouton summarized this unspoken, innate confidence in his classic autobiographical baseball chronicle, *Ball Four*, when he wrote, "I've had some thoughts on what separates a professional athlete from other mortals. In a tight situation the amateur says, 'I've failed in this situation many times. I'll probably do so again.' In a tight situation the professional says (and means it), 'I've failed in this situation and I've succeeded. Since each situation is a separate test of my abilities, there's no reason I shouldn't succeed this time.'"

Sabean noted that injuries prevented the Giants from establishing a consistent lineup, as reflected by the 58 different lineups Bochy used in the team's first 76 games.

"If we can get some continuity with the lineup—who's going to be out there every day, where are you going to hit—I think in time that everyday group will have a chance to get more relaxed and build some confidence," Sabean said.

Unfortunately, that continuity would prove unattainable. The Giants were less than halfway to the 126 different lineups they would end up using. Relaxation and confidence would have to be found despite continued change. Fortunately, those qualities are not primarily dependent on external circumstances: They're an internal discipline, first and foremost, although affected by performance and other contextual factors.

It was also becoming clear to Sabean and others that even The Freak, The Franchise himself, would have to step up his game in the shadows despite his early career dominance. As July began, Lincecum's training limits were beginning to show.

"He knows he's going to have to take his offseason training to another level," Sabean said. "The guys who have longevity don't do it on natural ability alone. And he's smart enough to understand that.

So he's in the process of having to make some mental and physical adjustments."

The Giants would have to make other adjustments as well. Besides hitting into prodigious amounts of double plays—within range of setting a major league record for doing so—they were last in the league in stolen bases. (The team's overall lack of speed connected those two statistics.) Their offense was still minimal. The team was also being soundly beaten by its own division rivals. A large number of reliable statistics piled up against San Francisco.

At least the Giants were leading the league's offense in one category: pinch hitting. It's a small category in the grand scheme of things, but it's better than a large dark cloud with no silver lining at all. Travis Ishikawa and Nate Schierholtz were leading the charge off the bench, both with pinch-hitting averages at or above .500. The entire team was hitting well over .300 in pinch-hitting situations—a lesson in collective readiness and focus. Since Ishikawa and Schierholtz had their greatest strengths as defensive replacements, this gave Bochy some fine and flexible options in the late innings—a particularly valuable commodity on a team as constantly involved in tight, stressful games as the Giants.

No panic. Equanimity still reigned.

The Exact Guy We Need

Maybe big leaguers don't panic in June. But after being swept by the Dodgers, the calendar read July 1. The Giants trailed San Diego by five-and-a-half games in the West, having lost four games in the standings in just eight days. Sensing he needed to speak up, Bochy held a team meeting before the Giants opened a four-game series at Denver against the Colorado Rockies, beseeching them to maintain a dedicated effort.

Two losses in a row to the Rockies prompted Bochy to call another huddle. This one involved only the pitchers and catchers. "We have to get this pitching on track. It's kind of gotten contagious," Bochy said. ("Contagious" seemed to be a word he had cause to use too frequently.)

If that was the case, then Lincecum needed some serious antibiotics. The night before, he had improved on his Boston outing by lasting six innings, but he'd allowed 13 baserunners, matching a personal worst. Four of them scored, propelling Colorado to a 6-3 victory and San Francisco to its seventh loss in a row and ninth in 10 games.

From different corners of the visitors' clubhouse, Aubrey Huff and left-hander Jeremy Affeldt made the same brave statement: "There's a lot of season left." Translation: Time's on our side, but pretty soon that won't matter if we keep playing like this. During their losing streak, the Giants had been outscored 38-15 while hitting .209.

Lincecum articulated the growing apprehension among his teammates. "We have to cut that tension that we have going on in the locker room right now, just relax and play the game that we all know we're here for," he said. "There's a lot of pressing for us right now just because we have to get out of that hole."

The hole more closely resembled a bottomless pit, given that Colorado would start Ubaldo Jimenez the next night. Jimenez had continued to win since blanking San Francisco on Memorial Day and now owned a 14-1 record. Knee-jerk prediction: The Giants would lose, fall to .500 (40-40) and wouldn't be heard from again until spring training 2011.

Huff's attitude? Bring Jimenez on. "Just come out and let it all hang out," Huff said. "He's one of the best pitchers. Let's go have some fun. I've seen crazier things in this game. When you're really down and out and you face a guy like this, you never know what might happen. This could be the exact guy we need to get out of it." It's a wild and beautiful concept that when you're at your worst, the cure is to face the best.

Huff's words should have been recorded and played on continuous loop over Coors Field's public-address system during the third inning the next evening.

The Giants needed a crooked number (baseball argot for multiple-run totals, typically in a single inning) to straighten themselves out, and they got one against the suddenly vulnerable Jimenez: Seven. *Seven!* Travis Ishikawa's first career grand slam turned what had been a productive inning into a stunning one.

And still, it almost wasn't enough. Barry Zito and the Giants couldn't hold the lead: Colorado inched back ahead 8-7, but Huff's third homer in two games—a two-run drive in the ninth inning—finally sealed an 11-8 victory.

"Break out the pom-poms!" exclaimed Aaron Rowand, whose double began the third-inning outburst.

Right fielder Nate Schierholtz spoke more seriously. "After losing so many in a row, we weren't going to roll over and die," he said. Personally, he had contributed a key seventh-inning triple.

The final words from this game could only be delivered by Huff. "Even though we were facing Ubaldo tonight and the odds were against us, we had to have this one," he said. "I think this is a game you have to have, or it's going to get ugly quick. It gives the offense the confidence to know that if you can hit this guy, you can hit anybody."

The Giants had been establishing all year that although they might struggle against the unknown and the purportedly weak, they could beat the best. They'd done it again. Huff was right. The cure for playing their worst was to beat the best. Perhaps.

Worse Than Dorothy's Storm

The Giants' resurgence lasted less than 24 hours. An excruciating 4-3, 15-inning loss to Colorado dealt them their fifth consecutive series defeat and left them a season-high seven-and-a-half games behind San Diego. With that loss, the Giants reached the season's halfway mark with a 41-40 record, stuck in fourth place.

One night earlier, observers saw the best of the Giants—equally powerful and plucky, capable of subduing the most challenging of opponents. This latest setback amplified their shortcomings, such as their inability to hit effectively with runners in scoring position. They went 1-for-9 in those situations in the Rockies finale, lapsing worst in the 13th inning when Huff tripled leading off and was stranded.

The Giants also continued to flounder against their NL West brethren, the opponents they needed to defeat the most. To this point, they were 9-20 against division foes. That's no way to win a division title. (In contrast, the Dodgers were 20-5 against NL West teams after sweeping the Giants.)

The Giants had much to dwell on as they headed for the airport to fly to Milwaukee. If they could depart, that is. A massive storm swirled around them, making air travel a questionable activity.

"Trust me—this storm was worse than the one that took the little girl and the dog," Giants broadcaster Duane Kuiper said, referring to *The Wizard of Oz.* "I'm telling you, it was worse than Dorothy's storm. There were low clouds that were rolling like boulders, and the wind had to be 40 miles an hour."

The Giants took off anyway—in more ways than one.

Halfway

Baseball's constancy is a fan's pleasure and a player's challenge. The daily game schedule means that, as Jon Miller has said on Giants broadcasts, "Baseball is always there for you." When you need it as a refuge from the rest of the world's rough edges, it's there more than any other sport. The annual schedule of 162 games is double that of any other major sport and 10 times that of professional football. So, as with other relationships, its steadiness makes for reliability and presence that makes commitment to it rewarding. The daily relationship a fan has with a baseball team is unique in that way.

For the players, however, the same factor makes baseball relentless. The flip side of Jon Miller's observation is that, from the player's perspective, you always have to be there for baseball. Even the number "162" is an underestimation of the true annual game count, for it doesn't include the approximately 35 more games in spring or the post-season playoffs, which can stretch up to another 20 games. The true total for a World Series winner is as high as 215. Even that doesn't count the intrasquad games before the actual spring games begin. And then there is winter ball in between—for those players still needing to establish themselves or hone their game further. Sheer physical training before and beyond all that—and game skill practice on the sidelines—are required to compete at the highest level of human capabilities. There is rarely a day off. It may not be the grunt work life of a man who tars roofs, but it's a legitimately grueling schedule. Body and mind go through dead zones, and no player gets to apply for a two-week vacation to go sun on Hawaiian beaches in the middle of the season. There's a plane to catch, a game starting in an exact number of hours, another pitch that needs to be made without regard to circumstance.

That constancy does require equanimity for successful survival. When the Giants left Colorado after their brutal 15-inning loss on Independence Day, the season was only half over. Exactly 81 of the 162 regulation games were now in the history books. It wasn't yet to the dog days of August—the most common stretch for fatigue and other body wear-and-tear to truly set in—but it was already pushing five months since pitchers and catchers had reported to midwinter "spring" training.

In other words, although it might be wearying, it was early yet. There was a plane to catch to Milwaukee right after the lengthy, excruciating loss to the Rockies. There was no day off. There was another series to begin immediately. They were only halfway to the finish line—or less, if things went well and they reached the playoffs.

They would never get to the playoffs if they didn't resume winning right away. That was obvious, of course. But timing is everything. If the Giants dropped farther behind as the July 31 trade deadline approached, they could be expected to trade some of their useful players and resign themselves to missing out on a World Series triumph for a 56th consecutive year.

Make or break. Do or die. And do it with a sputtering squad, against a hard-hitting team in their own hitters' park? Bookmakers would've given good odds against it. But odds never apply in the individual case. Especially not in 2010 San Francisco.

Chapter 9

Beginnings of Transcendence

Summerfest in Milwaukee

Dorothy's storm did not claim the Giants. They did not end up in Oz instead of Milwaukee. Nonetheless, in the place where they ended up, things were just as strange and beautiful. It isn't conventional wisdom that the way for a team to get back on track is to endure a stretch during which 16 of 22 games are played on the road—which was the challenge facing the Giants, beginning with a tough series in Colorado. But just as Aubrey Huff had correctly theorized that facing the league's best pitcher could be what the team needed to correct course, so the difficult schedule proved to be exactly the cure for what had ailed them.

The Milwaukee series also offered the Giants another opportunity for payback. Although Barry Zito had artfully settled the team's score with Prince Fielder in spring training, the only way to settle it with the entire team that had participated in the surrounding antics was to beat them on the field. And this was the first regular season match between the two teams since that Fielder home run spectacle in 2009. No one mentioned this, but no one needed to. Baseball players have solid memories of events like that one.

The Giants had far more important things on their mind, anyway. No matter their fourth-place standing, they were only interested in finishing first. College teammates Aubrey Huff and Pat Burrell were coalescing into one leadership force, and Burrell brought the right vision to Huff that first day in Milwaukee.

Huff said, "Pat Burrell told me before the game, 'Let's make up one game a week.' It makes sense. That way, it doesn't seem so overwhelming." There were more than seven weeks left to make up those seven-and-a-half games. Celebrations of summer were only beginning.

One of the nation's greatest summer festivals had just ended when the Giants arrived in Milwaukee. Summerfest, Milwaukee's annual celebration of music and cherished good weather, showcased its final acts on July 4, ending an 11-day run that had featured performers such as Tim McGraw, Carrie Underwood, Tom Petty, Justin Bieber, Eric Clapton, Weird Al Yankovic, Colbie Caillat, Uriah Heep, Pitbull, Usher, B.B. King, The Moody Blues, Rush and Kool and the Gang. Something for nearly every musical taste.

Another Summerfest performer was Carlos Santana, Barry Zito's hero and former San Franciscan. Had the great Santana stuck around a few more days, he could have serenaded the Giants with his 1981 hit "Winning"—because that's pretty much all they did for the rest of July.

In Milwaukee, the Giants staged their own version of Summerfest. They got their payback and transitioned into momentum—and they did it with force, power and decisiveness. It was dominance, not torture, from start to finish.

Well, that's the Hollywood version of it. In truth, it wasn't always as simple and dominant as the final scores. The first game was beautiful torture until the Giants broke it open in the seventh, aided by a critical Milwaukee error. For the first six innings, Jonathan Sanchez had shown his traditional mix of brilliance and wildness, walking six and throwing three wild pitches while also striking out six, hanging tough to hold the Brewers' heavy hitters to a single run. The Giants' offense had been equally languid, trailing 1-0 until tying the score in the sixth.

But in the seventh, dominance began with a Buster Posey leadoff single. That christened a four-run uprising that broke the 1-1 tie. Aubrey Huff contributed the rally's biggest hit, a two-run single that capped a 3-for-4 afternoon. Another Posey hit—an opposite field home run in the eighth—completed the scoring in the 6-1 victory as the bullpen combination of Santiago Casilla, the newly acquired Chris Ray and Dan Runzler completely stifled the Brewers. The Giants bullpen was now proven and deep; The team was solidifying.

Although Aubrey Huff led the offense for the second game in a row, he was also exhausted afterwards. "The whole game I was running on fumes," he said. "If I don't get [the next game] off, I'll be worthless until the All-Star break. I never felt that tired in a game in my life. . . . Those five-and-a-half hours got to me," he said, referring to the dispiriting marathon loss the night before in Denver. Huff had now played in 80 of the first 82 Giants games, as had Pablo Sandoval—more than any other Giants. Wisely, Bruce Bochy acknowledged

Huff's exhaustion and gave him Tuesday off. Huff's honesty served the team better than playing on fumes and pretense.

Had Huff played the next night, he might have been able to relax, anyway.

The Giants' defenders could have played their positions in rocking chairs, given the ease of Madison Bumgarner's effort. The rookie recorded his first major league victory in another 6-1 decision. At 20 years and 340 days of age, Bumgarner was the youngest Giant to earn a win since Matt Cain, who had been two days younger when he defeated Arizona on Sept. 4, 2005.

Huff's replacement, Travis Ishikawa, lashed a two-run single during a five-run sixth inning that shattered a scoreless deadlock. But the evening belonged to Bumgarner, whose pitching line reflected his dominance: eight innings, three hits, no runs, three walks and five strikeouts. He would virtually duplicate that effort under much more auspicious circumstances nearly four months later.

Confusion momentarily reigned in the clubhouse afterwards as players wondered, Is it legal to pour beer over the head of a man who is too young to drink it?

"They [the players] were saying they don't think that can happen," reported Bruce Bochy. But the beer-by-committee's decision was yes, and the dousing commenced. Given baseball's bizarre tradition of spraying or dumping good beverages over heads at key moments, it's possible to measure a season's success by the amount of alcohol that is worn rather than consumed.

This first occasion showed Bumgarner had arrived, although he was legally forced to drink only what the world calls a "sports beverage," while the beer was left to soak in through his scalp. Fittingly, this all occurred at Miller Park, named after a company making the very substance in question—in the town most famous for the same.

"That's as good as I've seen him, I think," Buster Posey said, referring to Bumgarner's pitching performance—not the sudsy look of his hair. It was a comment with more depth of perspective than their collective major league experience, since Posey had also caught the Mad Bum in the minors.

In the third game against Milwaukee, the team could not have made a more obvious announcement of arrival than if they'd stood naked on a train platform with a bullhorn. They hit three home runs—in the first inning. And the three who hit them were only beginning a month of transcendence. In retrospect, Torres, Huff and Posey's collaborative bullhorn proclamation might be recorded as

"Now Hear Ye, O Disbelievers, We Three Kings are About to KICK YOUR ASS for a Month. Amen."

In the Giants' Good Book, you can prove things like that—but you can't say them. Those three (and most of their teammates) would never dare make predictions like that. Just shut up and perform, one moment at a time: That perennial wisdom would become relevant—entirely too much so—down the line, when a teammate would later let unwise words slip.

While Torres, Huff and Posey were launching a dominant month with their first-inning home runs, Tim Lincecum followed the example set by Bumgarner. In losing his past two starts, The Franchise had only lasted a total of nine innings, while allowing eight runs, 14 hits and seven walks. Ugly. But he rebounded on a night when the Giants might have raised expectations for themselves. The three initial homers were only the beginning of a 15-2 thrashing of the Brewers. As the Giants rapped 18 hits, Lincecum struck out 10 in seven innings.

"That's not just some geek off the street out there throwing," Brewers third baseman Casey McGehee said. Here stood the ballclub at the beginning of transcendence, supplementing its typically stifling pitching with atypical hitting.

"We're not a team that has many games like this," Bochy said. Yet in Milwaukee, the Giants seemed to sustain this offense so easily, having now scored 27 runs in three games. Shouldn't this happen more often?

It seemed like it should indeed happen more often, particularly since Buster Posey was at the forefront of this display, appearing settled in by his 41st major league game. In the 15-2 win, he went 4-for-4 with two home runs, including a grand slam. With six RBIs, Posey became the first Giant to amass that many in a game since Barry Bonds had collected seven on July 19, 2007, at Chicago. Posey called being mentioned with Bonds "surreal," saying, "He's probably the best hitter of all time."

Posey's one-day output was also the most impressive by a Giant in Milwaukee since Willie Mays socked four homers there on April 30, 1961. Suddenly, Posey's name was being mentioned in the context of the greats. No one was rushing to place his bronze statue alongside those of Willie Mays, Willie McCovey, Juan Marichal and Orlando Cepeda outside AT&T Park, but with Posey in the middle of the order, the Giants seemed destined for many more big nights.

Unlike many of his teammates, Posey was no castoff, and he didn't match a misfit's description. He was what every franchise wanted—

a young catcher who cast a formidable presence, whether he stood in the batter's box or squatted behind home plate. That he was charismatic and marketable in an all-American way was a bonus for the Giants, who'd noticed Posey had begun prompting the kind of cheering that AT&T Park patrons usually reserved for Lincecum and Pablo Sandoval.

Among all of the great and popular Giants names, Willie Mays stood alone in being able to sustain a team almost by himself for weeks at a time. Posey might be able to do that, but he might never have to. And during July, the trio of Posey, Torres and Huff succeeded in sustaining the offense together, much as Mays had done so alone.

Indeed, Huff, Torres and Posey all homered again the next day—though not all in the same inning this time—as the Giants completed their first four-game sweep of the Brewers in another lopsided victory of 9-3. Huff paced the Giants with four RBIs, bolstering his candidacy as a late replacement for the All-Star team. The NL didn't prove to need him, but the Giants did. Huff went 6-for-10 with two homers, seven RBIs and four runs scored in the series. "I'm just trying to ride it out as long as I can," Huff said of his hot streak, properly staying in the moment.

Posey mimicked Huff by going 9-for-15 for the series with four home runs and eight RBIs. He said farewell to Miller Park for the year by smashing a leadoff homer off Trevor Hoffman to right-center field in the ninth inning, considered by many to be the greatest closer of all time.

"His opposite-field power is amazing," Huff said of Posey. "He stays through the ball. There's not too much you're going to see him get fooled on."

As lopsided as the final score again was, it wasn't a perfect afternoon for the Giants. Barry Zito couldn't capitalize on the scoring bonanza, working only 4 2/3 innings and falling one out short of being eligible for the win. Bochy removed him after he issued his fifth and sixth walks of the game to load the bases.

It wasn't always a lucky afternoon for the Giants either. As of that day, the team was carrying 13 pitchers on their squad—meaning that on a 25-man roster, more than half of the players were committed to playing the same position. Baseball players are notoriously superstitious, so it's hard to say whether that number 13 bothered anyone at all when Dan Runzler came to the plate in that fourth and final game in Milwaukee. That Runzler came to the plate at all was unlucky enough. As a late-inning relief pitcher, he was almost invariably pinch-hit for. But he'd pitched an excellent inning, and Bochy wanted him to pitch another. Since this was not the American League—where the Brewers had once been, before being asked to do the baseball equivalent of a sex-change operation and shift to the National League—there was no designated hitter, and Runzler would have to hit.

It was the first plate appearance of his major league career and the last time he would hit all year. Runzler did not even get to finish the at-bat. While fouling off a 1-2 pitch, he caught his spikes in the dirt—and dislocated his kneecap. He was done, although he was later credited with the win, having been deemed by the official scorer as the most effective reliever.

Losing a left-handed pitcher is a potentially devastating occurrence for a team. Unlike in the world at large—where left-handers are often regarded as somewhat odd and frequently struggle in a right-handed world—left-handers are considered a precious and coveted life form in baseball. Because of the direction their pitches break and the side of the body from which they release the pitches, left-handed pitchers are on average far more effective against left-handed hitters—who are often right-handed people hitting left-handed, which is another story altogether. In any case, woe to the baseball team without effective left-handed relievers.

Now the Giants were down to one left-handed reliever: Jeremy Affeldt, a man who had already struggled with injuries during the year and as a result had been plagued by inconsistency (he owned a 4.70 ERA at the time). If he went down, too, or even if he didn't, the Giants might have to make a move—if there was a move to be made. It's not like extra left-handed relief pitchers sit on the shelf at the local 7-Eleven, just waiting to be purchased. But general manager Brian Sabean and his lieutenants would now search a little more intently for another left-handed reliever.

Runzler's injury put a damper on what was otherwise a smashing success in Milwaukee—a four-game sweep that shed the pain of Colorado, collectively won by the overwhelming score of 36-7. ("The most significant series of the year," Duane Kuiper would call it.) Any ghosts of Prince Fielder's bowling-pin teammates had been exorcised, and the Giants could move on without another of Dorothy's storms to fly into. It was time to go to Washington, where the Nationals were barely functioning on a major league level, not unlike the government.

More Effective Than Congress

Changing venues did little to impede the Giants' ascent, although the first game against the Nationals was not an auspicious beginning—and anyone too quick to project the moment onto the future according to the tenets of Burrell's Law would've cried about another passing of the torch, just as in the season's early scorching of Lincecum by Ubaldo Jimenez. The latest matchup of young aces was Matt Cain against Nationals rookie Stephen Strasburg, who was saddled with the immense weight of being The Next Big Thing. He was even more heralded than Buster Posey and had come to the majors after a mere 11 outings in the minors. He was drawing huge crowds, and his early results were worthy of the attention. He was blowing hitters away, and the Giants (except for Andres Torres) would be among them. But being The Next Big Thing in baseball—like being called "the next Bob Dylan" as a songwriter—is a heavy weight to bear. After only 12 games, the all-too-human Strasburg was fated to suffer an injury that would shelve him for at least a year.

For now, however, Strasburg was shelving the Giants—in an 8-1 stifling that found Matt Cain ineffective again. The game started beautifully from the Giants' perspective, when Andres Torres commanded respect by turning on a 97 mph fastball from Strasburg on the fifth pitch of the game, roping a tremendous game-opening homer for the second time in three days. But that was the extent of the offense. Matt Cain ended up giving up all eight runs despite having good stuff, and if the game was a human, Giants mourners would've lined up to gaze at it in a casket before walking away sadly.

But the first-place Padres lost, too. The Giants had lost no ground.

If Strasburg helped his Rookie of the Year prospects by stifling the Giants, Posey stole his momentum the next night by going 4-for-5 with a homer and three RBIs as well as starring on defense. Meanwhile, Jonathan Sanchez struggled and came out in the fourth, losing, but the Giants' bullpen continued on a trend of being excellent as a unit. Joe Martinez—recently recalled again from Fresno—was the only one of five relievers who allowed even a hit or a walk. He was followed with uniform brilliance by Casilla, Ray, Romo and Affeldt, who held the Nationals to a performance as devoid of results as Congress. The Giants slowly chipped away at the Nationals' 5-3 lead. Aaron Rowand's seventh-inning homer tied the score 5-5 before Posey hit an RBI single and Juan Uribe ended an 0-for-23 skid with a two-run double to complete the four-run surge. "On Uribe's back," indeed. He was batting only .251 and his on-base percentage was a mere .321, but he had 49 RBIs, a figure eclipsed among the Giants only by Huff. Uribe always seemed to come through when it counted, and in the end, the Giants slammed a 10-5 win on the board. They made up another game against the Padres—their third in the first week since Pat Burrell had said one per week would do.

Now all that separated the Giants from the All-Star break was their July 11 series finale at Washington. Relatively few of the Giants would watch the All-Star Game, preferring instead to purge themselves of baseball during the three-day hiatus. Those who felt inclined to tune into the Midsummer Classic would have seen their nemesis, Colorado's Ubaldo Jimenez, start for the NL. So what? The Giants were fresh off roughing up Jimenez at Coors Field on the previous Saturday, led by Ishikawa's grand slam.

At 26, Ishikawa was young to be limited to reserve duty. But he handled his role with a veteran's aplomb, mustering all the patience he could while awaiting his next opportunity—and then seizing that chance when it came. He was another skilled practitioner of that aspect of the Giants Way.

A quasi-regular in 2009 when he appeared in 120 games and accumulated 326 at-bats, Ishikawa saw others usurp his playing time at first base in 2010—initially Huff, then Posey. Bochy fed Ishikawa little else but morsels of pinch-hitting appearances. Ishikawa still fattened his batting average, collecting 10 hits in his first 21 at-bats (.476) off the bench. Nevertheless, he had totaled only 37 at-bats through July 2.

Bengie Molina's departure for Texas temporarily increased Ishikawa's activity, since Posey moved behind the plate and Huff, during this period, was more likely to man an outfield corner than first base. The Jimenez game began a 12-for-28, 11-RBI binge for Ishikawa, who completed this stretch by driving in three runs as the Giants captured the rubber game against Washington 6-2.

Ishikawa attributed his productivity to a relative absence of stress.

"I went in there with no expectations, with no pressure," Ishikawa said. "Just to be able to go out and play and have fun and help the team as best I could. . . . Whether or not I was going to play after that wasn't up to me to decide."

Besides Ishikawa, it was Posey who again did the offensive damage as the Giants finished the road trip behind Madison Bumgarner's second major league win, which was not an occasion for a beer hairdo. An effective Romo and Wilson closed it out, giving Wilson 23 saves and a 1.91 ERA heading into the All-Star Game, where he would represent the Giants along with Lincecum. Delivering a positively saintly performance—although Huff was no longer referring to him as Jesus Christ—Posey finished the road trip hitting an even .500 (20-for-40).

Coming back to win six out of seven after the grueling finish in Colorado established the team's resilience, giving them an excellent mindset for the All-Star break—the season's only deep pause, where all players except the All-Stars tend to hop planes and quickly scatter across the world, reconnecting with whomever they vaguely remember their family might be or doing whatever else is generally impossible during the all-consuming season. It's a well-earned break—and often a dangerous one with a team carrying momentum, for even a three-day break in baseball is often enough to turn the tides.

The View from the Break

While the Giants were in the midst of their series against the Nationals—beating everyone except Ninth Wonder of the World Stephen Strasburg—Giants GM Brian Sabean offered a high-level view of the team to date.

He took the pitching staff to task, saying they hadn't been "as advertised," which is to say they lacked the consistent strength expected of them. They were now third in the league in ERA—a most vital statistic—but last in the league in walks, which was as galling as a massive zit on a self-conscious teenager's face.

Sabean was clear about the team needing to throw strikes. Not that they didn't know that. And Posey's rookie nature behind the plate was not an accepted excuse.

"[The pitchers] have to take it upon themselves," Sabean said. "They're the ones throwing the baseball." It was a time in which restating the obvious was necessary.

Sabean also addressed the continued hitting struggles of Pablo Sandoval, who was still having trouble keeping a disciplined approach at the plate (both home and dinner plates). Sabean offered him support and patience.

"Attitude-wise, I think he really has been able to keep a good perspective," Sabean said. "He gets his work in, including after the game from a conditioning standpoint. He's played really well at third base, which is heartening." One measure of a player's concentration is if difficulties in one aspect of his game begin to affect another. Sandoval's hitting struggles had not, to this point, affected his defense. That was a relief. "So you just hope that maybe with the off-days over the break and some of the adjustments we're trying to make now with him, it gets him in a better position to start the second half in a way he can finish much stronger and really help us in August and September."

Sabean was unwilling to proclaim the team good enough to make the playoffs, especially if they couldn't improve before the July 31 trade deadline. "I don't know," he said. But he added that his opinion was not the one that mattered. "Put it this way: They think they're good enough to get to the playoffs, which is important. It really doesn't make any difference what I think. They have to think they have a chance. And I have every reason to believe that's their attitude."

One game a week, as Pat Burrell said. That was their attitude.

As he detailed at the break, Sabean had complicated issues to worry about when seeking assistance for the Giants. "The one blanket statement I'll make is, like most organizations these days, we're really not interested in or going to pursue 'rental' scenarios," Sabean said, referring to the late-July trades where losing teams deal top players to be lost anyway at season's end due to impending free agency. Teams in the win-now-at-any-cost mode would sometimes deal away their future by trading hot prospects for such rent-a-players, knowing they'd only have their services for a few months before the players would move on again to where the money was best or they really wanted to be. The Giants would not do that, as Sabean made clear in his skilled, blunt way.

"Prospects are too valuable; [contractually] controllable players are too valuable. [It's a] roll of the dice of finding somebody who may or may not make as big a difference as we might need," said Sabean. "The downside is you end up with a free agent-to-be and either no chance to re-sign him or not wanting to re-sign him, and then you've got the prospects lost in the deal."

Sabean was now the longest-tenured general manager in the majors, and although he had his detractors, he had a razor-sharp mind and an overall track record with the Giants that stood above his lesser-tenured (and fired) counterparts. He played hardball in the truest sense of the word, even if some general managers complained he was hard to reach. Before his tenure with the Giants, Sabean was deeply involved in scouting for the Yankees. He was the man responsible for that team signing Derek Jeter, among others. No matter what he said, it mattered what he thought.

A Bright Orange Win

The All-Star game is one of baseball's strangest spectacles. It's an indi-vidual-focused event in what is usually a team game. The best players from each league are trotted out for display much like fashion models on a catwalk, except (fortunately) there is no swimsuit competition.

While being selected to the All-Star squad remains one of the most coveted individual honors, the game itself had begun to lose audience over the decades. This led to the addition of the Home Run Derby, which invites the power hitters of the game to tempt fate by changing their usual healthy approach of *not* trying to hit home runs. Displaying their prowess at hitting as many balls as possible over the fence, these players risked the rhythm of their swing in time for the season's second half.

Declining viewership also inspired the new rule that whichever league wins the game has home-field advantage during the World Series. It was an attempt to return relevance to the spectacle—and from the Giants' perspective, the relevance would turn out to be, as Brian Wilson would say, delicious.

Despite the many heartaches Wilson's penchant for pitching into trouble brought to Bruce Bochy and the majority of San Francisco residents, his consistency in pitching back out earned him an un-questioned place on the All-Star squad. Wilson was humble in ac-cepting the honor, acknowledging the equal candidacy of others. He also imagined his All-Star role as helping to give the Giants them-selves home-field advantage in the World Series.

"That would be just epic," he said, adding that he envisioned the Giants capitalizing on that edge, although the team was still only in fourth place in its own division. Yet Wilson was exactly right: It would be indeed be epic.

The other All-Star Giants player was less sure of deserving his place. Tim Lincecum had been struggling mightily at times—not The Freak and Franchise he was expected to be. His own stats looked a lot better than his erratic performance sometimes did: Despite the ups and downs, he was leading the league in strikeouts with 121, and his 8-4 record with a 3.28 ERA still kept him prominent if not dominant.

Lincecum did not end up getting into the game, but he served up entertainment in the unfamiliar land of the bullpen. According to Wilson, Lincecum spent part of the game providing comic relief by tying his long mane into a ponytail with a hair tie.

"He kept the mood light," Wilson said. "He did his Steven Seagal impersonation. It was delicious."

The comedy wasn't as delicious as the result. The National League won a tight game, 3-1, breaking a terrible losing streak in the All-Star Game. The NL hadn't won in 14 years, despite having garnered several World Series titles in this span—a more relevant statistic in terms of league balance.

Now sporting ragged facial stubble, Wilson was summoned to pitch the eighth inning instead of his usual ninth. He set down the American League hitters in a tidy manner, needing only 10 pitches to retire the side in order.

"One-two-three. What's up with that?" Wilson said to All-Star coach Bochy on reaching the dugout.

"Why can't I see that [in the regular season]?" Bochy asked in reply.

Bochy later had an explanation for Wilson's dominance. "I think the shoes were blinding the hitters," he theorized. Wilson had come out on the mound wearing a pair of brilliant neon orange cleats.

"They were magical," Wilson said of his new shoes, which he had never worn in a regular season game. His reason for not doing so was, "I don't think they're MLB-approved," which would prove rather expensively correct.

Regardless, Wilson's perfect eighth set up a save for the Dodgers' Jonathan Broxton, a massive man who led the league in butt size and who was ferociously difficult to hit when at his best, but who would falter in the season's second half. Broxton finished off the American League, and the NL had their first All-Star victory since 1996.

Odd, a Giant setting up a Dodger for a save, which would prove to benefit the Giants later.

"I wonder how the fans felt about that," spectator Lincecum pondered.

In retrospect, the fans were probably quite happy, for it isn't often a Dodger getting a skilled save benefits the Giants in the World Series. And Broxton would have another more painful moment coming against his San Francisco rivals a few weeks later—one that would in fact be magical, epic and even more delicious than a pair of illegal shoes.

Home at Last

Although Tim Lincecum had languished in the All-Star bullpen—Philadelphia manager Charlie Manuel planned to use him only if the game went into extra innings—he vented his frustration in the most constructive manner possible by channeling it into his next pitching assignment. In the first game after the All-Star break, Lincecum notched his 50th career victory and fourth shutout in a 2-0 verdict against the New York Mets at AT&T Park.

While Lincecum yielded six hits and recorded just three 1-2-3 innings, only three runners reached scoring position. Presto! The tidy game required just two hours and 11 minutes to complete.

"I would have guessed there would have been more [perfect innings], the way he was working," Ishikawa said. "Even when he had guys on base, he'd get that big out. There was a great rhythm to the game. It was a lot of fun."

Mets center fielder Carlos Beltran noticed Lincecum was throwing "cut" fastballs more often. This reinforced the notion that Lincecum's evolution as a pitcher was continuing.

"He didn't have that before," Beltran said, referring to the cutter. "He threw me a couple cutters inside, and I wasn't able to recognize the pitch well."

That was new. However, Beltran's assessment of Lincecum sounded familiar: "He's one of the best out there."

Entering 2010, Barry Zito had been one of the best at pitching in the second half, posting a 75-40 record. He appeared destined to maintain this pattern by nearly matching Lincecum the next day in a 1-0 triumph. Working eight innings, Zito surrendered just two hits, walked two and struck out 10. Bruce Bochy had high praise for Zito and his ballclub. "These are the kind of games you have to win if you think you're going to be a contender," the skipper said. By combining to walk only three in 17 innings, Lincecum and Zito had put into practice the exhortations of Bochy and pitching coach Dave Righetti, who met with the pitchers shortly before the All-Star break to cite their inflated walk totals and urge them to follow the most basic element of their craft: Throw strikes. That echoed Sabean's basic words.

After Zito shut down the Mets, Aubrey Huff commented on the energy now gathering at AT&T Park. "It was a nice atmosphere at the yard tonight. It kind of felt like a playoff-game atmosphere." Poking fun at his career full of losing teams, Huff wryly added, "Not that I would know what it feels like."

When the Giants again subdued the Mets 8-4 the next afternoon, it marked the second time all season that Lincecum, Zito and Matt Cain had won consecutive games. It also would be the last. But, at least for now, the Giants' corporate leaders were mollified, and their success momentarily answered Sabean's concerns. It also put distance between the team and their 2-10 stretch in late June and early July, during which San Francisco had yielded 63 runs. The rotation that boasted Cy Young Award winners Lincecum and Zito, a 2009 All-Star in Cain and Jonathan Sanchez—a guy who might possess better pure stuff than any of them—had been effective more often than not. But Lincecum, Zito and Sanchez had been prone to wild fluctuations in performance, and although Cain was consistent, he remained under .500 (7-8) after beating the Mets. Sabean knew the Giants needed excellence, not just effectiveness, to guarantee an escape from mediocrity.

For their part, the pitchers simply plunged ahead. What were they going to do, start a war of words with their boss? "I'm not aware of what he said, personally," Zito said, referring to Sabean's recent remarks. "We grind every day. We're trying to throw strikes, and sometimes it's not that easy."

Yet winning still seemed easy for the Giants, who had captured nine of 10 games. But professional athletes are voraciously competitive. They'd want to win 11 of 10 games if such an occurrence were mathematically possible. So after New York salvaged a 4-3, 10-inning victory in the series finale, the Giants didn't content themselves with the knowledge that they had taken the series 3-1—particularly after Ishikawa appeared to score the winning run in the bottom of the ninth inning.

In that inning, the Giants made a last-minute comeback from a 3-1 deficit, tying it on a two-run single by Travis Ishikawa. After Andres Torres doubled Ishikawa to third, the winning run was 90 feet away with one out. Freddy Sanchez grounded one to David Wright at third, and his high throw to the plate allowed Ishikawa to slide under Henry Blanco's tag for the winning run—except plate umpire Phil Cuzzi saw something other than reality and called Ishikawa out. Even Blanco—an admirable fellow who'd be a charter inductee if a Hall of Fame existed for backup catchers—said later, "He was safe all the way."

It was painful, but such judgment calls are just a part of the game, as Ishikawa noted.

"To feel like I was so sure the game was over was just a satisfying feeling, and then I started celebrating early because I thought I beat it. But when he raised his hand for the out, my emotions got the best of me, and I started arguing with him a little bit," he said. "But I calmed down a little bit. . . . These guys, they have a tough job to do."

Closers, who are accustomed to protecting slender leads, seem most vulnerable when summoned with the score tied. Such was the case with Brian Wilson, who yielded Ike Davis' go-ahead RBI double in the 10th on a two-out, full-count pitch.

"Whatever the umpire calls I feel is the right call; I don't really second-guess that," Wilson said of the umpiring mistake. "But ultimately, I take full responsibility for that loss. I still could have made a good 3-2 pitch."

Neither Wilson nor the Giants would dwell on the costly bad call. These things tend to even out in time. And they did not have to wait long for redemption.

The Thinker Reigns Supreme

After one home series against the Mets, it was on to Los Angeles for the latest installment of the fierce rivalry. Dodger Stadium had also been the site of Bruce Bochy's worst managerial nightmare. On Sept. 18, 2006—before he had joined the Giants—Bochy's San Diego Padres were leading Los Angeles 9-5 in the ninth inning. Then the Dodgers proceeded to tie the score with four consecutive home runs. San Diego scored in the 10th, but Kenny Lofton walked before Nomar Garciaparra lined another homer to win it for the Dodgers.

If Bochy felt any lingering demons needed to be exorcised from Chavez Ravine, the events of July 19–20 certainly satisfied him.

Virtually every move Bochy made in the series opener against the archrival Dodgers brought San Francisco closer to its eventual 5-2 victory. Right fielder Nate Schierholtz, starting his first game since the All-Star break, hit a two-run, fourth-inning homer that provided the ultimate stand-up runs. In his first exposure to the rivalry, Madison Bumgarner gave a gritty performance on the mound, but when he faltered in the sixth inning, Bochy used a sequence of relievers that blanked Los Angeles for the final 3 1/3 innings. The key figures were Jeremy Affeldt, who coaxed Andre Ethier's inning-ending groundout with the bases loaded in the seventh inning, and Wilson, who allowed the Dodgers to fill the bases again in the ninth before facing Casey Blake.

At this point, with the bases loaded (as usual) and the game on the line, we must pause the action for a wee bit of history.

One of the world's wise teachings is to not make fun of what you don't understand. Casey Blake of the Dodgers was reminded of this the hard way in 2009, when he mocked the crossed-arms gesture Brian Wilson uses to punctuate each save or win. It was captured on video, and Wilson was offended. Blake insisted he meant no disrespect towards Wilson, claiming not to know the relief ace's gesticulations honor his deceased father and his faith.

For the sake of Blake and any who might mock, let the record note that Wilson's gesture has complex roots. He turns his back to the plate after sealing a victory so he's not facing (or showing up) his opponent, then he crosses his arms with his left hand in a fist, his right hand with index finger extended. The crossed arms are a warrior's gesture, taken from the Ultimate Fighting Championship world and a company that uses it as a symbol—represented also on a t-shirt Wilson wears under his uniform. The single extended finger represents the lone warrior Wilson is, taking on the battle on the mound—which he does for reasons more than his personal triumph. That closed fist? It represents the unbroken circle of the Holy Trinity the devoutly Christian Wilson deeply believes in as well as the strength his God gives him. It also honors his own father, part of that unbroken circle, who died of kidney cancer when Wilson was only 17, causing him to abandon his Christian beliefs for a time. His faith later returned as fierce as his fastball and demeanor, and his gesture stands in humble honor to the greater forces for which he plays. Baseball for Wilson remains a privately spiritual honoring of Christ, and his gesture symbolizes that reverence. It may not be easy for outsiders to understand, but again, that's exactly *why* it shouldn't be made fun of.

Wilson struck out Casey Blake on three pitches to end the game, making it the fifth time he'd struck out Blake in nine matches. He made his point the right way: silently, on the field. Of course, he turned away to make his usual private gesture.

"I don't have a history with anybody," said Wilson afterwards. It was an effective way to head off any further discussion of the matter, but it simply wasn't true. History is history. Wilson and Blake had it.

The next night, Bochy "The Thinker" distinguished himself even more. It was another typically contentious game, with plenty of pitches thrown too close for comfort, warnings to the benches and an ejection or two. Trailing Los Angeles ace Clayton Kershaw 5-1, the Giants roused themselves for three sixth-inning runs.

Bochy precipitated the rest.

Still trailing by one, the Giants loaded the bases with one out in the ninth against Dodgers closer Jonathan Broxton. Los Angeles hitting coach Don Mattingly, substituting for ejected manager Joe Torre, visited the mound to discuss strategy with Broxton. Barely after leaving the mound, Mattingly spun around and conveyed more thoughts to the reliever.

Bochy instantly noticed this and alerted the umpires. They quickly invoked Rule 8:06, which forbids managers or coaches who visit the mound from departing and returning. According to their interpretation, Broxton had to leave the game immediately, since Mattingly had technically visited the mound twice.

The Dodgers' new pitcher was George Sherrill, sporting a 7.48 ERA. He was no Jonathan Broxton, especially not without proper warm-up. In the confusion, he was only given eight pitches. He hadn't been warming up in the bullpen prior to the double mound visit, but he should've been given all the time he needed. He "guessed" he was ready, apparently as flummoxed as everyone else by the situation.

Sherrill wasn't ready enough for Andres Torres, whose two-run double put the Giants ahead before Buster Posey sliced an RBI single off Travis Schlichting. That brought Jeremy Affeldt on for a rare save. Final score: Giants 7, Dodgers 5.

During Bochy's Padres tenure in 2006, he prompted umpires to cite the same rule—also against the Dodgers, when he'd seen previous Dodgers manager Grady Little make a U-turn to chat with Brad Penny. Except for these two instances, Bochy said he had never seen the rule necessitated.

"It's an easy mistake to make," Bochy said charitably. "I saw it. Once he [Mattingly] went back to say a few more words, I'm sitting in a pretty good position there. What was important was Torres came through."

Bochy credits players as often as he can and avoids criticizing them publicly. It partly explains his popularity among players, who trust him to treat them fairly.

Bochy's alertness in spotting Mattingly's transgression can be traced to his playing background. As a catcher, Bochy was obliged to notice when a hitter altered his stance or a baserunner took an unusual lead. Even now, Bochy studies opposing catchers as they warm up pitchers between innings, looking for flaws to exploit.

To complicate matters, Major League Baseball declared the next day that the umpires had misinterpreted the rule. Mattingly should have been ejected for ignoring an umpire's warning (Adrian Johnson was yelling, "No, no, no," telling Mattingly not to go back to the mound), while Broxton should have been allowed to face the next batter and *then* been removed. But as with the call that fell against the Giants a few days earlier, the ruling stood. Human imperfection remains an elemental thread of the game. And these things do tend to even out over time.

Bochy's chess game with his personnel was a less obvious skill. But the fact that he still had to use so many different lineups even while the Giants flourished in July reflected his expertise with his players.

"Bochy never had a set hand all season long," managing general partner Bill Neukom said when it was all over. "He had to find ways to put guys in positions to be successful. And he was brilliant at that."

No series defined his brilliance more than this one in Los Angeles, even though the series closed on a losing note after Chad Billingsley—one of the toughest pitchers San Francisco had faced all year—spun a 2-0, five-hit shutout in the series finale. Sometimes, no amount of managerial acuity can outthink mastery on the mound.

Another Round of Payback, Please

The Giants' next stop was Arizona, where the Diamondbacks humbled them in a two-game sweep in May. Despite now languishing in last—the only team in the division out of the race—Arizona was hot, having just swept the Mets.

In the opener, Matt Cain's eight-inning three-hitter in a 3-0 victory opened the four-game set against the Diamondbacks and reinforced his essential presence. On a staff that included the spectacular Lincecum, a talented yet sometimes vulnerable Zito, the dazzling yet erratic Sanchez and a still-developing Bumgarner, Cain represented the backbone—reliable, resolute. His month-by-month ERAs in 2010 varied between 1.81 and 3.80. Even at his worst, he was good enough to win. Compare that with the monthly ranges of Lincecum (1.27 to 7.82), Zito (1.53 to 7.76) and Sanchez (1.85 to 4.50), and Cain's consistency stands out even more.

The Giants then provided further reminders that their offense could respond to challenges. They won 7-4 against Edwin Jackson, who had thrown an improbable eight-walk, 149-pitch no-hitter at Tampa Bay on June 25. Then they prevailed 10-4 in a game started by Ian Kennedy, who limited them to one run and three hits in eight innings on May 19.

In the fourth and final game, Ishikawa's two-out, 10th-inning RBI single followed Posey's leadoff double—his fourth hit of the afternoon—and helped the Giants finish the sweep and a 6-1 trip with a 3-2 win. Posey also hit a first-inning RBI double, extending his hitting streak to 18 games. It made Posey's streak the second-longest by a San Francisco Giants rookie. At 17, he had broken a tie with Hall of Famer Orlando Cepeda, whose binge occurred in 1958. One lone, imposing figure remained ahead of Posey: Willie McCovey, the Hall of Famer who had set the San Francisco-era rookie record of 22 games in 1959.

Four games, four wins—and one more game gained in the standings. Only three back now. And a strange thing was happening in the series: Fans in the stands were heard chanting "MVP" for Aubrey Huff all the way in Arizona, far from the Giants' home park, if close to their spring training digs. As Huff himself had said earlier, "You get things started in the most unlikely places." The unlikely was getting started in Arizona again, and this time, it was a wave of fan momentum that would soon grow wild and take root at home—through slogans and themes previously unimagined.

Desert Pains and Complications

Even the Arizona sweep was not without its price. First, the Giants' lone remaining left-hander in the bullpen, Jeremy Affeldt, tore his left oblique muscle while warming up in the bullpen during the second game of the series.

"It felt like somebody shot me in the side," he said. He went on the disabled list the next day, causing the yo-yo string on Joe Martinez to be yanked again, bringing him back from Fresno for his final encore.

That same day, it was announced that Pablo Sandoval would have to leave for Venezuela for "personal reasons," which quietly translated to the pain of having to deal with a mid-season divorce at the ripe old age of 23. He would only be physically gone for a few days, but it made any compassionate observer wonder how much his personal challenges were contributing to his continued struggles on the field. He kept his positive outward spirit intact, but his weight was still ballooning, and he was repeatedly being tempted far out of the strike zone by opposing pitchers. How much did that parallel his private issues? It was impossible to tell, and no one on the unified team was about to spill Pablo's secrets. It merely reminded of reality's constant intrusions upon the supposed refuge of the game.

The measure of a true major leaguer is not simply whether you can hit or pitch with uncommon skill, but whether you can do it while the rest of your life is imploding, you haven't had a decent night's sleep in weeks and you've changed hotels so often it's hard to remember which city you're in. If you can still consistently bring your top game then, be better than all of those around you and bring positive equanimity into the clubhouse besides, you're an enduring major leaguer.

You also have to endure whatever bad breaks come your way. Since the early season omen of his misspelled uniform, Eugenio Velez seemed destined for less than glory. In Arizona, he continued his trend of bad luck by taking a drink of a certain sports beverage. Debate on the usual health benefits of doing so are better left for another forum, but it can be stated without FDA approval that under normal circumstances, sipping from a cup will not result in a concussion. However, in Velez's case, he happened to take a sip just at the moment Pat Burrell hit a wicked line drive foul into the Giants dugout. The ball struck Velez squarely on the left side of the head and down he went, soon to be carted off on a stretcher to the hospital, where his concussion was confirmed and his latest bizarre misfortune chronicled.

In the wake of this, however, a small, caring act illustrated clearly and poignantly what the 2010 Giants were about.

The next day, Velez relaxed in an armchair in Chase Field's visitors' clubhouse after the series-ending win, looking none the worse for wear after his accidental beaning and a rough night in the hospital—although looks can deceive. When the music celebrating the series sweep blared over the clubhouse stereo, Matt Cain quickly approached Velez and murmured into his teammate's ear, "Is that too loud?" Velez grinned and said the band could play on, so to speak.

Cain struck the right chord with his caring regard. It was emblematic both of Cain's quiet role and of the oneness that had developed among the teammates—the intense closeness that had begun in the camps of spring. To be effective, closeness and personal regard had to keep expanding to embrace any who might be a part of the moment's ever-shifting team, even players on the fringes like Velez. Oneness always has to be inclusive, and it has to keep evolving. Without even thinking of it, the Giants were evolving along with it. That was at least as important as the wins, if also instrumental in creating them. Wins and spirit were coalescing into the beginnings of transcendence.

Chapter 10

Castoffs, Misfits and Oneness in the Booth

While Eugenio Velez was left pondering the effects of beverages on his career, announcer Jon Miller was pondering how a boyhood desire to eat French fries while working had landed him in the Baseball Hall of Fame.

As the Giants were sweeping Arizona, Miller was being honored with the Ford C. Frick Award for broadcasting—one of the field's most prestigious honors. He was inducted into the Hall of Fame in Cooperstown, New York. The ceremony featured John Fogerty singing "Centerfield" to recorded backing tracks, while commissioner Bud Selig sat directly behind him, arms folded, wearing a frown along with his suit. Among many Hall of Famers, Willie Mays also sat there, chewing on something. Miller, on the other hand, smiled broadly.

Miller had grown up in the Bay Area, where he'd spent his boyhood years at Candlestick Park, rooting for the Giants and intently monitoring the broadcast booth. Some people are just born for a calling.

In Miller's Hall of Fame acceptance speech, he recalled how, as a wide-eyed 10-year-old, he had witnessed an unnamed announcer simultaneously eat French fries and call the game without missing a pitch. "I thought, 'That's the life for me!'" And it was. He was broadcasting Oakland A's games by the time he was 22 years old, and 36 years later, he was an icon of national stature. Miller spent 21 years alongside Joe Morgan on ESPN as well as landing broadcasting tenures with the Texas Rangers, the Baltimore Orioles and, since 1997, his hometown Giants. He'd already been in the National Sportscasters and Sportswriters Hall of Fame for over a decade, yet his career appeared far from finished. He'd developed an eloquent, emphatic style that was as distinctive as it was passionate, informed and funny at the same time. He was among the game's masters at the subtle art of making things interesting when nothing was happening—a storyteller, voice imitator and movie aficionado who could spin verbal gold out of nothing. He deserved his place in the Hall of Fame.

Miller summarized his career in one sentence. "I just wanted a job where I could eat French fries while I was working, and here I am today." He was not eating French fries at the time.

In some ways, a team's announcers represent the franchise for its followers more closely than even the players do. After all, it's their voices with whom the fans daily connect via TV, the radio and now the Internet. A fan develops an intimate, if one-way, relationship with those announcers, who have to capture the character of the team as well as the action.

In that regard, the Giants were also successful at a level most franchises only dream of. Miller's culturally eclectic and intelligent style fit the Bay Area's own aesthetic perfectly. He had a fine young foil in Dave Flemming, a Stanford grad with skill in description and mastery at making every word count. Flemming was in his fifth season with the Giants, although he (like Lincecum) might have occasionally been mistaken for the batboy at first and still took merciless teasing from the other announcers about his baby-faced youth.

On the television side, the two-headed creature of Kruk and Kuip was definitely one being inhabiting two bodies. Mike Krukow and Duane Kuiper embodied San Francisco's approach to life and baseball as perfectly as Jon Miller: They brought an edgy, hard-working–but-still-partying ethic. As former Giants players who seemed like they hadn't quit, they had the inside knowledge and spirit of players who still rode the bench. They were great broadcasters for the same reason lesser players often make the greatest coaches and managers: When it doesn't all come easily, you have to work the hardest and observe the most deeply just to survive. You have to turn every tiny observation into advantage that overcomes others' greater natural skill. As players and now broadcasters, Kruk and Kuip did that with deep baseball knowledge and the constant hilarity only available to two best friends. They, too, seemed in some way to be castoffs and misfits, bound together by the greater power of oneness. They were unafraid to support brushback pitches or a few drinks after the game, and although you always knew which team they were on, they didn't hesitate to call that team out for its transgressions. After 20 years in the broadcast booth together, it was clear: If their own turn for the Hall of Fame came, as many felt it should, they could only go as one.

It was when the four joined together on air as Jon, Flem, Kruk and Kuip for the *Post-Game Wrap* that things often got the deepest and wildest. Woe to anyone who turned off the broadcast after the final pitch, for the best broadcast moments were often in that final segment—insightful, funny, outrageous and occasionally irrelevant, with Jon Miller frequently forgetting to turn his microphone on at first. It was beautifully raw and real, like nothing else in baseball broadcasting. It didn't matter if the game was a loss or win. Sometimes the most torturous losses inspired the best wraps. It was all as daring as San Francisco itself, and the Giants (along with their broadcast networks) wisely let them run free.

"I do give credit to our organization," said Duane Kuiper. "They have never, at one time, ever . . . asked me not to say something." He said this after the season, explaining how the potentially explosive use of the "torture" motif on air accidentally developed a life of its own. He acknowledged this was one theme that might have caused discomfort for the team. "I don't think the Giants were overly thrilled about it, to be honest with you," Kuiper said. "As much as they may have wanted to [tell us not to] with this, they were really, really good about it. I told them, this is not going to be something that we're going to beat, beat, beat into the ground. We're not trying to sell T-shirts. There's no agenda to this. So we never used it after a loss and we used it sparingly after certain wins. You never know how it works. The fans grabbed onto it, and off it went."

Off it went indeed. By now, the torture mantra had become a rallying cry for the year, showing up on signs in the stands. It was beautifully out of control, and no one knew where it would go. That was exactly like the season. The Boyz 'n the Booth captured it perfectly. French fries, torture and the Hall of Fame: They were all part of the same sweet and strange continuum.

Chapter 11

Transcendence Continues

The Diplomat

When the Giants came home to face the Florida Marlins after sweeping Arizona, they were soldiering on without a left-handed reliever, and weaknesses remained in the offense beyond Torres, Posey and Huff. Although Sabean and his crew were surely searching for help, Bochy insisted the team would be fine without help if need be. As with the moment just before Pat Burrell was signed, Bochy carefully reiterated faith in the team as it was, never disparaging the ones he had—nor counting on ones he might soon have. It was, as usual, the perfect bland way to keep speculation and discord from being seeded in the clubhouse or media.

Fish Bites

Of course, sometimes it's impossible to know who's going to help you, even if help is standing on your field. In the first game against the Marlins—shortly after Bochy had made those comments—Aaron Rowand hit a long flyball to left that appeared to be a home run, cutting the Marlins' lead to 3-2. Marlins' center fielder Cody Ross gestured to the umpires that a fan had interfered with left fielder Emilio Bonifacio's attempt to catch the ball. After five minutes of video review, Ross and the Marlins were overruled. But the Giants were staring at help right on the field, and no one in the universe then imagined whom that meant.

Nothing helped that night, though, as the Giants' ninth inning rally came up short in an eventual 4-3 loss. Forget it.

The next night, the Giants proved again they could beat the best. Josh Johnson, the Marlins' ace, began the game having not allowed more than two runs for 13 consecutive starts—one short of the major league record. The Giants touched him up for three. The game included yet another 3-for-4 performance from Andres Torres—who was given fine supporting hitting at the top of the order by Freddy Sanchez—and clutch eighth-inning homers from Juan Uribe and Edgar Renteria. Cody Ross hit one off of Matt Cain, as did Dan Uggla, who then hit a second one off of Brian Wilson. No matter: The 6-4 win balanced the series books.

The win didn't help balance Wilson's checkbook, however. He came in wearing the glaring orange cleats Bochy had joked about blinding the hitters in the All-Star game. Marlins' manager Edwin Rodriguez complained to the umpires. The league agreed and fined Wilson $1,000 for his nonconforming apparel.

Wilson was not convinced his cleats could have such an effect. He said drily, "The fact that he [Rodriguez] thinks these shoes throw 97 to 100 [mph] with cut might be a little far-fetched. I guess we should probably have these checked for performance-enhancing cleats."

Instead, Wilson spent time at his locker, assisted by the injured Dan Runzler, coloring half of the offending shoes with black felt pens. They had to be over half the team's dominant color, which was decreed to be black, although that was certainly arguable on Orange Fridays, one of which was coming up in another two days. Would Wilson wear them then—or ever again? No. Even in a warrior's world, some fights are just not worth picking.

That night seemed like an easy win coming for the Giants after Buster Posey extended his hitting streak to 21 games—now one shy of the Giants rookie record set by Willie McCovey. Andres Torres hit a home run deep into the water, giving the Giants a 9-2 lead. But Jonathan Sanchez and the Giants bullpen couldn't hold the lead, and the Marlins tied it when Dan Uggla hit a ground-rule double off of Wilson and his 53 percent black-felt–penned cleats with two outs in the ninth. The Giants had to come through again in the 10th, once more led by Andres Torres, whose fourth hit of the night finally sealed the 10-9 bargain.

Alas, in the series finale, the Giants were muffled completely. The Marlins' Anibal Sanchez pitched a one-hit complete-game shutout, the only blemish being a clean single to center by Pablo Sandoval. Posey's hit streak ended one short of McCovey's, and the series closed with a draw. The Giants gained no ground on San Diego and finished the set as they began, three-and-a-half back of the Padres.

July's Gold Lettering

Should Posey evolve into a perennial All-Star or even a Hall of Famer, July 2010 will always be embossed in gold lettering on his career résumé.

Posey's hitting was especially torrid during the first 10 games of his streak as he amassed 19 hits, six home runs and 13 RBIs. No other rookie in National League history had assembled such statistics for any 10-game span. His totals for the streak included a .440 batting average (37-for-84), six home runs, 23 RBIs and a 1.217 OBP (on-base plus slugging percentage).

His league-leading 43 hits for the month eclipsed Jim Ray Hart's July 1964 franchise rookie mark of 42. Posey's seven July homers were the most hit by a Giants rookie in a calendar month since Jack Clark's seven in June 1977.

Among NL performers overall, Posey tied for third in RBIs (24) and ranked third in batting (.417), fourth in on-base percentage (.466) and fifth in slugging (.699). Predictably, he was named the league's Player of the Month and Rookie of the Month as well as Major League Baseball's Clutch Performer of the Month, an award sponsored by a popular soft drink.

Posey's performance, not his expanding trophy case, prompted praise.

"He's got a gift," Bochy said. "Some catchers are known for their catching skills more than for their hitting skills. This kid happens to have both. But he also has the ability to separate them. When it's time to catch, that's where his priority is. He knows his biggest responsibility is handling the pitcher that day. When it comes time to hit, that's where his focus is."

Posey punctuated numerous attempts to analyze his swing by insisting he maintained the most basic of all hitting philosophies: See the ball, hit the ball.

All season, Posey remained spectacularly unimpressed with himself. Although after he was named NL Rookie of the Year in mid-November, he admitted being linked with Giants legends and fellow winners Cepeda, McCovey and Willie Mays "gives me chills."

Rookie of the Month? "Ask me to name the Rookie of the Month any time from last year," Posey said. "Nobody knows. It's a nice honor, though."

Player of the Month? "Same thing," Posey said.

Posey wasn't being at all rude or ungrateful. His focus on winning simply excluded almost everything else. That's how genuine competitors think.

On the Trio's Back

As spectacular as Posey's July was, he was nearly matched by Torres and Huff. While fans in Arizona were chanting "MVP" for Huff, Bochy was proclaiming Torres a "premier" leadoff hitter, quite an accomplishment after 11 years in the minors. Their statistics were staggering for the month both as individuals and as a trio, and they eclipsed the rest of the Giants' offense. Posey, Torres and Huff carried the Giants for July, much as Mays had once carried the club on his own famed shoulders. Together, the three hit 22 homers that month, while the rest of the team hit 10. Together, they hit .367, while the rest of the team hit .220. The trio equaled the rest of the team combined with 23 doubles and three triples, and they drove in 67 runs while the others only drove in 77. Their joint slugging percentage more than doubled that of the rest of the team (.679 to .307).

It was an amazing run. Yet in a way, it echoed a warning that sounded back through history—that individual dominance and three-run homers might not be the deciding factor in the race.

Little Fundamental Things

In many previous years for the Giants, winning a championship required beating the Dodgers, particularly before the advent of divisional play in 1969. "They were going for pennants then," said Bob Stevens, the *San Francisco Chronicle*'s eloquent Giants beat writer, in Mike Mandel's 1979 book, *SF Giants: An Oral History*.

With lineups featuring Mays, McCovey, Cepeda, Jim Ray Hart, Tom Haller, Ed Bailey and the Alou brothers among others, the Giants were always capable of thrashing the Dodgers. In 1958, the longtime rival's first season on the West Coast, the Giants scored 11 runs or more in seven of 22 games against Los Angeles. During the fabled 1962 season, the Giants pocketed a 19-8 triumph over the Dodgers and defeated them 12-3 and 10-3 on consecutive days later that year.

But between 1959 and 1966, the Dodgers secured four NL pennants; San Francisco captured only one.

"They weren't any better, but they did the little fundamental things the Giants didn't do," former Giants shortstop Hal Lanier said. "The Giants didn't hit-and-run; the Giants didn't bunt or squeeze; the Giants waited for the three-run home run."

Right-hander Bob Bolin, who pitched in numerous roles for the Giants from 1961 to 1969, echoed Lanier. "It came down to the breaks of the game, the 2-1, 3-2 games—who won the close ones," Bolin said.

Modern Fundamentalism

Shaking off their early season miseries, the 2010 Giants were now capable of beating the Dodgers at their traditional fundamental approach, whether the game was close, low-scoring or both.

The Giants ended their glorious July and ushered in August with a three-game series against the Dodgers at home featuring Tim Lincecum on the mound. Lincecum helped make the night memorable for a sell-out crowd at AT&T Park by revising his windup in what he described as a "twerk"—obviously a different kind of "tweak." Bringing his hands over his head as he wound up to throw, he allowed two runs and seven hits while striking out nine. Lincecum explained that he wanted to gain better balance by employing a motion he hadn't used since college.

On the surface, this seemed to serve as another example of Lincecum's brilliant ability to recognize his own flaws and adjust to them. It was indeed that. "Just so I could stay over my back foot longer," he explained. "Lately, I've had a tougher timing issue in my windup. [I wanted to] mess around with a little twerk. I guess, for me, it's a big twerk."

It also should have represented a big crimson flag for the Giants. Lincecum already had endured dips in his performance this season. His insistence on fiddling with his motion indicated he still didn't feel fully comfortable on the mound. "He was mechanically as messed up as anybody I've ever seen," said one Giants insider.

The game seemed like another relatively easy cruise for a while, as Aubrey Huff led on both offense and defense. His two-run double and 20th homer of the season paced San Francisco as part of an attack that included five extra-base hits. They led 6-2 in the ninth, but no win is easy—especially in 2010 in San Francisco. Brian Wilson, unavailable due to back spasms, paced the dugout, medically prohibited from intervening as the rest of the Giants bullpen allowed the lead to unwind. He looked ready to charge the mound.

"You guys know me by now," Wilson said afterward. "I want to pitch. I'll go out there with a broken leg."

Instead, a makeshift parade of relievers allowed the Dodgers to close to within 6-5, with the tying and go-ahead runs on base, before Chris Ray finally coaxed a game-ending groundout from Casey Blake, sealing the Giants' 18th victory in 23 games.

"It felt like Willie was in there, it was so exciting," Bochy said, half-joking as he referred to Wilson's usual way of creating trouble just before escaping at the end.

Aubrey Huff added, "That's the kind of atmosphere I've been waiting my whole life for." It was indeed a playoff atmosphere at last.

The next day was July 31—the culmination of the Giants' outstanding month and also the trade deadline (the last day on which teams can trade for players who will be eligible for postseason rosters). The Giants observed the latter by acquiring a pair of relievers. They cut the yo-yo string off of Joe Martinez and sent him to Pittsburgh, along with trading John Bowker for Pittsburgh lefty Javier Lopez, who had already helped the Giants by squandering a late-inning lead against them on June 6. And they acquired Boston right-hander Ramon Ramirez for a minor league prospect. Although the Giants needed a competent hitter more than capable relievers, they were unwilling to part with either of the two left-handers other teams inevitably requested in any deal involving a bat: Jonathan Sanchez or Madison Bumgarner. So the Giants chose to address the next item on their priority list. With Jeremy Affeldt and Dan Runzler sidelined by injuries until at least mid-August, they could use some bullpen reinforcements.

At this last moment of July, despite a beautiful outing by Barry Zito, the Giants trailed 1-0 entering the eighth inning. They might have felt ready to request an extension of the trade deadline so they could acquire a proven hitter, after all. With two outs in the eighth, though, Dodgers reliever Hong-Chih Kuo hit Posey with a pitch. This being a Dodgers-Giants game, both benches were immediately warned against retaliation, but it was obvious the hit was unintentional—and disastrous for the Dodgers. Up came Pat Burrell, who worked the count full before lining Jonathan Broxton's fastball over the left-field wall to lift the Giants to a 2-1 decision.

The score and its means of occurrence mirrored in reverse the April game when Manny Ramirez had similarly crushed the Giants. It was again payback, a change of momentum, evidence of evolution. Some came to call it the season's defining moment. At the very least, it was a hell of a thrill for the Giants and their fans.

"I really thought Huff was going to have an aneurysm in the dugout," Kuiper said of Burrell's enthusiastically cheering buddy.

"That's why Pat's here," Huff said after calming down. "Professional at-bats, situations like that, playoff experience—he doesn't panic, and he brought that up there." It was Burrell's eighth home run for the Giants and far from his last.

The excitement brought Barry Zito back out of the clubhouse in time to be a part of the thrills. He'd been removed after seven three-hit innings, allowing only a home run by the infamous Casey Blake. Zito was heading towards the showers when he pulled his uniform back on and returned.

"I wanted to be a part of it," Zito said. "That's how it is now. We're a team. You just want to be out here for the energy." The energy in the stadium, on the field and in the stands was becoming an entirely different beast now. Something was happening.

The finale was no less satisfying for the Giants, who'd mustered the game's only scoring on Edgar Renteria's two-run triple in the sixth inning—after the Dodgers had irritated Renteria by intentionally walking Aaron Rowand to face Edgar instead.

"I was pissed off when they did that," Renteria said. "I wanted to do something for the team. Don't wake up the baby."

Throwing more pitches than he had in a start all year, Matt Cain used off-speed pitches to effect and worked both sides of the place, achieving 7 2/3 shutout innings to complete the Giants' series sweep. He also earned his much-awaited first career victory over the Dodgers after losing eight decisions.

"I definitely wanted to go out and win," Cain said. "But we needed to do it more as a group, together. I think that's definitely what happened."

What happened in July revived the Giants. They were 20-8 during the month and 6-0-1 in series, beginning with the Milwaukee sweep. Outpacing the game-a-week Burrell Plan, San Francisco had gained six games in the standings since the 15-inning loss at Colorado on July 4, rising from fourth place in the NL West to second, now one-and-a-half games behind San Diego.

"You're at the stage now where every win is big," Bochy said.

A scheduled off-day and a return trip to Denver failed to cool off the Giants, who whipped Colorado 10-0 on Aug. 3 in a game that was full frontal excellence at its most exposed. Jonathan Sanchez approached his best, allowing three hits in six innings and striking out nine, including seven in a row from the second through fourth innings. That tied Juan Marichal's San Francisco–era record, which the Dominican Dandy had set in 1964. Meanwhile, the lineup epitomized balance as seven Giants rapped two hits or more.

Most importantly, the Giants had improved to 10-1 against NL West competition since the All-Star break. Before that, they'd lost 20 of 29 to division rivals. The Giants now trailed first-place San Diego by only one game, their smallest deficit since the Padres had led them by a half-game on June 17. The momentum was all in favor of the Giants. By every measure imaginable, it seemed the Giants had embarked on an inexorable climb. When did you say postseason tickets would go on sale?

The Giants pose as a team after receiving their championship rings in April, 2011.

At the instant of World Series victory, Pat Burrell appears to transcend gravity. Beside him, Bruce Bochy celebrates with equal lightness.

After eleven years in the minor leagues, Andres Torres holds one measure of his persistence on the path to success—the championship trophy, as Damaso Blanco looks on, doused in champagne.

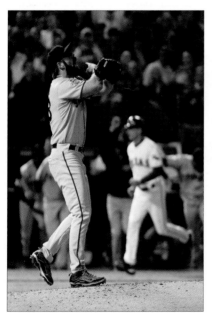

(Left) Brian Wilson uniquely honors greater forces, moments after striking out Nelson Cruz to complete the Giants' beautiful and improbable run to unity and victory. (Right) Brian Wilson's famed beard remains exceptionally focused as the 2011 season begins, perhaps with the assistance of the Red Bull beside him. No question, he flies his own flag.

Hoisting the World Championship trophy, Cody Ross sees his smiling reflection—perhaps reflecting himself on the unlikely path he took to the winner's circle.

Tim Lincecum returns to the mound after racking up the 11th strikeout of the night during his 14-strikeout, 2-hit shutout of the Atlanta Braves in the first game of the NLDS, beginning the Giants' classic run through the 2010 playoffs.

Tim Lincecum faces his former mentor Bengie Molina in the fourth inning of the first game of the World Series, inducing a groundout from the Texas catcher in a bittersweet moment of reunion.

Seven strikeouts and only four hits allowed isn't enough to carry Tim Lincecum to victory against Roy Halladay and the Phillies in Game Five of the National League Championship Series.

Buster Posey celebrates Halloween with a home run off of Darren O'Day of the Texas Rangers in Game Four of the World Series. Aubrey Huff looks uncommonly pensive behind Posey, as his teammates welcome Buster.

Javier Lopez and his teammates take a victory lap with teammates in AT&T Park after the Giants beat San Diego to win the National League Western Division on the final day of the regular season.

As one of the team leaders for four years, Bengie Molina guided the pitching staff, drove in key runs and always displayed grace and heart.

In the Giants' victory parade down San Francisco's Market Street, Aubrey Huff and Pat Burrell raise one of baseball's most memorable victory flags: Huff's famed Rally Thong, reputedly responsible for the Giants' strong finish in the regular season and subsequent championship run.

Announcer Jon Miller claims that he knows a bit of what it's like to be the Pope, as he blesses the assembled crowd in the name of Mays and McCovey at the Giants' victory parade in San Francisco.

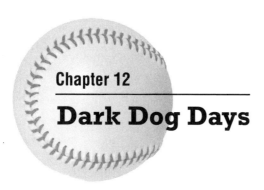

Chapter 12

Dark Dog Days

Little Resemblance

The schedule for August and September was loaded against the Giants—or at least loaded with intensity. August featured series after series against the league's strongest teams, frequently on the road. And September was packed with games against division rivals, meaning every game would drip with sweat and meaning.

"It's going to be two months of playoff games," Brian Sabean said from the front office. It would prove to be an exhausting understatement.

The Giants' performance in August barely resembled July's. After never losing two games in a row from July 3 through August 3, the Giants won back-to-back games only four times all month. In August, the team ranked unlucky 13th among National League teams with a 4.55 ERA, which for them was akin to the world spinning off its axis. They won only two series and were fortunate to have finished a still-unlucky 13-15. A five-game stretch late in the month typified the manic swings of San Francisco's fortunes. After Rookie of the Year candidate Jaime Garcia shut them out 9-0 at St. Louis, they returned home to score 11, 16 and 11 runs on consecutive nights against Cincinnati. Then they lost 6-0 to Arizona. "It was a long month," Brian Sabean concluded.

Through July, the Giants did what they needed to do. In August, two of the month's more notable events involved simply talking about what they had to do. One soliloquy proved more effective than the other. And doing is always more effective than talking.

The Allure of Agony

Throughout the manic strains of August, the team remained compelling to follow, no matter their struggles—or perhaps because of them. The combination of promise and uncertainty was riveting, and the energy in the AT&T Park stands began to swell.

What is it about combining mystery with passion that's simultaneously so enticing and so cruel? Is it because the word "passion" itself is so inextricably linked to the idea of "suffering," both in its linguistic and dramatic roots? Is that the reason the 2010 Giants season remained so compelling? The intermittent reinforcement the team gave through its performances kept that alluring, excruciating mystery alive until the end.

On the one hand, there were the enticements of July. There were promises like the easy 10-0 win in Colorado that made success seem inevitable. But there were also broken promises throughout much of August—like the year's perpetually futile attempts at stability. There were letdowns in equal numbers to breakthroughs. Hope and despair are two faces of the same coin, according to Buddhist wisdom, and the Giants kept inspiring both yin and yang without resolution.

Even in early August, the character of the team and season was yet to fully reveal itself. After that easy shutout, 107 of the 162 games had been played, and it still wasn't evident whether the Giants were winners, also-rans or merely a bunch of men who got along with uncommon unity and grace. Just one game away from first place, the Giants had been unable to take that final step to reach it. After scoring 10 runs in that first Colorado game, they scored fewer in the next five games combined. They started falling backwards into old, familiar ways. The Giants' grip began to slip one . . . painful . . . alluring . . . torturous . . . inch at a time.

Dog Days

It shouldn't be surprising that the Giants picked August to backslide. August is a rough month in the rhythms of the major league schedule. It's a long, long, long time since the team reported to camp in February. Bodies and spirits are worn, exhaustion sets in alongside the heat and the finish line is not close enough to provide inspiration. Neither is September 1, when major league rosters are allowed to expand, allowing minor leaguers to be called up as reinforcements. This serves as a reward for a job well-done in the small-time as well as offering a motivating, salivating glimpse at life in The Show, where the all-night bus rides to seedy hotels are finally over.

These hottest, most stagnant days of summer are known as the "dog days of summer," a reference dating back to the ancient Romans, who felt Sirius (the Dog Star) was responsible for said hot weather when it was in its closest apparent proximity to the sun. The Romans, in other words, were almost as superstitious as baseball players. The term can also refer to a period of time that is stagnant or marked by a dull lack of progress.

For the Giants of 2010, the dog days of August were not mere superstition but a stark truth. It was an exacting description and one that applied not only at the annual Dog Days of Summer game—during which fans are allowed to bring their dogs to AT&T Park (as long as each dog has a ticket). Dogs presumably understand the fundamentals of the game more than most animals: *See ball, catch ball.* And they are less prone than some human players to overthink it. This is perhaps a digression, but then, so was most of August.

Upsetting the Order

As noted by the jury, the Giants had begun slipping from the grace of their 10-0 Colorado shutout. Stuffed into a small container by Ubaldo Jimenez the next day, they moved on to Atlanta to lose three out of four, while scoring a total of eight tiny runs.

One baseball assumption is the runs are built on hits. But sometimes it doesn't work that way, and perhaps when it doesn't occur in a favorable fashion, the tiny handwriting of destiny can be read in retrospect.

On August 6, during the second game of the series, Zito pitched well. He appeared to be continuing his usual second-half surge by only allowing four hits, striking out ten and lowering his post–All-Star ERA to 2.02. Unfortunately, two of the four hits were home runs. Also unfortunately, the Giants only got four hits all night and found themselves losing 2-1 in the ninth inning. And they did not get a hit in the ninth inning. Nor the eleventh. And they won.

Destiny? It was built from efficiency, patient at-bats, execution of fundamentals, good fortune and a little assistance. That was the key to all three runs.

In the first inning, Andres Torres led off with a single. He stole second. He stole third. And Aubrey Huff brought him home with a ground out. "And that's all you need to do," said Duane Kuiper on the air.

Billy Wagner hit Aubrey Huff with a pitch to start the ninth. On Posey's following grounder, Alex Gonzalez threw wide to second, and both were safe. After Huff huffed over to third on Uribe's flyball, he bolted for the plate on Sandoval's grounder and scored when Chipper Jones booted it. Tie game.

In the eleventh, they were no more powerful, and no less successful. It was Huff and Posey to start again, and both walked. Uribe grounded out this time, again advancing Huff to third. Déjà-almost-vu. Showing rare discipline, Sandoval was walked semi-intentionally after taking the first two unintentional balls. And Pat Burrell hit a sacrifice fly to get Huff home, giving recent arrival Javier Lopez the win.

Brian Wilson came in and closed it out efficiently. "There's no messing around at 12:45 [a.m.]," Wilson said. "It was time to get the game over with." And a win was a win. Never mind what passed for offense.

The Giants had even less offense the next night, when they were shut out 3-0 by the Braves' Tim Hudson. And then came an outing from Jonathan Sanchez that would become infamous—not for what he did in losing, but for what he said after doing it.

A Predictable Outcome

Those who claimed Jonathan Sanchez never would amount to anything could feel smug on Aug. 8. He yielded four runs in four innings at Atlanta as the Giants dropped the finale of the desultory four-game series. When reporters gathered at Sanchez's dressing stall in the visitors' clubhouse afterward, however, the left-hander seemed oddly upbeat.

"I had my best stuff," Sanchez said. "I just couldn't make good pitches."

But Sanchez had more on his mind than that. Referring to the Giants' two-game deficit behind San Diego in the NL West, Sanchez said, "We've been losing a lot of games, and we're close. We're going to go back home and start winning now. We're going to face the Padres this weekend. Hopefully, we'll beat them three games."

Without the qualifier "hopefully," Sanchez's remark clearly would violate the you-gotta-play-'em-one-at-a-time mantra of team sports. Even as it was, his words came dangerously close to hubris. Sanchez

ignored the upcoming four-game set against the Chicago Cubs, probably because he wouldn't pitch until the opener of the Padres series.
But he wasn't done. "We *will* make the playoffs," he added without
qualification. Although time would prove Sanchez correct, he seemed
to be bandaging the wound of his subpar outing with bravado.

Sanchez *still* wasn't finished.

"We're going to play San Diego now, and we're going to beat them
three times," he declared. "If we get to first place, we're not going to
look back."

What about the Padres' seven victories in eight games against the
Giants thus far in the season?

"That was a long time ago," Sanchez said. "It doesn't matter. We
have a better team now."

You could almost hear the thumbtacks sinking into the cork backing of the Padres' bulletin board as a published copy of Sanchez's
comments was posted for each San Diego player to see. Publicly,
the Padres barely reacted to Sanchez's boasts, but there was still a
potential firestorm to head off. Sanchez actually incensed his teammates—who would have preferred to avoid a fuss—more than the
Padres.

"There were guys who were upset. There's no getting around it,"
Bochy reflected, during the calm of the offseason. "Something like
that can charge up your opponent. There's no reason to make yourself a target." Nothing motivates a competitive athlete more than
being told he's going to lose. Or as Edgar Renteria would say, "Don't
wake the baby."

Although some secrets remain within the sanctity of the clubhouse, one club insider felt certain veterans such as Pat Burrell, Edgar Renteria and Juan Uribe advised Sanchez to keep his mouth shut
from then on. "Those guys did not miss anything, and they were not
going to let this team be affected by any of that," Bochy said.

Sanchez wondered why he was perceived to have courted trouble
in the first place. According to Bochy, "He said, 'Well, I'd say that in
Puerto Rico, and it wouldn't be in the paper. It wouldn't be a big deal.'
Well, you're not in Puerto Rico."

Veteran baseball writer Manolo Hernandez explained that
Sanchez's boldness would indeed be standard operating procedure
in another country and culture.

"When he said that, people took it like you're bashing the rival
and saying something derogatory. It's not that way in Latin America,"
Hernandez said. "It's like a sign of confidence that his team is going

to accomplish this because it has the tools to do this. Most people took it the other way."

It can be explained as a cultural difference and misunderstanding—not exactly the first on Earth, nor the first in baseball, nor even the first that day. Still, in the culture of the United States, the baseball custom about predicting your own performance is clear and simple: *Don't.*

The culture also offers a simple corollary about predicting your *teammates'* performance: *Don't you dare, dude.*

When it comes to predicting personal performance, the American logic boils down to this: If you're truly confident in the impending outcome, you have no need to state it. You just do it. It's like predicting midnight's darkness or old age: Why bother? On the other hand, if the outcome isn't obvious, prediction holds no gain. Stating it will not improve its chances of becoming true. It only risks making you look like an idiot. Either way, talking about it distracts you from the actual doing. Nothing positive comes from it.

As much as it might have been a mere misunderstanding, Sanchez was alone on this one. Not that the team didn't believe they could do it. They just wouldn't be so foolish as to motivate the Padres by guaranteeing it. It is not the Giants Way.

Fortunately, the situation didn't escalate. "It turned out it was not as big a distraction as it could have been," Bochy later said about the controversy that wasn't. "I tried to tone it down with the media. Sometimes things are maybe taken out of context," he continued. "We all make mistakes how we word things. At the same time, Johnny's competitive. You don't want to take that away from him. [Pitching coach] Dave Righetti talked to him about it. I kind of tried to put a little touch of humor on it with Johnny because I didn't want to break his spirit, either. But I'm a believer, win or lose, you don't need to ever try to disrespect a club. You want to stay humble and play the game right. That doesn't mean you don't go out there and think you're not going to win or kick somebody's tail. But to go through the media is not the way to do it."

Fortunately, most Padres agreed—another reason the Giants had respect for them. Manager Bud Black, when asked about Sanchez's words, predicted nothing in return. "That's why we'll fly up there and see what happens," is all he would say. And what happens would have to wait until the Giants got home and got past Chicago.

Oneness Beyond the Uniforms

While the Giants were in Atlanta, they were also dragged out of the moment to discuss 2011 and Taiwan. Major League Baseball was proposing that the Giants and the Diamondbacks open the next season in Taiwan to continue spreading interest in baseball globally.

Aubrey Huff had participated in a similar venture in 2004, when his Tampa Bay team visited Taiwan to play against the Yankees. Huff said players felt like "zombies" for weeks afterwards. Some of their batting averages showed it, including the Yankees' great Derek Jeter. The long-term effects on the season were reason enough to question approving the trip, which the players would have to vote on.

Although evenly split about the trip, the players were firm on one issue regarding its terms: They would refuse to conduct the trip if coaches and non-uniformed team personnel, such as the traveling secretary, were not given the same additional pay the players were being offered.

"The staff is not getting the same treatment as we do," Huff said. The players were clear. Those people were team members, too, and deserved the same as they did. Equal treatment was a fundamental condition to their participation.

The statement spoke volumes. Months later—and for many reasons—the trip was vetoed. That was another victory of spirit that never graced the win column.

A Few Paces down the Corridor

Focusing on baseball instead of Jonathan Sanchez's gift of gab, the Giants returned home and captured three of four games from the Chicago Cubs. The team forged each victory by a one-run margin, developing the pluck and fortitude they'd need down the stretch. Pat Burrell played a significant role by hitting a sacrifice fly in the 11th inning to win the series opener, bashing a tie-breaking home run in the eighth inning two nights later and homering twice in the series finale, including a grand slam. This further underscored Burrell's impact. "He really changed the dynamic of the club with his big bat, his patience at plate and having won before," bench coach Ron Wotus said. It helped that Burrell felt comfortable in his surroundings. "It's just been such a great ride, being back in the Bay Area," he said. He was hitting like a veritable Machine.

The Best Player in a Supporting Role Award for the series went to Chicago's Mike Fontenot. The utility infielder threw out Travis Ishikawa at home plate in the 10th inning of the series opener to delay the Giants' triumph by an inning, then lined a two-run, pinch-hit single in the eighth inning the next night to help the Cubs record their lone win. The Giants admired Fontenot's performance so much that they traded for him before the series' third game on Aug. 11, sending Chicago a minor league outfielder.

The Giants needed Fontenot because they also needed depth. That same day, shortstop Edgar Renteria made his third trip of the season to the disabled list, this time with a left biceps strain.

Renteria had the gloom of a drowning man, going down for that third time. "Unbelievable," he muttered at his locker, thoroughly dismayed and disgusted with his luck—or lack of it. He was failing the expectations of his contract, and that disappointed no one more than him.

Still, he displayed the same quiet determination his leadership always showed in the face of adversity.

"I'll just get treatment and get strong again and hope in September everything's fine," Renteria said.

Although Renteria's frustration grew each time he was sidelined, other Giants sympathized with Renteria and continued to hope his faltering body would cooperate with his will.

"As far as team players, he's one of the best I've ever been around," right fielder Nate Schierholtz said.

"If you looked up the word 'professional' in the book, his picture would be right by it," center fielder Aaron Rowand added.

Other Giants infielders were also in less-than-optimal condition, hastening the Fontenot deal. A tight right hamstring had nagged Juan Uribe, San Francisco's primary shortstop in Renteria's absence. Freddy Sanchez and Pablo Sandoval weren't ailing physically, but their struggle to hit had been well-documented.

So Fontenot went on the move. Such is the itinerant nature of baseball. A few paces down the corridor makes such a huge difference and means an entirely different lifestyle. It's a turnoff to another world, with new opportunities awaiting.

Fontenot accepted Cubs handshakes, man hugs and kidding as he helped a clubhouse attendant empty his belongings into a cart. Realizing he was wearing blue Cubs workout shorts, Fontenot jokingly observed that putting on his jeans before reporting to the Giants' clubhouse might be a good idea.

"It's been a strange day so far," Fontenot said. He revealed no feelings of melancholy. "I'm excited for the opportunity to play here. I've been keeping up with baseball as much as anybody else does, and knowing that the Giants are in the thick of it really gets you pumped up."

Another Unhappy Lincecum Day

Typically a major pumping-up source for the Giants, Tim Lincecum had entered the most deflating period of his major league life. He absorbed the decision in the Giants' lone loss of the Cubs series, an 8-6 setback on Aug. 10. Lincecum yielded six runs and eight hits in four innings, including a career-worst four runs in the first inning. That dropped the Giants into a first-place tie with Cincinnati in the Wild Card Standings—after the Giants had maintained sole possession of the top spot for 19 days.

Nobody wanted to envision the worst-case scenario. But as one Giants insider said, "It was like, if he can't figure this out, this whole organization is in trouble the rest of the way." In the eyes of many, Lincecum was still The Franchise.

The numbers were disturbing enough. Lincecum plainly lacked "comfortability"—one of his manufactured words, which, like Stengelese or a Yogi Berra-ism, made perfect sense. Lincecum struggled with pitching's most basic aspect—how to propel the ball towards home plate. He ditched the hands-over-the-head motion again and pitched mostly from the stretch position, even with nobody on base. That ploy had worked for Lincecum previously, most notably on Aug. 17, 2008, when he allowed one run and three hits in 7 2/3 innings during a 3-1 triumph at Atlanta. Unable to find his proper rhythm despite muting the Braves' bats, Lincecum worked his final 1 2/3 innings from the stretch. Fewer "moving parts," he explained. That was the inventive, instinctive Lincecum at his best. This Lincecum simply didn't know what to do. He wasn't certain whether he'd begin his next start by using his old windup, his modified windup or the stretch.

Lincecum still spoke confidently afterward. "Everybody in here has high expectations of themselves, and when things like that happen, you kind of wear it. It's about bouncing back and staying mentally strong," he said.

That would bear repeating a few more times, for him and for others, in different times on different days ahead.

Setup Men and Straight Men

Meanwhile, in the bullpen, things were in better shape, even beyond the dramatic yet elite effectiveness of Brian Wilson. Setup men in the bullpen are like straight men in comedy: They don't get the glory, but they're just as essential. In the case of Sergio Romo, the Giants' setup man, he can hardly be called a straight man—except that next to Brian Wilson, anyone can be called that. By August, the estimable Mr. Romo was developing some very creative facial hair. He was also accumulating some interesting stories while catching the ceremonial first pitch each night during home games. And he was racking up some serious statistics in the shadows. Through the Chicago series, Romo had appeared in as many games as Wilson. He had only been scored upon in three of his last 34 appearances. His ERA was low; his reliability was high. His strikeout-to-walk ratio was one of the seven best in the National League. Romo was receiving high praise from Bochy, among others. He may not have been getting the glory closers get, but there is no ninth inning without an eighth, and Romo was getting the eighth done with grace. There was no question he was getting his due in the realm of the team, even if wider public glory eluded him.

Another Misfit

The Giants continued their desperate quest for offense by acquiring right fielder Jose Guillen from Kansas City on Aug. 13. The Royals outfielder they most coveted was David DeJesus, but DeJesus had sustained a season-ending thumb injury in late July. San Francisco instead settled for Guillen, possessor of an outstanding throwing arm and a penchant for hitting line drives. Reporters approaching Guillen often found him friendly and accommodating. That was the Guillen who said upon joining the Giants, "I like to win. I'm a very passionate guy, and I love to win. I hate losing. I think this is a great opportunity. I'm very motivated because I'm the type of player that likes this atmosphere, the playoff atmosphere." What type of player wouldn't?

Outwardly, neither Guillen's performance nor his demeanor explained why most employers felt compelled to show him the door after a little more than a year. San Francisco was Guillen's 10th team in 14 seasons. This castoff was a risk. Would adding Guillen to the mix disturb the precious clubhouse chemistry? Quiet concern was murmured outside of the clubhouse, but no discord emanated from within. Guillen was welcomed as enthusiastically as others before him.

Quiet as a Mime

Inevitably, the San Diego series arrived—the one Jonathan Sanchez had boldly predicted the Giants would sweep. The team was as quiet as a mime in terms of talking about the issue. The Padres had mostly done the right thing as well by not inflaming the issue further. If unwise words were allowed to dominate instead of the game, it would be a distraction to the Padres as much as to the Giants. The Giants had plenty of respect for the Padres, and both teams handled it well.

Unfortunately for Mr. Sanchez—or maybe fortunately, in the long run—his lessons quickly came on the field. Just as the wise ball seems to find its way towards the person most mentally unready to field it, the payback for his verbal miscues came immediately. In the first game against San Diego, Sanchez not only gave up three runs in 5 1/3 innings in taking the loss, but his failure to properly execute a sacrifice bunt also helped kill a key Giants opportunity on offense. The Padres did the little things right, and the Giants didn't. That was the difference in the game. That and the distance of the outfield wall, where Aubrey Huff hit one that would've escaped almost any other park but instead died for an out at the base of the bricks. Huff was clearly frustrated, believing it was gone when he hit it. But it wasn't, and it was the Giants who were gone in the end, along with the possibility of Sanchez's predictions coming true. Sanchez refused to regret his words. It was whatever it was, and what it was was over.

The next night was a more satisfying outcome from the Giants' perspective. With the initial loss already having swept Sanchez's predictions into history's dustbin, the team was free to get back to the true task at hand—winning one game at a time, without advance prediction.

Not that it appeared they would do that—for most of the game, anyway. Against young Padres ace Mat Latos, the Giants did absolutely nothing through six, striking out nine times and allowing the Padres to build a 2-0 lead despite the excellent efforts of Madison Bumgarner on the mound. But the Giants clawed back, one tiny run at a time. In the seventh, Pablo Sandoval greeted Latos with a line-drive homer that halved the lead. In the eighth, new arrival Mike Fontenot snuck a chopper through the infield, Huff doubled him to third and Pat Burrell got him home with a ground ball out. It was even. A parade of effective Giants relievers—Ray, Lopez, Wilson, Romo and Casilla—kept the Padres scoreless through the eleventh.

At that point, Buster Posey hit an infield chopper with pool-cue placement. It just escaped the pitcher's grasp, then threaded the needle between short and second, kicking off the second baseman's glove into left-center. Posey alertly showed no hesitation and took off for second as the ball slowly rolled, making his surprise attack safely with a head-first dive. That moment of daring proved the difference when Juan Uribe's soft single to right brought Posey home for the win. It was the little things again that were the difference, this time in the direction of the Giants.

If only the outcome of the next day would deliver an ending close enough to predictions. It began with promise when Lincecum struck out the side in the first. But soon he began to be flapped to death by moths—little bloops, soft liners, balls with exact placement to elude fielders. Lincecum only gave up two hard-hit balls all day, but after four runs crossed in the second, the lead was already deeper than the team could recover from. Posey called Lincecum's stuff "as good as I've seen it," but the unfreaky Freak only lasted 3 2/3 innings, giving up six of the Padres' eight runs as they scored in every inning from second through sixth. Posey was also the entirety of the Giants offense, producing three of the team's meager four hits, including a two-run home run that accounted for all of the scoring in an 8-2 loss.

It was a quiet loss—as quiet as the two teams were after the series. The Padres had no need to mention Jonathan Sanchez: They'd spoken their reply on the field, beating the Giants two out of three on their home turf. The Giants had even less to say.

A Bad Weekend to Be Named Sanchez

Maybe it was just a bad weekend to be named Sanchez. Giants second baseman Freddy Sanchez was dropped from second to seventh in the batting order and marked the occasion with intense self-criticism. The 2006 NL batting champion was hitting .258 with a .315 on-base percentage and a .324 slugging percentage. Each would be a career worst if he were to finish the season with those numbers. Sanchez made it clear that while the team's success stimulated him, his struggles sickened him. "I don't feel like I've done much to help this team win at all," he said. "It's frustrating and disappointing, obviously. You see everyone playing good baseball; I want to be a part of it. If I can get going, that'll help us even more."

Sanchez still stung from the 2009 season, when the Giants obtained him to bolster the offense down the stretch. He batted .284, but shoulder and knee injuries limited him to 25 games and two extra-base hits in that span. This year, he was bent on contributing.

He couldn't accomplish that with a faulty swing, but he found refuge in the confidence that shelters all accomplished athletes. "I know I'm going to come out of this," he said, repeating the wisdom Jim Bouton had once articulated: "I've failed in this situation and I've succeeded. Since each situation is a separate test of my abilities, there's no reason I shouldn't succeed this time."

Thirteen Again

As the Giants headed out on the road after losing the San Diego series—quietly beginning another stretch of 16 out of 25 games away from home—another unlucky 13 bit the Giants. With Barry Zito losing to Roy Oswalt of the Phillies—Oswalt had been traded from Houston and was not fated to face his nemesis Lincecum—the Giants endured their thirteenth consecutive game in which their starting pitcher did not get a win. On a team in which starting pitching is the central strength, that is somewhere between depressing and calamitous. "We have to do better, myself included," Zito said, winning the day's award for stating the obvious.

But Matt Cain didn't do any better the next day, running the streak to fourteen. Although victimized by a key error from Mike Fontenot, Cain still wasn't sharp, and neither was much else about the team's performance.

"We're kind of back to where we were a couple of months ago," said Bruce Bochy after the latest loss. Only a win in the final game by Jonathan Sanchez kept the Phillies from sweeping the Giants away.

Moving on to St. Louis proved initially more promising. Madison Bumgarner won the opener in assertive, effective fashion. He was now 21 years old and legal to drink a celebration beer if he chose— this time, in the beer palace of Busch Stadium.

"He doesn't scare," Aubrey Huff said. "He's a country redneck who goes out there and throws."

But the rest of the series provided only a view of more wreckage. Lincecum and Zito were hit again as the Giants mustered a total of one run in a final two games, which the team lost by a collective 14-1 score. Losing to playoff-capable teams in subdued fashion made the hopeful mailing of postseason ticket order forms to Giants season ticket holders seem only like wishful thinking—like a prediction as unwise and disconnected from reality as that of Jonathan Sanchez. The Giants were six back of the Padres and fading.

An Unpassable Torch

While the Giants were in Philadelphia, a torch was extinguished that could not be passed, and a memorable moment of history was replayed for a countless time.

Captured in grainy footage, the moment is every bit as iconic as the one of Willie Mays turning with graceful desperation towards the center-field wall, perfectly merging with the drive of Vic Wertz and sending it back to the infield. This moment is three years before that, however, and Willie Mays is in the on-deck circle—fated never to come to bat in the game. It's the culmination of one of the greatest comebacks ever: Despite being 13 games behind the Dodgers in August, the Giants had tied their rivals for the pennant on the last day, forcing a three-game playoff. It's the bottom of the ninth of the last playoff game, and the Dodgers are again ahead, 4-2, although the Giants have the tying run in scoring position.

In the grainy film, another unlucky 13 is the one on the back of Ralph Branca's uniform, which flashes as he winds and throws to Bobby Thomson, who sends the ball on its famous long arc, sailing into the Polo Grounds stands and baseball history. Branca throws the resin bag in disgust as Thomson leaps around the bases and the jubilant Giants converge. Russ Hodges screams over and over into the microphone: *"The Giants win the pennant! The Giants win the pennant! The Giants win the pennant!"* Like the clip of Mays, the replays of Thomson's home run are not over, even fifty years later. As long as baseball exists, they may never be.

But the life of Bobby Thomson is. He did not live to see the Giants win a World Series after 1954. On Aug. 16, Bobby Thomson passed away in Savannah, Georgia, at the age of 86, remembered beyond his baseball immortality as a true gentleman.

On the field, Thomson did many fine things. He was a multiple-time All-Star who hit 264 home runs, repeatedly drove in more than 100 runs and once led the league in triples. Yet throughout his entire career, his legacy in the enduring public eye has been distilled to that one astonishingly fluid swing. Most will only ever remember Thomson for "The Shot Heard 'Round the World." Strange, how five seconds of an 86-year life can come to define it. Stranger still, you never know just when those five seconds might occur.

Be ready for every one of those seconds within your own 86 years, if you are fortunate to get that many. That's what the legacy of Bobby Thomson says. Be prepared and present for every precious second. And be a gentle person in the process.

Lighting Another Torch

At the other end of the life cycle, a few days later, Santiago Casilla took a couple of days off from the Giants bullpen to witness the birth of his son.

Sons born into baseball families often excel at the game, although it isn't a family business passed down in the 19th century way. The legions of sons who have followed their fathers and surpassed them are numerous, from Ken Griffey Jr. to Barry Bonds. So, perhaps, after Bobby Thomson has been resting for a couple of decades, there may be a new Casilla who reaches the majors and provides the next transcendent moment to be replayed for decades. You never know when you're present at the birth of magic, the world whispers. So again, be prepared and present for every precious second. The cycles of life and death are too brief to choose otherwise.

Yet Another Castoff: The Accidental Outfielder

With Jose Guillen's arrival, it seemed inconceivable that the Giants would add yet another outfielder. The outfield was already as crowded as a Boston subway. Yet on Aug. 22, nine days after Guillen's acquisition, rumors materialized into fact as the Giants claimed Cody Ross off waivers from the Florida Marlins.

Remember Cody Ross? He was last seen standing in the AT&T Park outfield, pleading unsuccessfully to the umpires that Aaron Rowand's home run was actually a case of fan interference. He was just an anonymous opponent.

Ross's career had lately been in decline. After batting .270 with 24 home runs and 90 RBIs in 2009, Ross had slumped to .265 with 11 homers and 58 RBIs at the time the Giants obtained him. But the Marlins had other reasons to deem Ross expendable. He was eligible for salary arbitration after the season, guaranteeing him a seven-figure raise from his 2010 salary of $4.45 million. Moreover, Florida wanted to recall Cameron Maybin, a prospect viewed as a potential replacement for Ross.

It was widely believed that the Giants grabbed Ross mostly to prevent him from being awarded to the rival Padres, who had lost center fielder Tony Gwynn Jr. for the season with a broken hamate bone in his right hand. The Padres didn't complain, however, since playing tic-tac-toe with personnel has long been part of front office gamesmanship. San Diego was deep into a stretch of winning 13 out of 16 games, including 10 of 11, which extended its division lead to six-and-a-half games over the Giants on Aug. 25. The Padres' need for Ross was questionable, and the rumors of their interest in him were dispelled after the season.

For the Giants, even if they hadn't sought Ross, adding him meant more than just deepening the roster with a proven, all-around performer. Though Ross had never played in the postseason, he owned a reputation as a winner and a solid teammate. The Giants' chemistry—their intangible sense of oneness, camaraderie and team spirit—reached its zenith when Ross accidentally reached San Francisco.

Witness the reaction of Marlins second baseman Dan Uggla when he was forced to say farewell to Ross.

"The last five years, I've grown as close to him probably as any-body," Uggla told Marlins' beat reporters. "I've never had a better teammate, a better clubhouse guy. Everybody here in this organiza-tion is going to miss him. He's a huge fan favorite, just a big part of this organization [and] the core of this team for the last five years, and it's tough. It's really a sad day. His personality and his ability to lead and his ability to make the rest of us happy and in the right game mode. . . . He's going to be a huge asset to the Giants."

The Giants sensed that before Ross arrived.

A few days beforehand, Mike Krukow had sauntered past the batting cage, where Aubrey Huff and Pat Burrell stopped him. They briefly discussed the Ross speculation with Krukow, who confirmed it was legitimate. Burrell's reaction was at once immediate and defi-nite. "If we get that guy, we can do this," Burrell insisted. By "this," of course, he meant winning the division and beyond. Burrell's positive audacity persisted.

Asked a few months later to recall issuing that stamp of approval, Burrell wasn't certain about specifics but acknowledged, "I can see me saying that." He already had developed a friendship with Ross by training with him during the offseason (both live in the Phoenix area) and playing against each other in the NL East. Burrell added, "You get to know guys and what they bring to the table. When I found out we had a chance to grab him, I hoped we did. I have a pretty good feel for the clubhouse and what it takes to take it to the next level. I just felt like if we could get him involved, he would be a perfect fit."

The day the Ross move became official was otherwise dreary for the Giants, who had collected three hits off St. Louis rookie Jaime Garcia in a 9-0 loss at St. Louis. Afterward, Aaron Rowand looked up from his iPad and asked a reporter, "Are we getting Cody?" Rowand's tone was full of anticipation and eagerness, although his already-reduced playing time would dwindle more with Ross' presence. Rowand was looking beyond his self-interests, in accordance with the Bochy Paradox and the Giants Way.

As for Ross, he felt the soul of the Giants immediately on entering their clubhouse. "I didn't think I was going to be nervous because I had been traded before and been on different teams throughout my career. But I'm not going to lie. I walked in, and I was a little nervous," he said. "Especially when I walked up to Cain and he said, 'Do you think you could have flipped your bat a little higher when you hit that home run off me?'" Cain was referencing a tall ball Ross hit off the right-hander on July 27. "I knew that he was joking. Everyone welcomed me with open arms. From then on, I was part of the family."

Estranged Family

After losing three consecutive series to the Padres, Phillies and Cardinals—potential playoff rivals all—the Giants moved on to face the Reds.

Seeing Dusty Baker in the Reds dugout at AT&T Park still looked as incongruous as Winston Churchill doing strategy for the Germans. Baker hadn't managed the Giants for eight years now—with a four-year tenure managing the Cubs in between—but his association with the Giants had been so deep, his 10-year run there so successful and popular, that his Reds uniform still looked as glaring as Brian Wilson's famous orange cleats. It was not as unpalatable and tragic as watching Juan Marichal pitch two terrible games for the Dodgers in 1975, but it still induced that feeling of wanting to adjust the set to correct the colors.

Many Padres fans probably still felt the same way, watching Bochy guide the Giants. But a few steps down the corridor is indeed a turnoff to a different world. It's inescapable: Times and families change.

Temporary Nirvana

The current Giants family suddenly and briefly appeared to be direct descendants of the 1927 Yankees and their hard-hitting Murderers' Row. Facing Dusty Baker's Cincinnati Reds, the NL's ultimate Central Division champions, San Francisco rolled to 11-2 and 16-5 victories in the series' first two games on Aug. 23–24. As was the case at Candlestick Park, AT&T Park plays comparatively small on the rare occasions when warm weather reigns. Sure enough, game-time temperatures were 75 and 83 degrees, respectively, for these games. That genuine feeling of summer occurs so rarely in San Francisco *during* summer that when it happens, you allow yourself to bask in the delusion that it'll never end. The dog days of summer, in San Francisco, rarely give the dogs days warm enough to sit in the sun. The Giants added to the temporary nirvana by rapping a total of 35 hits, including seven extra-base hits each night. Freddy Sanchez, who had vowed a couple of weeks earlier to emerge from his funk at the plate, collected four hits in each game. By the end of the series, he had batted nearly .500 (17-for-35) in 10 games.

The Giants lost the series finale, yet it reflected what they were about more than the previous pair of games had. Trailing 10-1 entering the bottom of the fifth inning, they narrowed the difference to 10-5 before roaring ahead with a six-run eighth that featured Juan Uribe's three-run homer and Andres Torres' two-run double. But third baseman Pablo Sandoval, who was 10-for-16 in the series, committed a ninth-inning throwing error that created an unearned run and forced extra innings. The Giants ultimately lost 12-11 in 12 innings, although they had runners on the corners when Reds closer Francisco Cordero secured the last out.

Then the record-keepers took over. The 57 runs represented the most ever scored in a three-game series at AT&T Park. The Giants hadn't totaled 11 or more runs in three consecutive games since June 3–5, 1953. And they hadn't collected at least 17 hits in three games in a row since Aug. 2 and 4–5, 1933.

The Giants also set a franchise record for most players who felt as if they had won a game despite actually losing it. Nobody ever thought to keep track of that in baseball's archives, but it might have been the most important result.

"It sucks to lose, obviously, but you can't come in here down," Aubrey Huff said. "The game was lost. I mean, it was 10-1 in the fifth, and there shouldn't be one person hanging their head. A game like that shows a lot of character coming back like that, and this series showed a lot."

"It says a lot," Barry Zito added. "It was a tough loss, obviously, but we feel inspired, too, because we went out there and didn't throw in the towel. A lot of times when there's no momentum in your favor and you muster it back up, it says a lot about how much heart a team has."

Heart, this team did certainly have—a cohesion of the human spirit that was now complete for the unlikely run ahead. The human pieces were finally in place to transcend perceived limits.

Basement Ceiling

All of that inspiration didn't prevent the Giants from losing listlessly at times. The perceived limits were still as low as a basement ceiling. Even the jerseys on Orange Friday could do nothing to dispel the Giants' run of bad luck, bad performance, bad karma, bad all of the above. August was just an experience with a bitter aftertaste.

Nonetheless, to go with the old-fashioned orange jerseys, Lincecum went with old-style knee-high uniform stirrups and socks with three orange stripes—apparently in sufficient compliance with the league's color code regulations.

"And I seem taller," said Lincecum, to laughter.

But his performance induced no laughter. He concluded his 0-for-August performance (0-5, 7.82 ERA) by walking two batters in the first and then giving up a mammoth home run to Adam LaRoche of the Diamondbacks, the slugger the Giants had failed to sign in the offseason. It landed deep in the waters of San Francisco Bay, and the Giants were off and running backwards again in a 6-0 loss to the last-place team in their division.

"It's one of those punches you have to roll with," Lincecum said. "Obviously, it's not fun to go through. Nor do my teammates want to see me go through this. But it's part of the game, and you just have to fight through it, and that's what I'm trying to do. The last thing I want to do is give up or give in to what's going on right now."

Lincecum tried to remain positive, noting that the beginning of a new month might help him "hopefully start out fresh"—if not taller in striped orange socks.

Something beyond fashion would absolutely have to be done. But following Lincecum, Zito didn't do it either. The Giants rolled over as easily as a puppy for a tummy rub, while the Diamondbacks crushed them again 11-3. Zito yielded nine runs, including seven earned, while working a season-low 3 2/3 innings for the second outing in a row. That dropped the August record of San Francisco's starters to 5-13 with a 5.56 ERA. In five games on the home stand, they were 1-3 with a 9.12 ERA. Zito, the second-half performer par excellence, was now 0-6 with a 5.51 ERA in nine appearances since his last victory on July 16. There were excellent outings without reward at the beginning of that stretch, but suddenly even that silver lining had turned a dark, ugly grey.

Short and Direct

General manager Brian Sabean had seen enough. After the game, he ordered the four starting pitchers on the premises to gather for a closed-door meeting in Bochy's office. (Matt Cain, who was scheduled to pitch the next day, had gone home.) The exact contents of Sabean's soliloquy were kept in the inner sanctum, but the message was relatively short and extremely direct.

"They all need to step up," was Bochy's terse translation. "It's tough when you go through stretches like this. But the last thing we can do is accept it. You have to do something about it, individually, as a staff and as a team. These are all critical games. We're just not getting it done, and we know it." That was not acceptable to Sabean, Bochy or the failing starting pitchers themselves.

Said a chastened Zito, "We gotta do better. That's the bottom line."

At that juncture, the bottom line read that the Giants trailed San Diego by six games in the NL West and also trailed in the league's Wild Card race—the last remaining back door through which they might slip into the playoffs. Though neither margin was insurmountable, it was impossible to fathom reaching the postseason unless the pitchers acted on the message they heard.

After the closed-door meeting, when Bochy entered the interview room for his usual postgame session, he looked more furious than he ever had since joining the Giants in 2007. His face was flushed and frozen in a glare. Surely he had growled at the pitchers as well. Yet Bochy primarily elected to defer to his boss on this one. Had Bochy or pitching coach Dave Righetti dominated the discussion, the pitchers might have tuned out their all-too-familiar voices. "You almost become a parent," Bochy said.

So another family member stepped in. Sabean's direct voice provided a jolt that would prove far more effective than any empty prediction.

"We were really in a rut there," Bochy said. "Sometimes it's great, I think, for them to hear it from somebody else. For Brian to come in there and address the starters and tell them how much he is behind them but they're better than this, it was something they needed and something to help turn us around."

Time was of the essence. Defining "essence" as an odor, that meant: Time stinks. The Giants were running out of it. Almost eight weeks had now passed since Pat Burrell's one-game-a-week strategy was unveiled, and most of the early gains had unraveled. The Giants had gained only a game in those eight weeks. Less than five weeks remained. It would take different pitching, and yes, different under-wear to accomplish the feat ahead. It was time for the Rally Thong to change everything.

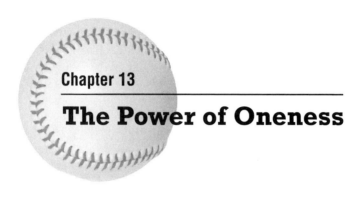

Chapter 13

The Power of Oneness

Swarm Intelligence

No pennant race was ever more vivid or unique than the Giants' wild run through 2010's final weeks. There will be other singular chapters of the Giants' Good Book, but there will never be another combination of baseball and human context like this team offered, often transpiring beyond conscious design.

Watching these Giants in their edgy, scintillating glory felt like watching one of the automobile ads that punctuated playoff games, with the caption spun below feats of daring driving: *Professional drivers on closed course. Do not attempt.*

This glorious spectacle also embodied the mysterious concept of swarm intelligence—collective wisdom that transcends the minds of its individual members. A single ant is dim and lost on its own, yet in the context of the colony, its tiny contribution magically adds up to a complex, smart system of living.

Not that the Giants were individually dim-witted ants—on the contrary, there were many fine minds on the squad. But in September and October, the cohesion that rose to transcendence on the team as well as in the organization and the surrounding stands was swarm intelligence at its highest—and sometimes strangest.

The circle of Giants unity drew tighter as the season lengthened. By September, nothing would tear them asunder. As Sergio Romo later observed, "Every personality in the clubhouse made the overall personality that much better."

Others agreed. "There's not a guy in here you wouldn't go to bat for every day," said first baseman Aubrey Huff, employing an entirely fitting baseball metaphor.

"The chemistry we have as a team is second to none," second baseman Freddy Sanchez said. "We have a great group of guys who all look out for one another and pull for one another. That's definitely big at this time of the year when you know everybody's on the same page and knows what our plan is."

Developing this oneness and tapping into its power requires players deft at nurturing positivity. It requires players who are willing to accept each other's differences and who don't become too intoxicated by winning or too dismayed over losing. It essentially requires a team of 25 men possessing basic interpersonal skills. In theory, that shouldn't be difficult to achieve. But in a realm where egos can rage unchecked and some players care more about money than winning, it's all too rare to find clubs that have truly jelled into a *team*. These Giants were such a rare team.

Nobody appreciated this more than Bruce Bochy. He said, "It makes the task of managing a lot less daunting when you have guys in there all on the same page, pulling on the same rope, very supportive of their teammates and having the ability to set aside their own agenda and ask, 'What's best for the team?' And these guys did it. It's one of the toughest things to get with a team, to have that mentality from *all* your players. To think team first—sometimes it can be tough, and it does sometimes separate a team from having a good year or a bad year."

From the third-base coaching box, Tim Flannery recognized the rarity of what the Giants had accomplished, which he described after the season. "In this day and age of professional sports, there's so much personal agenda. . . . The reality is, [with players,] I'm arbitration-eligible this year, and you're a free agent this year, and you might be playing with somebody else next year so you've gotta get your numbers up, and if you're not playing, you can't get your numbers up . . . " He paused for a sigh and a celebration. "This team, *nobody cared who got the credit*, and it was a total pocket of purity of baseball. I wasn't 100 percent sure it was still alive anymore, and as a coach, to be able to get that jolt, that dose of it, it really inspired me to keep coaching and keep going. And the players . . . all of a sudden they saw this is kind of beyond ourselves, beyond our coaches and our managers. And the whole thing of it was: *If you honor the game, the game will honor you*. And these guys who had been released, been castoffs and all the other stuff, they regained great power from this spirit of the sacred game of baseball by just honoring it and getting out of the way of it. [Giants fan] Carlos Santana said to me one night,

'Sometimes you have to get out of the way of yourself.' And I think that's what a lot of this was."

It was swarm intelligence at its finest.

The Long Journey to Purity

The Giants had been struggling to attain that purity for years. Barry Bonds' final seasons illustrated what baseball is like when the team becomes secondary. Make no mistake—Bonds wanted to win, and so did his teammates. But as the organization devoted attention and energy to Bonds' pursuit of Hank Aaron's all-time home run record, distraction became inevitable. Matt Morris, a gritty competitor who would have fit in well with the 2010 club, said as much on July 19, 2007, when the Giants performed sloppily at Chicago's Wrigley Field and lost 9-8, despite Bonds' two homers.

"I don't know what the goal is here, winning games or is it—I don't even want to say it," said Morris, a mentor to Cain and Lincecum who would be traded to Pittsburgh 12 days later. Referring to Bonds, Morris added, "We need him out there, we need him playing, he's our biggest threat—today he produced, and we still weren't good enough."

Moreover, Bonds' hulking, glowering presence intimidated other Giants, inhibited their self-expression and dampened their enjoyment of the game. In other words, none of the brilliant humor of September 2010 would likely have occurred if No. 25 were still occupying his three-locker acreage in the AT&T Park clubhouse. The lighthearted oneness would've found no habitable climate.

In 2008, during the Giants' first spring training without Bonds since 1992, Barry Zito predicted that players "will have more say in the clubhouse. You don't have a presence like a Barry Bonds. You're going to see some leadership roles forming that didn't exist last year. And I think that's good for the team."

Zito was right. The binding of the Giants accelerated in 2009. Lincecum won his second consecutive Cy Young Award, raising his profile as the face of the franchise. Pablo Sandoval established himself as one of the most fun players to watch in the majors, batting .330 and playing lively defense while inspiring Zito to nickname him "Kung Fu Panda" after the animated film's title character, a rotund panda who aspires to be a martial arts master and ultimately becomes the Dragon Warrior who brings peace to the valley.

The apt nickname stuck. Fans began to wear Panda masks and hats and all other manner of paraphernalia. Sandoval, like Uribe, always seemed to be up no matter the outcome. And throughout 2009 (unlike 2010), he continued to amaze by hitting screaming line drives off of pitches far enough out of the strike zone that other batters wouldn't touch them. As much as his personality as a team leader was the antithesis of Bonds, so was his strike zone—Bonds had exceptionally acute eyes for the zone and a disciplined willingness to take a record-breaking number of walks.

Led by Sandoval, Lincecum and others, San Francisco finished 88-74 in 2009, breaking a spell of four consecutive losing seasons and conjuring genuine hope.

"Going through the transition from the Barry Bonds era—and what a tremendous era that was for San Francisco baseball—this team had really gotten its own identity now with the young pitching staff, a great closer and our young players coming up," Bochy said. "I think they were just coming into their own as far as being a team that believed they could go out there and win."

They fully came into their own in September and October of 2010, and the journey to purity was complete for one transcendent time.

Do Not Attempt

In some ways, those two months became what the Giants had been striving for without success since the last World Championship 56 years earlier. The months became magical in a way that drew in viewers and listeners far beyond the team's usual faithful, beyond the Bay Area to communities that (like too many American towns at the time) desperately needed to celebrate an underdog winner in times of deep economic turmoil. The Giants began to attract interest countrywide as new audiences became fascinated by their unique and inspiring saga. That occurrence is the dream of every organization and its marketing department.

Yet the Giants were also doing it right out along the risky edge of personality, with expressions and occurrences that brought the "only in San Francisco" kinds of comments—both from those who said it with adoration and those who said it with offended yet titillated scorn. No team's marketing department would dare feature skimpy rhinestone-studded underwear, equally skimpy yet villainous leather apparel, pro-marijuana T-shirts, false beards (on women as well as men) and rallying cries involving the word "torture." But the Giants and their fans did, despite every cold sweat it must have induced in the front office wishing to carefully craft a family experience from the sport.

And they got away with it. *Professional drivers on closed course. Do not attempt.*

August almost ended tamely enough, after the closed-door meeting Bruce Bochy and Brian Sabean called with the starting pitchers. That critical meeting proved a catalyst for a run by the entire pitching staff swarm that was not only of championship quality but was unprecedented in modern baseball. The results were not quite immediate, however. The night after that meeting, Matt Cain and the Giants started out with a lead against last-place Arizona, but after Cain came out in the seventh, the bullpen experienced a rare unraveling, and the Giants had to scrape through a few rallies and a long, tense save by Wilson to emerge with a battered 9-7 victory.

The offense failed the next night as Colorado came to town and began a critical series by handing the Giants a 2-1 loss. Was it the bullpen that had failed? Or the defense? Or the collective swarm? Or luck? The yes to all questions didn't matter in the win column. Jonathan Sanchez was brilliant and took a shutout into the ninth but was removed for Wilson after walking the leadoff batter. Wilson shattered the bat of Carlos Gonzalez, but Gonzalez still hit a triple over a deceived Cody Ross, who had instinctively broken in at the shattering of the bat.

"He's a good outfielder," Gonzalez said afterwards. "It was crazy because I hit the ball on the barrel, and I didn't know how that bat broke. I guess it was meant to be." For the Giants, it was meant to be even worse when Freddy Sanchez's relay throw hit Gonzalez and skipped away, scoring Gonzalez and giving the Rockies the late lead. Three Giants hit the ball hard in the bottom of the ninth for no gain, and an uncharacteristically frustrated Buster Posey slammed his helmet down at the bitter last-minute loss.

The Giants now had 30 games left to play. Aubrey Huff surmised they would need to win 20 of them to take the division with 92 wins. That was a very tall order but, aiming to keep the clubhouse light, Huff had a solution.

Clad only in a ridiculous red rhinestone-studded thong, Huff pointed at his underwear. "Guys, here's 20 wins right here," he reportedly said. The Rally Thong was born, and Huff would keep wearing it if the Giants started and kept winning.

It was an edgy form of baseball superstition. It was a supposedly private joke, a clubhouse moment that maybe should've stayed that way. But it was also audaciously funny, and the thong's existence was reported in a baseball blog connected to the *San Jose Mercury News*.

The truth was out. And it was a perfect truth for the racy sexual sensibilities of San Francisco. The Rally Thong was a hit—at least with those who didn't have to see Huff parading around in the clubhouse wearing nothing else. Even while playing, Huff wore the thong under his uniform.

Surely if Major League Baseball had disliked Wilson's orange cleats so much they'd fined him $1,000, they couldn't possibly have liked Huff's rhinestone-studded thong. But there are no rules about what you wear *under* your uniform, where it's unlikely (usually) to affect the game's public image. There was nothing the league could say. Wisely, the team let Huff be Huff. He was a key team leader and stifling his personality would have only stifled the team's unified spirit.

If Jonathan Sanchez had been mystified by the cultural firestorm surrounding his predictions, he must've been even more bewildered now. Predicting three wins because of confidence in your team pales in comparison to predicting 20 wins because of the magic of skimpy, tacky underwear. Yet Huff took no heat for it at all. Cultural misunderstanding? Maybe all of American culture is a misunderstanding—or at least a mystery. And you can get away with a lot more jokes if you're winning.

Unlike with Sanchez's predictions, the Giants backed up the joke with eerie accuracy. After Huff donned his thong, the Giants won exactly 20 games the rest of the way, finishing with precisely 92 wins. As the team then rose into the intense spotlight of the playoffs and World Series, the tale of the Rally Thong and its perfect prediction rose to legendary status.

Even Huff's thong appeared sedate compared with what happened the day after its first appearance. Brian Wilson had become a regular guest on the Fox Sports television program *The Cheap Seats*, hosted by Chris Rose. Wilson's combination of high intelligence, odd humor and sheer intensity made for strangely compelling television, including the intriguing mystery of trying to figure out what was real in Wilson's mind. He (and his invented personas) also made televised appearances elsewhere. Speaking with ESPN's Jim Rome, Wilson claimed to be a "certified ninja," his certification supposedly having come to him in a dream. It was hard to remember that underneath Wilson's inscrutable character was a deeply religious man with workout habits few could equal.

Chris Rose probably deserved what he got moments after *The Cheap Seats* showed a photograph comparing Wilson's Mohawk-and-beard appearance to that of an obscure barnyard animal. While

Rose was suggesting to Wilson that he give a similar hairdo to his dog—with Wilson broadcasting from home via webcam—a silent figure suddenly walked through the background of Wilson's broadcast. It was a large man wearing a hooded, minimal leather costume straight out of a B-movie or bondage catalog—or the scariest place of all: Wilson's imagination.

Rose came unglued while Wilson remained deadpan, claiming not to know what Rose was talking about. Rose ended up nearly shouting, "That's just *mean*! That can ruin people's *careers* right there!" Wilson almost kept a straight face before finally saying casually, "That guy? Oh, that's The Machine. He lives next door. He doesn't say much. . . . He comes over for sugar once in a while."

"Where do we go after that?" Rose finally asked, completely at a loss for composure. Wilson had trumped Rose's ribbing brilliantly. It was perfectly executed payback.

Backing It Up

Wilson was backing it up. He was raising the bar for all sorts of personal performance records while remaining in position to lead the league in saves, the key stat for a closer. That wasn't his concern, however. His interest was that he was poised to lead the team to the place he believed they were going—into the October playoffs.

At this late point in the exhausting year, most players were stuck in physical survival and maintenance mode. Not Wilson. He already had a workout regimen that was beyond punishing, and when September began, he *increased* his regimen beyond its already almost-inhuman levels.

"I gotta amp it up, workout-wise," said Wilson, with emphasis on his cardiovascular routine. "We have a chance to go into October. I haven't played baseball in October before, so I gotta work out a little harder. A lot of people back off, but have those people been working out the whole year? I can't just back off. This is when your body needs it the most, I feel. I don't need rest."

The Giants were working Wilson hard, too, often pitching him for longer than most closers. He was leading the league in saves longer than one inning—something once common in baseball but now rare in the Age of Specialization.

"Another manly-man save on a ship of manly men," as Duane Kuiper said on a *Post-Game Wrap* after another lengthy September save from Wilson.

Typically, Wilson loved working that hard. He should have been the one called The Machine, not his silent accomplice. "For me, I don't mind pitching three days in a row, then taking a day off, pitching two more days, then another day off," Wilson said. "You get acclimated with your motion, your mechanics and baseball as a whole. You get out on the mound and have a good feel for what's going on."

Wilson had a great feel for what was going on, and the results were there, even if they often produced as much anxiety as The Machine had for Chris Rose.

One Slump Is Too Many

The Giants could not afford to lose a series to Colorado, especially at home, and they'd already lost the first torturous game. Undaunted, the Giants rallied past Colorado 5-2 as Andres Torres homered leading off the eighth inning. Buster Posey then added a two-run double. This would become the first of the 20 victories Huff's thong had predicted and a positive note on which to end August.

Meanwhile, the Padres were finally losing. Again and again and again. They'd been all year without a slump until late August—an incredible feat by a low-payroll team mistakenly presumed to be cellar dwellers all year. As August ended, the Padres' losing streak climbed to six games with a 7-4 setback at Arizona.

At six games, the Padres' losing streak wasn't over yet. And things kept happening for the Giants that would keep the momentum turning in the clubhouse and on the field.

The Franchise Returns

The start of a new month signaled a new beginning for the Giants and their embattled ace, Tim Lincecum. On Sept. 1, he again opposed Colorado ace Ubaldo Jimenez, who had thoroughly humbled the Giants on May 31. But that had been Lincecum at less than his best. August, of course, saw Lincecum at *far* less than his best. In September, Lincecum was neither. This was the Giants ace in full glory, having fortified himself with a revised between-starts workout regimen that included running stadium stairs and playing long-distance catch, commonly known as "long toss."

Against the Rockies, Lincecum played quick toss. He worked eight impressive innings, faltering only when Gonzalez homered leading off the fourth inning. As if for emphasis, Lincecum concluded five separate innings with strikeouts. Meanwhile, Jimenez limited San Francisco to three hits in seven innings, resulting in a 1-1 tie.

Mike Fontenot coaxed a walk from Jimenez to christen the Giants' eighth. In came Darren Ford, who had been recalled that day from Double-A Richmond to run for Fontenot. Ford probably was the organization's fastest player. He immediately showed that "probably" should have been changed to "definitely." After Ford took second base on Lincecum's sacrifice bunt, Jimenez flung a split-finger fastball in the dirt to Andres Torres. The ball bounced just a few feet away from catcher Miguel Olivo, but the fearless Ford dashed for third and made it safely. The hurried throw from Olivo slipped away into very short left field, and the daring Ford again took off for the plate and scored what proved to be the game-winning run. *Professional drivers on closed course. Do not attempt.*

In the dugout, the elation was unbridled. A television camera caught Huff and Burrell, grinning like kids on the last day of school as they punched each other in the torso out of sheer glee.

Bochy was full of praise for Ford. "He wasn't afraid to make a mistake, which is how you want your guys to play," Bochy said.

The Padres then suffered their seventh loss in a row—a 5-2 decision in Arizona—trimming San Diego's lead over San Francisco to three games.

In total, the Giants pitchers gave up only five runs in three games to the Rockies, despite losing the opener. That stellar performance was only a warm-up for the collective pitching mastery of the three weeks to come.

Freedom!

Again, the mastery wasn't immediately evident. In Los Angeles—where things frequently seem to begin and end against the rival Dodgers—the Giants quietly lost the first game as both Zito and the offense were ineffective. Zito's pitching line was consistent in ugliness: four innings, four hits, four runs (all earned), four walks. His five strikeouts didn't help salvage his second consecutive short ineffective outing, in which he was nibbling at the strike zone instead of asserting himself in it. Making the ugliness even harder to look at, his final two walks were cashed in when opposing pitcher Chad Billingsley raised his average to .137 with a 2-RBI single. Meanwhile, the Giants managed only two hits total in the 4-2 loss. It was not an acceptable way to begin a critical 10-day road trip against division rivals.

So the next day, it was time for a closed-door clubhouse meeting. Tim Flannery recalls it as one of the key moments of the season: "Boch told all the media and all the players that, Hey, there's a players association meeting, so all the media had to leave the clubhouse. And all the players are thinking . . . we're going to talk about collective bargaining or going to Taiwan. And LA's such a small, old-school clubhouse, where everybody's right on top of each other and everybody's looking at each other, and Bochy came out, and he started talking about the history of Scotland and a man called William Wallace. Then he says to our video guy, 'Danny, bring out the monitor!' And he brings out a monitor, and he pushes [play on] the movie *Braveheart*, right when Mel Gibson is going up and down the line, firing up his castoffs, his misfits, the guys who were going to go fight this battle. . . . [Bochy] got guys so fired up that from that night on, they were yelling 'Freedom!' every time something happened. You yelled, 'Freedom! This is our time! This is our time!' And from that moment on . . . we knew that we were up against the clock . . . we had to win every game. That was the mentality."

The message, said Sergio Romo, was that "It's not about us as individuals. It's about the cause in general." He, too, tells of how the players ran around yelling "Freedom!" afterward, echoing Mel Gibson's character. "We got a good chuckle, but at the same time, we understood the message."

Jon Miller—part of the media not allowed in the clubhouse for the meeting—didn't know what had transpired inside. But he knew *something* important had, for as he related on the *Post-Game Wrap* that night, "When the closed-door meeting ended before the game, Pat Burrell turned to Bruce Bochy and said to him, 'That was beautiful!' And Huff added, 'That was the best ever! I have a man crush!'"

What a classic game it became—one that would have done Mays, McCovey, Cepeda and Jim Ray Hart proud. The Giants entered the seventh inning of the game trailing 4-0, having collected only one hit off Los Angeles left-hander Ted Lilly. Then Posey drilled a leadoff homer. *Freedom!* Edgar Renteria and Burrell christened the eighth with back-to-back homers, the latter done as a pinch hitter. *Freedom!* And with one out in the ninth, Cody Ross beat out an infield hit before Juan Uribe—always cool in the clutch—delivered the crushing blow, the fourth Giants home run in three innings, a deep no-doubter. *This is our time!*

Uribe's concluding blast, which gave the Giants a 5-4 win, was hit off of Jonathan Broxton, who'd already been victimized in classic fashion earlier in the season by Pat Burrell. Broxton had since lost his closer's job to Hong-Chih Kuo, but Kuo had been removed early in this game, and Broxton was still throwing hard.

"Broxton was throwing 97 [mph]," Mike Krukow reported. "It wasn't like he was out there naked throwing prayers." His pitch to Uribe was the 14th pitch he'd thrown—and the first breaking ball among them. When it vanished deep into the left-center field bleachers, the stadium noise vanished, too.

"This was the best stomach punch to a crowd on the road I think I've ever seen," Krukow added. "You could hear the Giants fans right over the top of a very quiet Dodgers crowd. It was one of the coolest things I've ever heard!" Downright cold, in the view of Los Angeles.

But of course, it still wasn't easy. Brian Wilson allowed runners to reach the corners with one out and had to do another high-wire escape act to preserve the win.

"It couldn't end any other way," Jon Miller concluded on the broadcast. "It's the Giants and Dodgers. They always end . . . about to have a heart attack."

For his own heart, Bochy claimed otherwise, saying, "Willie's put me through this many times. We're kind of used to this."

Starter Matt Cain had one bad inning—in which all four Dodgers' runs scored—but otherwise pitched well. Still, in allowing four runs in one game while the Padres were losing their ninth straight, he did something the entire Giants team would not do again for a long, long time. What was about to transpire on the pitching staff would do *Braveheart* proud. *Freedom! This is our time!*

Next came the series finale, and with it the eternal guessing game: Which Jonathan Sanchez would show up? The imperturbable strikeout machine who would flirt with another no-hitter? Or the shaky 27-year-old who'd walk the ballpark and struggle to last four innings?

Pitching before a nationwide TV audience furnished by ESPN, Sanchez the Brilliant stepped forward. Benefiting from the twilight—the game's scheduled starting time was 5:05 p.m.—and Los Angeles' overeager hitters, Sanchez walked only one and struck out nine while yielding three hits in seven innings. Uribe's slugging again proved essential as he belted a two-run, seventh-inning homer. Sergio Romo and Brian Wilson struck out two batters apiece while pitching perfect innings as the Giants prevailed 3-0.

Just as importantly, San Francisco's NL West deficit was down to one game because the Padres kept on losing. Their losing streak reached 10 games as Colorado recorded a three-game weekend sweep at San Diego.

More awaited the Giants at Arizona, where Nate Schierholtz's 11th-inning triple won the Sept. 6 series opener 2-0. Huff, Freddy Sanchez and Burrell each swatted first-pitch homers the next night to back the resurgent Lincecum in a 6-3 triumph. The Padres, whose losing streak had finally stopped, suddenly changed directions and continued a three-game sweep of Los Angeles. They led the Giants by two games entering a four-game showdown at San Diego.

By this time, the Giants had started their own streak, which continued despite a hard-luck 3-1 loss in the Arizona series finale. The game began with promise, when Freddy Sanchez homered in the top of the first. An effective Barry Zito allowed only four hits and struck out seven, yet came out losing again. The Giants could not rally and lost their chance for the sweep, despite pitching excellence. No one yet considered it historically significant that the team had allowed three or fewer runs in four consecutive games.

A Closer Call

As the San Diego series began, horrifying reality intruded—much as it had done in 1989, when the the Loma Prieta earthquake interrupted the World Series between the Giants and A's.

This disaster was more localized. During the season, Pablo Sandoval and his beloved mother, Amelia Sandoval, lived in San Bruno—in close proximity to an aging natural gas pipeline. With devastating consequences, the gas line exploded, lethally destroying an entire neighborhood.

"Everybody told me my neighborhood's on fire," Pablo said later. He was not there, busy as he was with the Giants. Amelia Sandoval was unscathed in the initial blast, but she had to escape quickly. Unable to speak English and with no experience driving a car in the United States, Amelia fled to safety, negotiating Bay Area freeways and attempting to scale communication barriers. Fortunately, she did both successfully, ending up in San Jose at the home of another Sandoval, Pablo's older brother, Michael.

Pablo and his mother moved into a San Francisco hotel for the remainder of the season. That they were not among the ones truly devastated offered faint consolation.

"I feel sad that this happened," said Pablo. "I care about the people who lost members of their family."

The Giants dedicated a game to the victims when the team got home, raising $120,000 that night to assist with the recovery. But what recovery can there be for lives and houses that are gone?

Home Field Advantage . . . on the Road

Despite the Padres' surprising seasonal success, the atmosphere at San Diego's PETCO Park wasn't exactly charged with down-the-stretch intensity. The paid crowd of 28,456 for the four-game series opener on Sept. 9 was decent for a Thursday night but not overwhelming.

However, the audience did possess a distinctive trait, which became evident immediately when Andres Torres tripled to open the game and scored on Freddy Sanchez's single. The Giants fans present were numerous and loud enough to give San Francisco what amounted to a home-field advantage. The team's traveling fans, who had earlier chanted "MVP" for Aubrey Huff in Arizona and had outshouted the quieted Dodger crowd in LA the previous week, were now in San Diego with volume and force.

The Giants responded to the fans' serenade with one of their most assertive performances of the season. They were dominant in a 7-3 win, scoring in five of the first six innings while Matt Cain took a three-hitter into the ninth. Cain received a standing ovation upon leaving the game. A standing ovation *in San Diego*, it's worth repeating.

"To be able to hear those guys on the road is definitely fun," said Cain.

The Giants hit four home runs that night as Huff, Uribe, Posey and Burrell all connected. The Giants had never hit that many homers in any of their previous 60 games at PETCO Park since it had opened in 2004. The most impressive was by Pat Burrell, who nearly hit one over the Western Metal Supply Company building adjacent to the left-field foul pole. Mike Krukow expressed hushed awe.

Another Giant was nearly as hushed before the series began.

"I have nothing to say," said Jonathan Sanchez wisely. The Giants and their traveling fans said everything that needed to be said. Loudly.

The Giants indeed captured the attention of the Padres. San Diego starter Jon Garland, who had teamed with Uribe and Aaron Rowand on the 2005 World Series champion White Sox, knew the look of a winner when he saw it.

"They have an unbelievable lineup over there, especially with some of the moves that they've made," Garland said after allowing six runs and eight hits in five innings. "It seems like they just keep stacking it and stacking it. They're hungry. They haven't been to the playoffs in a long time, and they want to do some things, and they've shown they're going to go out and try to do it."

Still, the offense had aroused legitimate skepticism all year. It almost always struggled to "keep the line moving," one of Bochy's favorite phrases, by stringing together walks and base hits. But as the season lengthened, the Giants recaptured their classic method of scoring: power. The team was historically built on the home run, from Ott to Mays to McCovey to Bonds, and in 2010, the Giants shared the National League lead in that category with 80 after the All-Star break, tying Cincinnati and Arizona. The Giants would deliver a league-high 36 of those homers in September alone.

After their four-homer opener, the Giants were now only a single game back again—in both the Western Division and the Wild Card race—and the Padres had to be hearing their footsteps.

The Giants caught them the next night, in the first of three 1-0 games within the next four. They survived the best and worst of Jonathan Sanchez, who allowed only one hit but walked seven in five innings. Five relievers then combined to surrender just two singles and one walk in four innings—most notably Brian Wilson, who recorded his ninth save of four outs or more by working the final 1 2/3 innings.

After muscling up on the previous night, the Giants employed by-any-means-necessary desperation to score their lone run. Huff was hit by a pitch and literally ran away from the Giants' assistant trainer on the way to first base before stealing second. Violating baseball gospel, Huff then took off for third on a grounder hit ahead of him and beat shortstop Miguel Tejada's throw. "It was actually a dumb play on my part," said Huff. But he got away with it—another good omen of fortune. Huff scored when Uribe beat the throw to first on a potential double-play grounder. It was enough.

After the game, Wilson praised the tenacity of Sanchez in keeping the shutout alive under constantly tense conditions. "He didn't give in. As a starter in those kinds of situations, he knows that it's September and we have plenty of arms in the bullpen. He went 100 percent every single pitch, every single hitter, gave it everything he had and came out in our eyes a winner." The Giants were a winner in the standings and in everyone's eyes. They were tied for first. They hadn't climbed that high since May 6, when they led the division by a half-game. It had been a long time coming.

But it was a short time lasting. Another 1-0 game the next night went the opposite direction. The Giants wasted a beautiful effort by

Madison Bumgarner, who only faced two batters over the minimum but lost when one of the three hits he gave up was a home run to former Giant catcher Yorvit Torrealba.

Back to second place.

Then back to first as the resurgent Lincecum outdueled Padres ace Mat Latos in a decisive 6-1 rendering. Latos opened the game with a pair of strikeouts, hoping to establish immediate dominance. But Huff's single prolonged the inning for Posey, who displayed his opposite-field hitting skill by directing his 13th homer of the season towards the porch in right. Maintaining the aggressiveness they had displayed in the series opener, the Giants scored in three of the first four innings to chase Latos, tagging him for five runs in those four innings—including a two-run single by Lincecum. The Giants thus ended Latos' major league record string of 15 consecutive starts of five innings or more in which he gave up two or fewer runs. His young arm—unlike Bumgarner's or Lincecum's—appeared to be tiring as September wore on. It was the first late season for both Latos and Bumgarner, but while Bumgarner was saying, "I feel like it's the spring of the year right now"—and proving it with performance—Latos was suddenly showing vulnerability.

By contrast, Lincecum allowed just two balls to be hit out of the infield and struck out five in the same four-inning span. At game's end, Lincecum was 3-0 with a 2.08 ERA in September, far from his August doldrums, and he reached 200 strikeouts for the third straight year—the first Giant to do so since Juan Marichal had a four-year run from 1963 to 1966. Lincecum was figuring it out. With confidence.

The win concluded a 10-game, three-city trip, which the Giants finished 7-3. During that stretch, the Giants occasionally outslugged their opponents. They usually outpitched their foes. Almost always, as general manager Brian Sabean would ultimately declare, they'd outcompete the other ballclub.

Those 10 games made an impression on Bochy that lingered weeks after the season ended. "That's when I really felt there was something special about this team," he said.

One of the things special about the team was they had now allowed three runs or fewer in eight straight games. Noticeable now. Consistent. But not yet amazing.

The Giants left town with a lot of "fun" games ahead, as Posey put it. They were coming home to face Los Angeles. And there's never an easy Giants-Dodgers match in September.

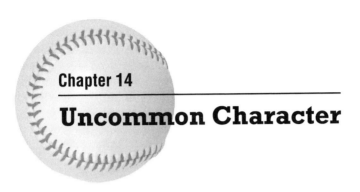

Chapter 14

Uncommon Character

Hairy Attitude

Down in the bullpen, things were getting truly hairy. The origins of the relievers' odd facial hair is another tale shrouded in embellished legend and the unfathomable recesses of Brian Wilson's mind. Sergio Romo was getting facially creative by July, and Wilson followed suit in August. By September, a new legend was born. As in most things bullpen, Wilson was the leader soon enough.

Wilson had become the *attitude* of the bullpen. As the pennant race unfolded, that attitude manifested itself in a frightening form. Not only did Wilson's beard grow thicker and thicker alongside the baseball tension, but it also turned blacker and blacker—as black as the darkest corners of his imagination. His beard got as black as if, say, he'd colored it with a felt pen, just as he'd done with his brilliant orange cleats. It soon looked so unnatural—especially alongside the lighter brown of his Mohawk—that even the reality of the hair itself came into question. At one point, Dave Flemming reported on the air that he had tugged on Wilson's beard in the clubhouse to see if it would come off. (It didn't.) Even Brian Sabean reportedly called the beard "ridiculous." It was perfectly obvious that Wilson was coloring it, but even as the playoffs and World Series unfolded, he refused to admit that to the media hordes, claiming his beard was simply "tan" from all the day games the Giants had been playing. "It's just *focused*," he added.

It was also ungovernable by league officials, like a red thong under a uniform. Furthermore, league officials had already deemed black the Giants' primary color, so Wilson's beard was in perfect keeping with his uniform—especially if you consider his true uniform to be eccentricity. He wore that uniform daily, and he wore it with such accomplished ferocity and humor that, somehow, it became exceptionally cool. Wilson backed it up with his fearless approach and searing fastball: That was the ultimate key.

Fans in the stands soon began to follow suit, with facial hair that was unquestionably false. "Fear the Beard!" signs and T-shirts began appearing in the stands alongside the equally ridiculous beards that had materialized on men, women, Wilson volleyballs and beyond. It was unity, solidarity, as much a symbol of oneness as the more invisible thongs some in the stands were surely wearing. It was suddenly another emblem of a team that was drawing a whole different kind of crowd now. The stadium noise was changing. The city was adopting the esoteric castoffs and misfits as its own.

It was game on, now, as September and its beards unfolded, paralleling the pitching staff's historically unprecedented run of dominance. Priceless baseball, beards and attitude coalesced, and pretty much every reliever had some personal form of facial hair by the time the playoffs arrived, even if not all were necessarily enamored of their own whiskers. (With a sigh of relief, Jeremy Affeldt immediately shaved his beard off after the World Series—before the victory parade even commenced.)

During the playoffs, Wilson was asked by yet another man with a microphone when Lincecum and Cain would join in the beard parade.

"When they can," Wilson replied, with humor or accuracy.

Professional drivers on closed course. Do not attempt.

Body Breakdown

Unfortunately, the Giants had to come home to face LA without one of their best. Andres Torres had been feeling pains in his side and was mired in a sudden slump. The two seemed connected, and Torres was rushed to the hospital on the last day of the Padres series. An emergency appendectomy was performed, putting Torres out of commission for 10 days . . . or two weeks . . . or for the rest of the year. No one knew. Suddenly, the Giants were lacking speed at the top of the lineup as well as their best center field defense. The team missed his surprising power and—perhaps most importantly—the intangible spark of energy with which Torres led off every game. It was a potentially crushing blow.

Bochy refused to take the woe-is-us outlook. "You feel terrible for Andres with the year he's having and the great job he's done," Bochy said clearly. "But these guys [the other outfielders] need to look at this as a great opportunity, and you move on. This is a good club with a lot of depth." It was back to the lineup game for Bochy and the coaches. And the team had a surfeit of outfielders, even if none had Torres' particular skills.

Bochy said the majority of center field duties would be handled by Cody Ross and Aaron Rowand. "You'll see one of those two out there for the most part. Right now, we need experience, and these guys have been through it and know how to play and are looking forward to getting some opportunities."

Beat LA?

In the first game against the Dodgers, Ross was in right hitting lead-off, Rowand was in center hitting eighth, and Torres was back in the clubhouse showing off his new scar to his teammates.

With the latest capable patchwork outfield behind him, Barry Zito and four relievers continued the team's run of pitching excellence—now the ninth consecutive game in which they'd allowed three runs or fewer—but for no gain. Clayton Kershaw of the Dodgers was simply better, apparently, than the one-hitter upon which the five Giants pitchers collaborated. The only run was unearned, and the Dodgers' lone hit didn't figure in it. A hit batsman and two walks by Zito preceded an error by Juan Uribe, and that was that. The Giants dropped another game to the Padres, who'd beaten the Rockies 7-6. The Giants now trailed again by a game and a half.

The lineup game produced a new one the next day, with Nate Schierholtz and star-crossed Eugenio Velez in the outfield, while Mike Fontenot gave Freddy Sanchez a rest at second.

Did it help the beleaguered offense? Not much.

Did that matter? No.

Matt Cain and Chad Billingsley provided the latest brilliant pitching duel, slinging zeroes for six innings. Travis Ishikawa hit for Cain in the seventh and broke a small slump with a double.

"Don't ask me what pitch it was," Ishikawa said. "I have no idea."

Mike Fontenot hit a broken-bat single that scored pinch runner Emmanuel Burriss—back at last from his second broken foot—and the Giants were ahead 1-0.

"Went down a hero," said Fontenot of his deceased bat.

The Giants got an insurance run in the eighth. Thus Andre Ethier's home run off of Brian Wilson in the ninth amounted to inconsequential noise. 2-1 final, with Cain reaching 200 innings pitched for the fourth consecutive year. Only four other Giants had built a streak that long since the franchise's move West in 1958: Juan Marichal (10 years in a row, 1962–71), Gaylord Perry (six, 1966–71), Jim Barr (five, 1973–77) and Jack Sanford (four, 1960–63). None of those streaks had occurred within the past three decades—with starting pitchers now used only every fifth day, the mark was even harder to attain.

"Invaluable," Bochy said of Cain's stamina. "To have a guy like this who's so strong; he's a horse. He's one guy I don't get concerned with as far as pitch count. He's in incredible shape. It's a credit to how hard he works. Even in the seventh inning, he had the same stuff he started with."

End result: Series tied.

San Francisco's 10-2 win in the finale was a rarity, since the Giants-Dodgers series rarely produces such routs. But it wasn't a fluke. The Giants were heading for history; the Dodgers were bound for a sub-.500, fourth-place finish. Then again, the Giants' commanding performance would have subdued most clubs. Edgar Renteria won the lineup game and led off, producing four key hits, including a triple. Aubrey Huff hit a three-run homer. Jose Guillen—back in the lineup after an epidural to take care of a neck problem—had a perfect night, including a home run. Posey homered, too, and others contributed to the offense in a 15-hit attack that included eight extra-base hits. Jonathan Sanchez was in a zone of transcendence on the hill, not only striking out 12 but, more significantly, walking no one.

This game actually magnified a looming problem: It was an aberration. The Giants had scored two runs or fewer in five of seven games preceding this laugher. Then they scored *one* run or fewer in four of their next five games. For the offense, it continued to be all or nothing.

Nonetheless, the 10-2 crushing of the Dodgers was a fine way to finish the season's rivalry, overcoming early season woes to finish with a winning record against the Dodgers for the first time in five years.

Bruce Bochy was not impressed. "We're not into season series," he said, thinking with his usual clarity.

More importantly, the Padres lost their second game in a row. So the final win against the Dodgers vaulted the Giants into first place, alone there at last. Would they stay there and not look back as Sanchez had once predicted?

Changing the Mind-Set

On the few occasions when a ballclub is likened to a college team, the comparison usually places the college team in a favorable light. Recalling his years at the University of Miami, Huff spread his arms and brought them together as he said, "In college, we pounded people, and the team was like this. Everybody. I think that translates on the field, and this team has that feel."

Hardly shy, Huff contributed to that atmosphere early in the season. After the arrival of Pat Burrell, his college teammate, Huff found his voice even more. By adding one legitimate leader, the Giants had ultimately gained two.

"Maybe it's nice to have somebody around you can be a little more comfortable with," Burrell said, trying to summarize his effect on Huff.

Sergio Romo described a typical scene following frustrating defeats. Huff or Burrell, Romo said, would burst into the clubhouse and holler, "Hey, way to battle. Keep your heads up high. That was a great effort we put forth." Added Romo, "Those guys have us look at the bigger picture. Or at least they help make it more visible. It's not just individual effort. It's all of us put together for the same goal. You look at the clubhouse, or the dugout during a game, and we're not down. We always seem to have a pep in our step, and I think guys like Huff and Burrell, as veterans, mesh well with the younger guys, and they match that energy. Or they're the ones with more energy."

As a rookie in Tampa Bay, Huff had been hazed in negative, destructive ways, and he swore he would be a leader in positivity when it came time for him to inhabit a veteran's place. He was backing up that vision—uniquely.

Juan Uribe and Edgar Renteria complemented Burrell and Huff—and not just as leaders of the Latin players on the team. Uribe relaxed everybody with his exuberance and steadfast refusal to act defeated, even after a loss. "He always came in with a smile on his face," first baseman Travis Ishikawa said. "If he was hitting well or in a little bit of a slump, you never could tell."

Meanwhile, Renteria was a true paragon—the hero of the 1997 World Series, a five-time All-Star, three-time Silver Slugger recipient and two-time Gold Glove winner who remained mostly silent—except behind the scenes, where he opened up to teammates needing advice.

"When things aren't going well on defense or something, then he'll come up to you," said Freddy Sanchez, Renteria's double-play partner. "Little things. Nothing major, but a few words that might help you when you're going through a little slump or not feeling good. He has so much experience and knowledge about the game. You can go up and talk to him at any time. He's approachable and somebody you can learn a lot from."

Everyone who encountered Renteria appreciated his unblinking honesty. "You get to be a leader when you respect everybody, and you tell everybody the truth to their face," he said. "That's my responsibility—to let him know what he's doing bad and learn to be successful in the future." To tell the truth with compassion: This was another core principle of many a spiritual practice, and Renteria was living it.

Although not as renowned as Renteria, right-hander Guillermo Mota also helped unite the club. "He's a great dude," left-hander Jeremy Affeldt said. "A guy like Guillermo is phenomenal."

Mota's friendship with Jose Guillen led the Giants to consult him before acquiring the right fielder. Mota vouched for Guillen, whose reputation had buckled under the strain of playing for nine teams. "We are like family here," Mota said. "If somebody asks me, I'm going to try to help."

The acquisition of Ross sealed the circle for good. No wonder Rowand and Burrell, both veterans of World Series winners, welcomed his arrival.

Ross, Burrell noted, played for some decent teams in Florida. But, Burrell added, "There's a difference when you have a chance to *really* win. For a guy who played five or six years or whatever it was down there and is hungry, and his whole career's in front of him, and you get somebody like that on a team like we had, you're going to see the best of him. And we did."

The hungry confluence of Giants yearning for a World Series title couldn't be stemmed. There were simply too many of them.

Huff had spent most of his previous 10 seasons with the Tampa Bay Rays before they were good and the Baltimore Orioles after they were good.

The considerable respect commanded by Ross clashed with his zero playoff appearances in four seasons.

Andres Torres, raised in poverty in Puerto Rico and coping with ADHD, could do little to make his unlikely personal saga more compelling—unless he played for a big winner.

Playing for Pittsburgh, Freddy Sanchez won the 2006 National League batting title and, except for admirers of his intensity, nothing else.

Juan Uribe earned a World Series ring with the 2005 Chicago White Sox and remained productive. Yet when he was a free agent in the 2009–10 offseason, he didn't prompt a bidding war.

Pat Burrell hadn't forgotten what it felt like to be in limbo earlier in the season after Tampa Bay had released him.

And the proud Renteria, who turned 35 shortly before going on the disabled list for the third time this season, was sensing his baseball mortality.

Some of these players and several others could have opted to gripe about not playing regularly. Given Ross' postseason production, it's mildly stunning to realize he started only 17 of a possible 37 games after joining the Giants. Even when healthy, Renteria frequently sat while Uribe played shortstop and Pablo Sandoval played third base. Accustomed to being a regular, Rowand started just 27 of San Francisco's final 87 games. Ishikawa, named to the Topps Major League Rookie All-Star Team in 2009, started 25 games in 2010. Schierholtz received 41 starts in right field after entering spring training with an apparently solid chance of cracking the opening day lineup.

Meager numbers all. Yet egos, which fill the baggage of numerous pro athletes, were a no-no among the Giants. They had other priorities.

"Winning was important," Burrell said. "Sometimes you're not fortunate enough to be in a place where that's possible."

It seemed the Giants had conducted a secret meeting and taken a blood oath not to complain about playing time.

"There was no meeting, but I think everyone had that sort of thought process," Ross said. "Throughout the clubhouse, guys would say, 'Hey, this isn't about each individual, it's about us. Let's go after this.' Obviously, everybody was on board. I've never been on a team where you didn't have at least *one* selfish person—except for this one."

Noticing his players' uncommon character in September—particularly after Guillen and Ross joined the club to complement the likes of Burrell and Huff—Bochy believed the Giants could do more than merely challenge for the Wild Card berth.

"These guys were men," Bochy said. "They were all about winning, and they really changed the mind-set in that clubhouse."

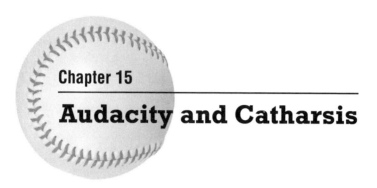

Chapter 15

Audacity and Catharsis

Nothing, Nothing, Everything

An invisible, intangible line separates good pitching and bad hitting. A great offense can be shut down by a greater pitcher, and a meager offense can make a journeyman pitcher look like he has "Koufax" written across his back.

The Giants offense was a conundrum along this intangible line. All year, they'd risen to beat great pitchers while falling to lesser ones. It was maddening, yet riveting, because on a daily basis it was unclear what kind of team the Giants would be.

The Milwaukee series that commenced in San Francisco on Sept. 17 was a perfect example. The first night, journeyman Randy Wolf was the pitcher the Giants made look like Koufax. He pitched a complete-game three-hit shutout against the Giants, not even giving up a hit after the fifth. The Giants made two errors on defense and looked extremely sloppy in their orange jerseys. The early-season magic of Orange Fridays had long ago worn off. The 3-0 loss was miserable, despite a gutsy and effective outing by Madison Bumgarner on the mound.

Seeing the beauty within challenge, the strength within resistance, Bumgarner said, "It's good to have games like that where you have to battle and fight instead of just going out there and it coming easy every time."

But it's bad to have games where you play poorly and lose. And the next night, the Giants lost their grip on first as they faced a man of more consistent excellence on the hill: Yovani Gallardo, hard-throwing 24-year-old right-hander on his way to his second consecutive 200-strikeout season. Gallardo held the Giants completely in check until the bottom of the fifth, when they mustered what attempted to be a rally. Given the Giants' desperation to score, Bochy angered Tim Lincecum by hitting for him in the fifth. Lincecum was visibly upset in the dugout and kept a frozen stare as Bochy talked to him about his removal. But he calmed down later and understood. The moment vanished without leaving a wound or scar.

Figuring in Bochy's decision was his supreme confidence in the bullpen. That confidence proved justified—the latest parade of relievers did not allow the Brewers a single hit the rest of the way. Gallardo and the Milwaukee bullpen were equally and legitimately effective, however, shutting the Giants down in a 2-1 loss.

That was 13 games in a row now that the Giants had allowed three or fewer runs. The statisticians were interested. But would it matter if the team lost anyway?

Needing to salvage one game of the series to avoid being swept at home, the third form of the Giants showed up on Sunday—the one with overpowering offense and excellent pitching turned to dominance. For the third series in a row, the Giants followed two games of zero offense with an explosion.

The Giants' offense appeared star-crossed in the first when lead-off batter Cody Ross had an apparent home run taken away by left-fielder Ryan Braun in one of the finest catches ever at AT&T Park. This setback became irrelevant later in the same inning, when Jose Guillen connected for a long grand slam. The Giants were off and running, on their way to piling up more runs than they needed in a 9-2 crushing of the Brewers. It was decisive, it was *done* and it took the Giants back into first by a half-game. The Padres had lost to St. Louis 4-1.

The Brewers series marked three consecutive three-game series where the Giants' offensive pattern was nothing, nothing, everything. In even more extreme style, the Giants were about to make it four in Chicago.

Trust the Guy Behind You

Inherently, Wrigley Field's an all-or-nothing place. When the wind is blowing out in Chicago, scores resembling football are common. When the wind is howling in, home runs are fantasies. The Giants didn't need any extra help with unpredictability—their performances were already as wildly divergent as the Chicago winds.

The first game was delayed by rain. When they did play, the heavy air held balls down. The dampness didn't seem to bother the two aces pitching, Matt Cain and Carlos Zambrano, who matched zeroes for six innings. Cain allowed only two hits and one runner to reach second base. His reward? Bochy hit for him to begin the seventh inning of a scoreless tie.

As usual, Cain was not disturbed. "Anybody can be a better hitter than I am to lead off the inning," he said amiably. But Travis Ishikawa's groundout was in fact no better. Zambrano walked five Giants and kept the tension high, striking out eight as he and Cain dueled to no decision.

The Giants bullpen took over as Ramirez, Romo and Wilson allowed absolutely nothing the rest of the way—not a hit, not a walk, not a hit batsman, not a hair off of their furry chins.

Their effort still wouldn't have been good enough were it not for Buster Posey. In the eighth, Posey lifted one into the mist to absolute dead center, just over the wall directly above the 400-foot sign. 1-0 Giants, final.

Posey also demonstrated his "cannon" arm while throwing out a runner trying to steal, and he guided the four pitchers through their latest collaborative masterpiece, a two-hit shutout. They'd reached 15 games in a row now with three runs or fewer.

"It's hard to have a better game than that," Bochy said about Posey, praising his great growth and leadership in every department. Posey was now in serious national contention for Rookie of the Year.

This team—Posey's team—didn't head for the showers after the game. They stayed in uniform, glued to the television in the cramped, ancient Wrigley clubhouse, watching the Padres shut out the Dodgers and the Rockies lose to Arizona. The team was beginning to look forward to their own final series to come—after Chicago, just Colorado, Arizona and San Diego remained.

Under those conditions, Posey almost lost his focus on the moment. His accidental Zen mastery slipped. "It's almost like you want to go ahead and skip to the last two or three games," he said. "You figure it's going to come down to the last two or three games."

You can't do that, though—think about the last two or three games when there are still 10 left to play. Then it *won't* come down to the last two or three because you'll lose focus, lose games and be out of the running for good.

The ongoing intensity was good training for the team, though.

"This is like boot camp for the playoffs," Mike Krukow said on the *Post-Game Wrap*. "Every game is like nine ninth innings." After comparing the game's relentless drama to an episode of the television program *24*, he talked about Wilson's calm three-up, three-down save in the ninth to make the 1-0 lead stand. "We didn't *need* any more torture, we didn't *need* any more drama."

What they did still need was offense. The Giants were impatient the next night, blanked for 7 2/3 innings by the Cubs' Randy Wells— who owned a 7-13 record and a 4.46 ERA entering the game—and finished off by Carlos Marmol, who recorded strikeouts in all four outs he needed for the save. The Giants were back to old habits, striking out 10 times in the 2-0 shutout loss. They often struck *themselves* out.

Huff believed the solution was oneness in patience. "It can't be one or two guys. It has to be *everybody*"—working counts deeper, selecting better pitches and capitalizing on them.

Now mired in a 3-for-27 slump in a largely lost year, Pablo Sandoval owned his guilt. "I tried to drive in a runner from scoring position three times in one AB [at-bat]," he admitted. He'd gone from being one of the league's most fearsome offensive stars in 2009 to being pinch-hit for by Mike Fontenot in the eighth inning of this game. It was a tragic fall.

After the ugly loss put the Giants back in second place again— despite yet another night of pitching excellence—Bochy decided one more meeting was in order. Before the Sept. 23 series finale at Wrigley Field, he gathered the position players by the batting cage underneath the right-field bleachers. Bochy kept his message simple. "We're better than this, and it's going to take everybody being focused. Trust the guy behind you," he said.

After Bochy's simple but central reminder, he and hitting coach Hensley Meulens departed. But the keynote speaker remained on the Giants' agenda: Renteria, the most revered player among his peers. Standing in the bowels of the grand old ballpark, Renteria sensed his own history. He would forever carry his World Series–winning hit against Cleveland in 1997 as well as his numerous other awards and accolades. Right now, however, Renteria most acutely felt his baseball mortality. His three trips to the disabled list dismayed him. His career-low .250 batting average for the Giants in 2009 still stung. Now he would sit out 13 of San Francisco's final 14 regular season games, hampered partly by a sore right elbow. Listening to Renteria, right fielder Nate Schierholtz read Renteria's frustration as stemming from his injuries. "I think he was hinting it might have been his last year," Schierholtz said.

Renteria didn't dwell on himself as he spoke. The veteran of six postseasons wanted the Giants to understand the opportunity to play deep into October remained within their grasp—but they would have to seize it.

"Edgar wasn't sure how much longer he was going to be in the game. He wanted to go out a winner," Aaron Rowand said. "It was motivational stuff about pulling together as a team."

Said Freddy Sanchez, "I remember Edgar coming into the cage. It was emotional. Edgar never said that much, as far as to the team. So when he did, everyone was listening. Whenever Edgar speaks, it's from the heart."

"You could tell he really cared about the team," Schierholtz said.

Once Renteria finished, the Giants would have gladly tried to sprint back to their clubhouse through Wrigley Field's ivy-covered brick outfield wall. "Everyone got fired up over his speech," Sanchez said as the rest of the team echoed Renteria's sentiments.

"Everybody put their two cents in," Rowand said.

That's how the Giants approached the subsequent game. They matched a season high with 19 hits, scoring nine runs in the second inning alone (another 2010 best). Juan Uribe contributed two homers to that big inning, including a grand slam. Freddy Sanchez added four hits for the day, quietly raising his average to .296, now contributing in key ways to the team on defense as well. In the end, the 13-0 pasting enabled San Francisco to leapfrog San Diego and regain a half-game lead in the West.

"There was a little bit more fire in everybody," said Posey, who collected two hits along with his 16th homer. "Hopefully, that's something we can continue for the next nine games."

They would need to do so *consistently*. The offense for the three games of the Chicago series was one more nothing, nothing, everything pattern. Bizarrely, the Giants had scored a respectable 43 runs in the past 12 games—yet only four times had they scored higher than 2. And they'd scored either 1 or 0 in *seven* of those 12 games. Ouch.

Meanwhile, the pitching staff kept its incredible streak alive. Madison Bumgarner—showing late-season strength despite pitching more innings for the year than his young arm ever had—threw seven brilliant shutout innings with nine strikeouts. As ever, the bullpen was equally brilliant behind him: zero hits off of Runzler and Mota as they closed it out. It had been an amazing 17 games in a row with only three runs or fewer allowed. More than statisticians were paying attention now.

Defy Trends, Deflect Power

Still, the Padres wouldn't go away. They took two of three from Cincinnati during the regular season's next-to-last weekend.

The Giants, too, refused to falter, although they had to endure a trio of games against the Colorado Rockies at Coors Field, which is never a comfortable place for visiting teams. True, out-of-town hitters might relish the chance to drive balls through the thin, mile-high atmosphere or into the gaps of the spacious outfield. But the Rockies simply were more acclimated to the elevation. From 2007 to 2010, they exceeded 50 victories (in 81 games) three times during those four seasons.

But a performer such as Lincecum can defy trends and deflect power. He did both before a paid crowd of 49,071 on Sept. 24, maintaining a perfect game for five innings before finishing with a two-hitter over eight innings. Pat Burrell hit a two-run homer, and Brian Wilson recorded his 45th save in a tidy 2-1 victory.

"You can give it all you've got, or you can give in," Wilson said. "We're not the team to give in."

Lincecum certainly didn't give in after his awful August. This decision improved his September mark to 4-1 with a 2.08 ERA. "It's more valuable to me just because of what I went through in August," Lincecum said of his dramatic improvement. "But in September, it's not about me. It's about the team and wins." Spoken by many, that's an empty cliché. Here it was just plain truth. And the tough truth was the Giants still needed more. Even with Lincecum's dominance, they were still only half a game ahead of the Padres, with eight left to play.

Without Precedent

Lincecum's ace effort in Colorado—where he'd faced the most difficult pitching conditions in the country—made it the 18th straight game in which the team had held opponents to three runs or fewer. That meant *not a single pitcher—no starter, no reliever—had a bad day for three straight weeks*. To a man, they coalesced into a unit of such stunning brilliance and consistency that it nearly took archaeologists to dig far enough back into the history books to find precedent. The pages flew back past the steroids era, past the 1980s and 1970s, past the Year of the Pitcher in 1968, then past the McCarthy Era, World War II, the Great Depression, the heyday of Babe Ruth and the beginning of the "live-ball" era of increased scores that had begun in 1920. It wasn't until the record-keepers had scraped off the layers of dust to reach

1917—in the midst of World War I—that they unearthed a precedent. It had been 93 years since a team had accomplished the unified run of excellence the Giants had, allowing three runs or fewer for that many consecutive games. The 1917 Chicago White Sox had done it during the "dead-ball" era, when average scores were far lower, and they did it in May and June—not in the heat and pressure of a late-season pennant race. What the Giants achieved in that 18-game stretch was unprecedented in modern baseball and may never be duplicated.

Yet here was the trouble: The Giants still lost six of those 18 games, including two 1-0 losses in the span of three days. Their offense—now bolstered and with home run capabilities throughout the lineup—was still feast or famine. In September, almost two-thirds of their runs were scored by home runs—far off the usual charts. Even unprecedented communal pitching brilliance couldn't put an end to the anxiety-ridden games in which the Giants specialized. As many as 10 of those 18 games were decided by two runs or fewer. It was easy only on the rarest of sweet occasions.

On the night when the streak finally ended, the Giants dropped back into second place behind the Padres by half a game. They were only half a game closer to winning their division than they had been before the streak began. With one week to go, the outcome remained certain. Nothing could be taken even slightly for granted.

All Things Must Pass

If there was a soundtrack for the Giants' game against Colorado on Sept. 25, it would have been George Harrison's "All Things Must Pass." It was inevitable that someday the team's pitching staff would give up more than three runs, ending the best pitching streak baseball had seen in nearly a century.

That it happened in Colorado with Barry Zito on the hill was not surprising—not only because Zito's starts had ranged from brilliant to miserable in the season's second half. The thin, high-altitude air of Denver is hardest for pitchers who rely on breaking balls for their success—less air means less air resistance against the ball, which means less break in a curveball. Zito has one of the finest curveballs in the game, but its rainbow arc is handicapped in Denver even on a good day. And Zito did not have a good day. Again lacking control, he was gone in the bottom of the fifth, followed by Chris Ray getting no one out. At the end of the inning, the Giants were losing 6-4. The streak was over.

But the Giants were not finished. They roared back with five runs in the top of the sixth to get Zito off the hook, reestablishing a 9-6 lead. Cody Ross hit the Giants' fourth home run of the night to help reach that score, following earlier blasts by Freddy Sanchez, Aubrey Huff and Andres Torres.

It was Andres Torres' first game back after his emergency appendectomy just 13 days prior.

"It's good to have him back. It's a credit to the shape he's in," Bochy said.

He wasn't back for long, though. After following his third-inning home run with a great sliding catch in the fourth, he felt tightness in the place of his surgery and was removed from the game as a precaution.

Freddy Sanchez was also removed after suffering a mild right shoulder strain. The team could scarcely afford to lose Sanchez, who had hit .389 in his last 27 games and was often playing inspired defense as well. He was finally performing up to his level of capability, making contributions that had earlier eluded him.

The win also eluded the Giants. The usually reliable bullpen—which had allowed only two earned runs in the entire month of September to this point—faltered this time. They had no solution for Colorado's Troy Tulowitzki, who rapped a two-out RBI single in the sixth inning, a two-out two-run double in the eighth inning off Wilson to tie the score and a game-winning RBI single off Wilson again in the 10th.

Asked in cliché terms if he "tipped his cap" to Tulowitzki for the clutch hitting, Wilson said bluntly, "I don't tip my cap. They beat us. That's fine." The loss dropped the Giants back into second place once more, which wasn't fine.

After his 1 2/3-inning ordeal, Wilson needed a rest in the finale. He received it thanks to Matt Cain, who continued to defy single-season actuarial tables by taking a no-hitter into the eighth inning. It was broken by a ground ball to short that Uribe couldn't get out of his glove—the runner might have beaten it anyway, although Uribe didn't think so.

Cain didn't care. He gestured supportively to Uribe and went right back to work, finishing with his fourth complete game of the season as the Giants won 4-2. The offense was provided by (big surprise) homers from Freddy Sanchez and Cody Ross.

Asked if he was disappointed about losing the no-hitter, Cain was as calm as always. "Disappointed in what? Not at all," he replied. "I couldn't care less. We needed a win today." And they got it—as Cain's gem improved his post–All-Star–break record to 7-2 with a 2.48 ERA.

"No lead is safe here [in Colorado]," said Cody Ross, whose seventh-inning homer helped the Giants crawl a half-game in front of San Diego in the NL West. "But with Cain on the mound, it was game over."

It was series over, too, with the Giants having taken two out of three in one of the most critical, hostile environments at an essential time. The game served as a microcosm of the 2010 Giants' ability to fend off rivals such as the Rockies, who'd beaten them out for the Wild Card postseason berth in 2009. And it started yet another run of pitching dominance—this time a four-game streak in which the team allowed *two* runs or fewer. With the offense back in all-or-nothing mode—never to score more than four runs again in the regular season—would that be enough?

Only six games remained, all at home—three against Arizona, three against San Diego. Everything was on the line.

The Audacity of Dope

The audacity of dope: That was the side circus to the season's finale. As the Giants were completing their season, California was preparing to vote on a referendum to legalize marijuana. Both campaigns were ramping up.

Cannabis is rarely a baseball issue, but given Tim Lincecum's preseason arrest on a minor pot charge, he had become a legend among Bay Area stoners, of which there were large numbers. For reasons having nothing to do with baseball, legions of new fans had begun to root for Lincecum.

Inevitably, the unofficial T-shirts proliferated, especially as the season climaxed. "Let Tim Smoke!" proclaimed the most popular one, the bold Giants orange melding with a green cannabis leaf. The shirt-wearers often added stickers that said, "Yes we cannabis!" supporting the Proposition 19 legalization bill with a takeoff on President Obama's 2008 campaign slogan.

There was, however, no evidence that Lincecum even desired to smoke, especially during the season. Performance-detracting drugs are not part of his in-season regimen and would interfere with his intensely competitive desire to excel. He wanted to win, not smoke. The T-shirts, of course, really translated to "Let *Me* Smoke!"

It was another edgy headache for Giants management, but with just a few games remaining, they had more important things to worry about.

Pretty Cathartic

While the Giants rested on Monday, Sept. 27—their final scheduled off-day of the season—San Diego lost 1-0 to the Cubs, boosting San Francisco's lead to a full game.

The Giants could see the finish line. They tweaked the starting rotation to bring it closer. (The move worked, as was the case with virtually everything the Giants tried late in the season.) They flip-flopped Lincecum with Bumgarner. This gave Lincecum his regular four days' rest while simultaneously creating the possibility that he could pitch the Sunday, Oct. 3, regular season finale against San Diego on a three-day break. It would also align Lincecum to pitch a one-game tiebreaker on Monday, Oct. 4, if necessary.

Looking ahead that far was potentially lethal to their division hopes, however. The constant lesson of spirit returned: *Stay in the moment.* The Diamondbacks might be in distant last place, but they could still end the Giants' own hopes.

Before the first game, the Giants organization broadcasted an extremely pumped-up season highlight film on the massive AT&T Park video board, aiming to boost energy in the stadium. It worked—to excess.

"Mike and I put on our jockstraps after that one," Duane Kuiper said on the *Post-Game Wrap,* referring to Krukow and the desire it gave them to suit back up.

Jonathan Sanchez was overly amped up, too, throwing too hard in the early going. It took the young mastery of Buster Posey to bring the game back in control, who slowed it down and controlled the rhythm. The resulting 4-2 victory helped the Giants gain another game on San Diego—now two ahead with five to play.

The win also helped the Giants reach another milestone: 89 victories for the year, one more than in 2009—irrefutable evidence that doubters of the team's legitimacy were mistaken.

Krukow summed this up with precision and eloquence on the broadcast. "For all the pre-season prognosticators who said that [the Giants] wouldn't come close to winning 88 games this year," he said, "*Ppppffffffffffffffffffftttt!!!!*" Or some loud, messy approximation thereof. He then completed the dedication by singing with an intentionally pained country music twang, "From the bottom of maaaaaahhhh heart!"

"Sounds pretty cathartic," Dave Flemming responded. "Want to do it again?" Krukow did. It *was* pretty cathartic.

So were the next two games against Arizona, in which the reordered Lincecum and Bumgarner gained wins in 3-1 and 4-1 victories, respectively. In the first game, Lincecum allowed a home run to the first batter of the game, Stephen Drew, before settling down to earn his final win of the season, courtesy of another enormous three-run homer by Pat Burrell. Lincecum's 11 strikeouts clinched not only his 16th victory but also his lead in the league's strikeout totals for the third consecutive year—not bad for an off year.

Bumgarner continued to show arm strength. The team had considered shutting him down at the beginning of September to preserve his valuable young arm, but he just kept getting stronger and more effective instead. Throwing a slider Krukow described as "lethal," Bumgarner struck out seven in five innings before turning it over to the trio of Casillo, Romo and Ramirez, none of whom allowed a single hit while striking out five more of their own.

Continuing their reliance on the long ball, Torres, Posey and Sandoval all hit homers. Sandoval's landed in the water beyond the stadium.

In total, the Giants allowed just four runs in three games while sweeping Arizona. Although each game's starting pitcher recorded the decision, the relievers truly excelled by allowing just four hits and walking two in nine shutout innings.

This illustrated the bullpen's handsome contribution to San Francisco's 1.78 team ERA in September, the lowest compiled by any club in a month of at least 20 games since Cleveland's 1.42 in May 1968. But the Indians hadn't done it at the close of a pennant race. Statisticians had to go back to the pennant-winning 1965 Dodgers to find precedent for such a September run.

And yet the bullpen's stellar ERA *still* wasn't enough. The Padres lost three of four to Chicago, but that lone victory was enough to keep them alive as they arrived in San Francisco for their season-ending three-game series. The Giants owned a three-game lead, but they'd have to win once to secure the division title.

That was fine with them.

"We want San Diego to come in," Brian Wilson said. "We want to play good baseball, and that's what we're going to get. That's the way the story's been written this year."

Ominous signs still lingered in the Giants' torturous story. Homers accounted for eight of their 11 runs against Arizona. They remained overly reliant on power, a fact noted by Burrell—a primary source of San Francisco's slugging but also a keen observer of the big picture.

"We have to find a way to manufacture more runs," Burrell said. "It's tough to always rely on the big hit. . . . The deeper this thing goes, the harder it's going to be for that to happen, the three-run homer."

Nevertheless, the scene was set for a hell of a party at AT&T Park—a party that would still have to wait.

The Audacity of Being a Dope

After serving as one of the league's young elite for most of the year, Padres pitcher Mat Latos seemed to lose his sense along with his strength as his late-September performance plummeted. Having apparently learned nothing from Jonathan Sanchez's previous faux pas, Latos took the opportunity of the impending final series in San Francisco to motivate the Giants via the media.

His first sentence to CBS Sports.com was a truthful cliché. "Baseball works in funny ways," he said. So far, so what? But then came the mistake pitch: "The only way I could honestly put it is we could be like the Giants and go and change our whole lineup, put guys with 'San Francisco Giants' across their jerseys. We didn't. We added two guys. We've been the same team all year. We haven't just gone and grabbed guys from other teams." Was he saying he wished Miguel Tejada and Ryan Ludwick—the Padres' two valuable late-season additions—gone?

Sure, consistency is a laudable goal, and the Giants had failed to achieve it in their daily starting eight. Such is the nature of baseball. What did Latos expect the Giants to do under their uncertain circumstances? And what would he want his own team to do if the Padres had been similarly inflicted? Stand pat and lose?

What the Giants had achieved instead of consistency was flexibility—an ability to change positions, places in the order, surrounding faces and everything else without losing the magical team chemistry that kept them moving forward as one. Just how far that attitude went is summarized by what pitcher Sergio Romo said about being ready for the outfield, above and beyond the call of duty: "I practiced shagging flyballs during batting practice in case they needed me." They needed him—to stay in the bullpen, where he belonged and excelled.

The bulk of the Giants' starting rotation and bullpen—the core of the team—had come up through the Giants minor league system. To say the Giants had all been "grabbed from other teams" was as inaccurate as painting them all as castoffs and misfits.

It was Cody Ross—one of the guys "grabbed from other teams," who fired back at Latos. He told the *San Francisco Chronicle*, "It's asinine to say, 'We're a close-knit group, and this is our team.' Every team goes out at the trading deadline and tries to make a deal. It's very rare for an organization to say, 'We don't need any improvements. We're as good as we're going to be.' Every team looks to improve, whether it's one, three or five guys."

Latos should've been focused on self-improvement rather than criticizing the Giants for improving from both without and within. Coming into the final series against the Giants, he had lost his last four starts, giving up 20 runs in 16 innings. He was slated to pitch the last day of the season against (whom else?) Jonathan Sanchez. Poetic justice was loose—and stalking Latos.

Chapter 16

Let the Party Begin!

Andres and Willie Mac

The night after Latos made his "asinine" comments about the Giants, the team held a ceremony that silently illustrated how incorrect Latos was.

Every year, the team votes to honor its most inspirational member with the Willie Mac Award, named after the inspirational Willie McCovey. It's an award of the heart as much as of performance, and it's one of the most coveted tributes a Giants player can ever receive.

Choosing among the 2010 Giants was difficult because inspiration abounded, but there was jubilation and harmony when Andres Torres was selected by his teammates to join the honored ranks. Torres had overcome abject childhood poverty, 11 years in the minor leagues, attention deficit disorder, release by five teams, the perception that it was too late at age 32 for *anyone*'s career to blossom and, most recently, that pesky appendectomy. Through it all, Torres conveyed gratitude and constant friendliness while working as hard as anyone in his rigorous conditioning. It had paid off beautifully as he became an elite leadoff hitter and joined the league's leaders in extra-base hits. Torres also led the team in steals, hitting home runs beyond expectation and becoming one of the league's most accomplished defenders in center field—one of the game's most challenging defensive positions. Torres had done it all with grace and spirit, and it brought tears to many eyes to see him accept the 2010 Willie Mac Award. He'd earned it the hard way. Torres not only inspired the team by what he had overcome as an individual, but he *symbolized* the team and all of the other stories of inspiration and overcoming contained within its collective soul.

That it was so difficult to choose a Willie Mac Award candidate—even with the compelling beauty of Torres' story—also spoke to the team's unified nature. The Giants were indeed the very essence of what a team is supposed to be. Every player inspired, whether a veteran or newcomer with suitcase in hand.

Equally impossibile was the task of selecting a Most Valuable Player. Would that be Torres again, offering the spark at the top of the lineup the Giants had desperately needed? Would it be Aubrey Huff, who'd provided leadership in the clubhouse and was at the center of the team's power production—all while cheerfully moving from first to left to right to back to first to wherever the team needed him? He was definitely the MVT—Most Valuable Thong—but the MVP? Maybe. Would the MVP instead be Juan Uribe, whose positive spirit and power production was equally transcendent as he, too, shifted positions wherever and whenever necessary? Was it Buster Posey behind the plate, going from minor leaguer to one of the league's best catchers on offense, defense and attitude in a mere matter of months? Or was it one of the starting pitching staff, who were at the core of what the team accomplished, even though they'd had periods of struggle? Tim Lincecum or Matt Cain then, perhaps? Or was it Brian Wilson, the heart and soul and beard of the bullpen, leading the charge at the end? But how could you name a single individual from the pitching staff, when the unprecedented run they had just accomplished was achieved *as a team*—not because of any one man but because of *all* of them? And then what about the other regulars and semi-regulars and those people who'd made key contributions off the bench? The race came down so close to the wire that with even one fewer win, the Giants wouldn't have made it. So every game contribution from every player had been essential. They were *all* MVPs—including those who contributed in spirit when they couldn't even contribute physically. Mark DeRosa, for example, who'd provided key leadership from the bench despite being injured most of the year. Aaron Rowand, Pablo Sandoval and Barry Zito all kept up relentless positive energy and never complained when their performances and playing time declined. That, too, was most valuable.

Equally valuable were the contributors who weren't players: Bruce Bochy pulling the strategic strings, Brian Sabean in the front office giving him strings to pull, the coaches and trainers staying focused on fundamentals and keeping the pitching staff extraordinarily healthy. Who was more valuable than Mike Murphy in the clubhouse or the rest of the support crew who'd been so critical to the team that the players wouldn't go to Taiwan unless the staff received equal compensation? Every team member viewed even the ones *off* the field as both players and equals. That is a *team*, Mr. Latos—team enough to be collectively nominated for Sportsman of the Year. Team enough to do what no other Giants team could accomplish in over half a century. Team enough to stand as an example for at least another half-century to come.

In Clemente's Footsteps

Sometimes you see the best of a player in places beyond the field. It's beyond—yet within—the Giants Way to give back to the community in ways that are deeper than baseball: It's the Human Way. To be in a position of advantage and opportunity for contribution without making that contribution is tragic, and nearly everyone experiences, in some small way, an opportunity for contribution. Stories abound about people in impoverished cultures who have nearly nothing but who still give to a stranger at the doorstep, and perhaps that's because in the poorest places, there's a greater awareness of need. Contribution is service—it's a spiritual principle, and it's essential to harmonious survival. It's been part of baseball tradition as long as baseball has been a part of life, but as affluence and public attention have climbed with baseball salaries, players can now do more for others. Not that all do, however, since money and fame offer temptations away from service. Riches buy vices. Wealth can purchase waste. It's easy.

The Roberto Clemente Award honors commitment to service alongside baseball excellence. Hall of Famer Clemente exemplified that sacrifice even in his death, as his plane went down on the way to delivering aid to Nicaraguan earthquake refugees on New Year's Eve, 1972, a couple of short months after Clemente had finished the season with exactly his 3,000th hit. Clemente's beauty and tragedy are immortalized in that award, which ensures his legacy of community service will be carried on. (It was originally called the Commissioner's Award, with Willie Mays being its first recipient in 1971. but the award was renamed in honor of Clemente a scant two years later.)

Every year, one member of each of the majors' 30 teams is nominated for the award, and in 2010, it was one of the Giants' less public members who received the nomination: reliever Jeremy Affeldt. His commitment to service comes out of a deep Christian devotion, and although he does make performance-based contributions, his efforts transcend mere financial ones. Ministry and the gospel form his core motivations, but his efforts go beyond work with a spiritual focus. Affeldt has become active in efforts against human trafficking through the Not For Sale campaign, a Bay Area-based charity he personally approached a mere two weeks after signing with San Francisco. Not For Sale has been active in the fight against atrocities in Thailand, Cambodia, Uganda, Peru and Romania, among other places. Through partnership with Living Water International, Affeldt has helped bring clean drinking water to Uganda and other areas where there was none, and he has assisted with providing food to the impoverished in numerous locations. By involving youth in service projects through his Generation Alive program, he's shown extraordinary commitment to inspiring a strong tradition of service in the coming generation. Because of those and many other contributions, Affeldt was the Giants' nominee for placing his own soles in Clemente's immortal footsteps. Although Tim Wakefield of the Red Sox was eventually selected as the year's winner, the nomination alone is an honor—and pales in significance next to the service it represents.

Stay in the Moment

Beyond the half-century to come and the larger service work to be done, there was still a pennant race hanging in the balance. Heading into the season's final series, the Giants contemplated the most critical principle to keep in mind.

"Being able to stay in the moment," Mike Krukow said after the final Arizona win. "I didn't hear one guy talk about the Padres this weekend. Maybe it's all the torture . . . you can't look ahead." He reported that Pat Burrell walked around the batting cage before the Friday night game, repeating that mantra: "*Stay in the moment. Stay in the moment. Stay in the moment.*"

That was another area in which Buster Posey clearly excelled. Bochy explained it this way: "He's got a gift. Some catchers are known for their catching skills more than for their hitting skills. This kid happens to have both. But he also has the ability to separate them. When it's time to catch, that's where his priority is. He knows his biggest responsibility is handling the pitcher that day. When it comes time to hit, that's where his focus is." *Stay in the moment.*

Running Through Mud

In the moment, the Giants entered the final San Diego series opener brimming with confidence as Cain took the mound. He had gone 3-0 with a 2.19 ERA in five September starts, and the Giants had won each of his last seven outings.

It was Oct. 1 now, however, and the Padres also believed they had the right man pitching. Clayton Richard was 3-1 with a 1.95 ERA in five starts this season against the Giants. Advantage: Padres—at least on this evening.

While Richard blanked the Giants on three hits through four innings, Cain allowed home runs to Ryan Ludwick, Adrian Gonzalez and Matt Stairs during the same span (Ludwick being one of the guys whom the Padres had, ahem, "grabbed from other teams"). After Cain's early exit, the Giants were down 6-0, and they never recovered before the game's 6-4 loss. The resilience of their late rallies, although good for their spirit, netted nothing else. The result necessitated a take two on Saturday afternoon.

The number of fans stuffing themselves inside AT&T Park grew from Friday's 42,409 to 42,653 that Saturday. Anticipation merged with pure, intoxicating, boundless love in the hearts of Giants fans. But once again, they went home wondering what to do with all this emotion. The Giants *still* only needed one win against San Diego to clinch the division, but they . . . just . . . couldn't . . . seem . . . to . . . get it. To the fans, it must've felt like running through mud.

In his last start of the year—one that would leave painful, lingering memories and consequences—Zito was no more able than Cain to provide leadership. Zito was on his way to completing his worst season statistically, but a division-clinching victory would salve that wound. Alas, it was quickly evident that very little would go right for him. As was the pattern in most of his weaker games, his control and strike-zone assertiveness deserted him at a critical juncture. Bases-loaded first-inning walks to Yorvit Torrealba and Scott Hairston put the Giants in an emotional 2-0 hole. The hole was 4-0 when Zito vanished before he could record an out in the fourth. The Giants again staged insufficient late-inning rallies: They brought the potentially winning run to the plate in the ninth inning against Padres closer Heath Bell, but the rally died when Jose Guillen grounded into—what else?—a double play. It was the 157th time the Giants had grounded into a double play during the year, a horrific league-leading statistic that didn't even include the other forms of creative double plays they'd managed to hit and run into during the year. This one sealed their 4-2 loss. They still needed one win, and they had only one game left—one more double play to hit into.

Jackson Pollock Pennant Race

The National League playoff picture resembled a Jackson Pollock painting after San Diego's 4-2 victory. It illustrated how much baseball's process as well as its game had shifted since 1954. Back then, the team ending up with the most regular season wins went to the World Series. End of story. As with most other aspects of life, things were more complicated now—if also potentially more dramatic and exciting. Multiple possibilities existed for the season's closing that Sunday:

- If San Diego completed its three-game series sweep and Atlanta defeated Philadelphia, then the Giants, Padres and Braves would share 91-71 records. That would necessitate a Giants-Padres one-game playoff on Monday for the West title. The loser would visit Atlanta in a Wild Card playoff game on Tuesday. The Giants could end up playing three games in three cities over three days.

- If Philadelphia defeated Atlanta while the Padres prevailed again, San Diego would capture the West title and San Francisco would win the Wild Card. Why? The Padres' huge 12-5 advantage over the Giants in the season series would serve as the first tiebreaker between the teams.

- A Giants victory and a Braves defeat would force San Diego to visit Atlanta for a Wild Card playoff game Monday—but if the Braves won on Sunday, the Padres would be eliminated.

All of those possibilities were just to *get* to the playoffs. To get to the World Series from there would be an equally unmappable journey.

Bottom line for the Giants: They still needed just one victory. Facing this dizzying array of possibilities, they tried to simplify matters for themselves.

Bochy and Zito emphasized calmness. Said Bochy, "We're in a situation where we do have a little margin of error, but we certainly would like to win."

Zito's take was, "You can't look at it as six months of baseball coming down to one game. You just can't put that on your back."

"The only time we want to go back to San Diego now is if we're both in the playoffs," Sergio Romo said. "Realistically, we don't look past tomorrow." *Stay in the moment.*

Buster Posey dismissed the challenge with a laugh and said, "I don't even really want to think about it."

Neither Posey nor anyone else would have to think too long. Sunday's first pitch was less than 24 hours away.

The Most Meaningful Date

The sun rose in San Francisco, California, at 7:07 a.m. on Sunday, Oct. 3. Just as this day dawned with a number that read the same forwards or backwards, the omens for the Giants could be interpreted as good or ill.

Of all the dates on the calendar, Oct. 3 stood out as the most meaningful in the club's franchise history. That's when Bobby Thomson hit his immortal home run in 1951, giving the New York Giants a 5-4 victory over the Brooklyn Dodgers with the National League pennant on the line. It's also the date the Giants again stunned the Dodgers in 1962 by scoring four ninth-inning runs to claim a 6-4 win and pennant in yet another playoff finale. It's the anniversary of Joe Morgan's three-run homer in Game 162 of the 1982 season that denied the Dodgers a division title. And it's when Los Angeles gained a measure of revenge in 1993 by thrashing the Giants 12-1, eliminating them from the NL West race on the season's final day.

One way or another, this afternoon would add to Giants lore. Yet reading the baseball equivalent of tea leaves to divine how San Francisco would fare against the Padres yielded inconclusive data.

Whatever happened, it would be the most meaningful date of the year. Again.

Burning the Bridges

By 8:45 that morning, Sanchez had arisen. He fully intended to seize the day and subdue the Padres, whom he'd vowed the Giants would humble one month earlier.

"I felt good," he said. "I couldn't wait to get to the field, get the ball and start pitching. I knew that was going to be my game."

Sanchez followed his custom of stretching and performing various exercises for about 15 minutes. "I don't want to go to the field like my body's asleep," he said. Sanchez's routine included an old-school staple: jumping jacks. "To get the body going," he explained.

Sharing Sanchez's confidence, the Giants' brain trust made a symbolic but essential decision. They forbade players from bringing luggage to the ballpark, although the possibility existed for quick getaways to San Diego and/or Atlanta for playoff or postseason games.

Manager Bruce Bochy discussed the matter with general manager Brian Sabean after Saturday's loss before informing the players.

"We burned the bridges," said Bochy. "Brian and I talked. We said, 'Let's take care of tomorrow.'"

The Giants accomplished that by ignoring yesterday. *Stay in the moment.* They scored first, which they'd failed to do in the series' first two games. Every team increases its win probability significantly by opening the scoring. But with their stifling pitching and ferocious competitiveness, grabbing an immediate advantage was especially meaningful for the Giants. They'd finished 63-19, second-best in the majors, under these circumstances.

But nobody could have guessed they'd jump ahead of the Padres.

The Giants were facing Latos for the sixth time this year, which didn't portend doom as it might have earlier in the season. The right-hander was 0-4 with a 10.13 ERA in his previous four starts. Besides, the Padres had lost his last three outings against San Francisco.

Like the Giants, the raucous paid crowd of 42,822 brought no baggage to the ballpark. The spectators seemed refreshingly anxiety-free, ignoring the setbacks the Giants had absorbed the previous two days.

Pablo Sandoval opened the third inning with a drive that appeared destined for extra bases, but left fielder Scott Hairston ran it down. Sanchez, batting .125 for the season, startled one and all by lacing Latos' first pitch to the right-center field wall for a standup triple.

Sanchez's first career triple was a happy accident. Third-base coach Tim Flannery later informed Sanchez that Bochy was hollering orders from the dugout that would have restrained him. "I was supposed to take the first pitch," Sanchez said. "I didn't see the sign." Sanchez had a tiny sweet spot in his swing, which Latos had accidentally perfectly hit. Poetic justice was indeed stalking Latos—and vindicating Sanchez.

Up came Andres Torres, who soon sat back down as Latos struck him out. But Freddy Sanchez singled on an 0-1 pitch to break the scoreless tie. The crowd bellowed as if the Giants already had won. Aubrey Huff doubled beyond the diving reach of San Diego center fielder Chris Denorfia, widening the difference to 2-0.

Jonathan Sanchez preserved his shutout and composure, although he didn't throw a 1-2-3 inning until authoring an 11-pitch fifth. But

Adrian Gonzalez singled, and Ryan Ludwick walked to open the sixth. Although the bullpen had worked 11 innings in the previous two games, most relievers were relatively fresh, so Bochy didn't hesitate to summon reinforcements. Santiago Casilla, adept all season at marooning base runners, induced Yorvit Torrealba's grounder to third base. Sandoval stepped on the bag and, taking a risk, whipped the ball to second base in an attempt to retire the second lead runner instead of seeking the easy out at first. Sandoval indeed converted the double play as his throw beat Ludwick. Hairston hit a grounder towards the hole, and shortstop Juan Uribe grabbed it in shallow left field before whirling and jumping to throw out Torrealba at second. This sealed Casilla's stellar season totals at 47 runners inherited, 41 stranded.

It also froze Sanchez's pitching line. Five innings, three hits, five walks, five strikeouts—and zero runs. "I showed people I could do it," he said. "I talked s—t; I *had* to back it up."

The Giants invited trouble with two outs in the seventh. Chris Denorfia singled and David Eckstein—concluding an excruciating nine-pitch at-bat—hit a comebacker that rolled under Casilla's glove for an error. Ramon Ramirez relieved Casilla to face Tejada, who represented the potential go-ahead run. Since the Braves had already won, the Padres were now facing elimination from the postseason, and they could be expected to fight hard. Indeed, Tejada fouled off three two-strike pitches and worked the count full before flailing at a split-finger fastball and missing it.

Bochy left nothing to chance. He had Javier Lopez—who had become the league's most effective left-handed reliever against left-handed batters—face Gonzalez to open the eighth. Result: a harmless foul pop-up. With right-handers Ludwick and Torrealba due up, right-hander Sergio Romo replaced Lopez. Fly out, strikeout. Romo bellowed in exultation as he stalked off the mound. Romo's own screams were drowned out by the swelling din of the crowd, which whipped orange rally towels while greeting each scoreless inning with a standing ovation.

"At that moment, I kept thinking, 'Three outs away!'" Romo said.

Anxious souls might have wondered whether two runs would be enough to fend off the Padres. Given the excellence of San Diego's bullpen, which owned the NL's best relief ERA, the Giants seemed unlikely to score. They stranded two runners in the sixth during Latos' final inning and two more in the seventh against Luke Gregerson, San Diego's third reliever of the inning.

San Francisco's leadoff hitter in the eighth was Buster Posey, hit-less in the series' 12 at-bats. Months later, Posey admitted he was fatigued. "I was starting to feel it a little bit toward the end of the season," he said. "It was such a grind those last couple of weeks." Yet there would be another month to go!

Pitching for the fifth day in a row, Gregerson might have felt the same way. He hung a slider to Posey, who mashed it into the left-field seats for the 18th homer of his illustrious rookie year.

Only the ninth inning remained. Time for Brian Wilson to appear.

Wilson's first foe was Luis Durango, an impossibly fast runner. After Wilson jumped ahead 0-2, Durango took two balls before start-ing for first base, losing track of the count. Durango fouled off a 3-2 pitch before grounding out to shortstop.

Next was Chase Headley, who had reached base safely in six of his 11 previous plate appearances in the series. He grounded out to second base.

Up came Will Venable, who had absolutely no chance against Wilson. Called strike, foul tip, swing and a miss. The digital clocks at AT&T Park read 4:10 p.m.—not that anybody was paying attention to the time.

The Giants had ended the longest postseason drought among NL West teams by winning its first division title since 2003, and all any-body wanted to do was celebrate.

"LET THE PARTY BEGIN!" Duane Kuiper shouted on the air. And it did.

The Giants cavorted in the middle of the diamond. Almost un-noticed, Bochy found Jonathan Sanchez, placed his hands on the pitcher's shoulders and spoke to him as a father would a son. It was easy to guess what Bochy was saying: "I'm proud of you."

Said Bochy, "I was. He really had grown. He did, really, all year. To pitch a game like that on that stage after what happened, that's what I basically was telling him, how proud I was of how he handled himself."

Sanchez appreciated Bochy's gesture. "He had confidence in me," said Sanchez, who finished 4-1 with a 1.03 ERA in his last seven starts. "He knew I was going to do my best to win the game. When the manager knows what you can do out there, it makes you feel like you can do whatever you want, and you'll be successful."

Pablo Sandoval ended the euphoric monotony, breaking away from the group to don a preprinted "Division Champions" T-shirt. His teammates quickly followed suit.

Shortly after the wardrobe change, local product Pat Burrell exhorted teammates to thank the people in the stands who themselves felt so thankful. The Giants took a victory lap around the warning track, exchanging high fives with giddy fans along the way.

"Some of them wouldn't let go of our hands," Tim Lincecum said.

And why not? Nobody wanted to let go of this season. And now they never will. The champagne showers were waiting. The first parts of history were indelibly written, the Giants Way etched in stone. And as the banners outside the stadium said, "It's Magic Inside." It was. It was magic inside—forever.

Chapter 17

The Relentless Flow of the Positive River

Braving the Pitfalls

The playoff process and pitfalls have radically changed since the days of Bobby Thomson's glory. Although 1951 necessitated a three-game playoff between the tied Giants and Dodgers to determine the season's winner, that was an anomaly of the highest form. Normally, there was one clear winner from the only set of standings in each league who automatically reached the World Series. Simple, clear, direct.

By 2010, the path to the World Series was far more circuitous. The country's population had swelled—as had the population of major league teams.

The introduction of more teams into the playoffs added hope for suffering fans, whose chosen team had more opportunities to reach the playoffs. However, more ways *into* the playoffs necessarily meant more ways *out* of the playoffs as well.

No team more painfully understood this than the Atlanta Braves, who'd won their division for an astonishing 14 straight years from 1991 to 2005. Again and again, they bested every other team over the course of 162 grueling games, proving their superiority as clearly as any team possibly could. Yet in those 14 years, they had only reached the World Series five times, winning it just once. In the last four years of that run, they lost in the first round—the National League Division Series (NLDS)—and never even had the opportunity to play in the National League Championship Series (NLCS). After winning close to 100 games annually, they vanished from contention because of three short losses at the most critical time—not once, not twice, but four times straight.

To get that far and still have it not be far enough is a cruel outcome. Losing in the League Division Series leaves a bitter taste of waste on the tongue—the sense that the entire effort of the season has been thrown away by failure when it counted the most. Because the Division Series is shorter than other playoffs—best of five instead of best of seven—even more pressure is placed on the players. Some feel more pressure in the League Division Series than in the League Championship Series or even World Series. No one remembers who lost in the League Division Series—except you, if you lose. Then you can never forget.

In the League Division Series, the Giants were fated to face the team most cognizant of its pitfalls. The Braves were a hungry team now, too, having slipped from dominance to miss the playoffs entirely for four consecutive years after their record-setting run of dominance. They had only reached the playoffs this time by virtue of being the Wild Card—the second-place team with the best record.

The Braves had many fans outside of Atlanta rooting for them to go all the way in 2010. After all, these playoffs were the retirement ceremony for Bobby Cox, the great Braves manager who had led the team through their unprecedented 14-year stretch of division dominance as part of his remarkable 25-year managerial career with Atlanta. A certain Hall of Famer, Bobby Cox was revered by players and baseball people far beyond Atlanta. If the Braves were ever going to get the final monkey off his back—that weak playoff record—this was their absolute last chance. The Braves were motivated.

Full Strength

It all starts with pitching—especially in a short playoff series. All season long, none of the pitchers in their starting rotation had worked on fewer than the standard four days' rest, with minor exceptions occurring when Jonathan Sanchez and Barry Zito had made isolated relief appearances that did not disrupt their pitching routines. In the facet of the game that can render a team most vulnerable in the postseason—pitching—the Giants remained formidable. Everybody was strong. The skilled guidance of Dave Righetti, Bruce Bochy and the training staff kept it so—along with the diligent work of the pitchers themselves. As ever, good fortune also assisted.

Previous postseason qualifiers hadn't been so fortunate. Krukow cited the 1989 Giants, his last team, as an example. That club reached its zenith when Will Clark lined his go-ahead single off Mitch Williams in the Giants' NLCS clincher. San Francisco proceeded to absorb a four-game sweep at the hands of the Oakland A's in the World

Series. "By the time we got to the A's in '89, we were done. We were gassed," Krukow said. "We had shot our wad. We were tired, and we were burnt. The arms could not match up the legs. The everyday players were much stronger than our pitching staff."

These Giants faced no such problems. Tim Lincecum rested for a full seven days before confronting Atlanta in the Oct. 7 Division Series opener at AT&T Park.

"There's no need to put any added pressure on yourself," Lincecum said. The Franchise himself, the unfreaky Freak, was the leader of the staff once more.

The Roster Game

Critical decisions had to be made to set the 25-man active roster for the series.

In a mild reversal, Bochy opted to keep Cody Ross instead of Jose Guillen. Although Guillen had received a majority of the right-field playing time down the stretch, he'd developed neck pain that significantly hampered his hitting and made Ross a more solid alternative.

Guillen appeared in 42 of the Giants' final 45 games and started 38 of them, but his physical discomfort limited him to a .266 batting average with three home runs and 15 RBIs. After they'd claimed him during waivers on Aug. 22, Ross batted .288 with three homers and seven RBIs in 33 games with the Giants.

Referring to Guillen, Bochy said, "It's a tough decision when you have a guy who's been going out there pretty much every day, and you leave him off the roster. But I think he would agree that he wasn't quite 100 percent."

Another potential reason for Guillen's exclusion materialized later in the month, when *The New York Times* reported that Guillen had been linked to a federal investigation into shipments of performance-enhancing drugs.

In the story, several unidentified lawyers said federal authorities informed Major League Baseball of a probe into shipments of human growth hormone, allegedly sent to Guillen's wife in the Bay Area. The report also said Major League Baseball ordered the Giants to leave Guillen off their roster. Perhaps wisely, the Giants organization remained mum about this. They had worked hard to assemble a team clear of such allegations and wanted to stay clear now.

Another rumor became fact when Bochy announced Barry Zito would also be left off the roster. The Giants' highest-paid player and their opening day starter in 2007 and 2008, Zito had been eclipsed by Madison Bumgarner, the rookie whose 3.00 ERA since his June 26 recall was the fourth-best among NL lefties. By contrast, Zito had endured a nine-game losing streak from July 21 to Sept. 14. Although Zito's run support at times was faulty and his 19 quality starts were the most he'd thrown in a year for San Francisco, he finished 9-14 and failed to reach double-digits in victories for the first time in his 10 full seasons.

"Barry's such a good teammate and a stand-up guy," Bochy said. "I think it's fair to say that the other four [starters] are throwing a little bit better right now. And we weren't going to go with five starters. . . . Believe me, it's tough, when you have a guy who's the reason why you're here. . . . But he was great about it. He said, 'Hey, I understand. Right now, I'm not throwing quite as well as the rest of them.'" Zito's grace under humbling circumstances made a silent but significant contribution to the playoff team. It helped keep the harmony and oneness intact.

The Beautiful Essence of Mastery

Game One: game on. From the first instant, Lincecum's dominance was evident. The primary evidence wasn't in the regained velocity of his fastball, his devastating changeup, his newly mastered slider, his effective curveball or even his ability to use any of them at any time. It was in his eyes. The intense spotlight of the playoffs distilled him down to the beautiful essence of mastery. Its heat burned away all doubts, fears and extraneous thoughts and matters. Lincecum was as focused as Wilson's beard—and utterly in control.

Omar Infante, the Braves' All-Star utility man, doubled to open the game. And that, for all intents and purposes, was *it* for the Braves. Rookie of the Year candidate Jason Heyward flied out before Lincecum struck out the next five hitters, all on swings. Each of the nine strikes he threw while striking out the side in the second inning prompted swings.

The innings spun by in the compressed trance that happens when a player is truly in the zone, where everything else but mastery falls away. Lincecum was in the zone all night. His strikeout pace slowed from the third through fifth innings as he added "only" two strikeouts. But he picked up two more in the sixth and another to lead off the seventh by fanning Derrek Lee, his 10th strikeout victim of the night. After Brian McCann doubled to left-center field, Lincecum showed he could "pitch to contact"—letting batters get themselves out by connecting ineffectually—by erasing Alex Gonzalez on a comebacker and Matt Diaz on a flyball.

"He was giving us pitches to hit virtually every at-bat," Diaz said. "That's the thing with him and his delivery and his ability to mix pitches. He may give you a pitch to hit, but you're probably not going to hit it because you might not be looking for it, or it's just *funky*"—as devastatingly funky as the music of James Brown.

Having recorded most of his early-inning strikeouts on sliders or changeups, Lincecum reverted to pure power for the finish. Rick Ankiel and Eric Hinske went down flailing to end the eighth, causing mass delirium among the 43,936 AT&T Park patrons. Seeing the Giants end their seven-year postseason hiatus was enough of a treat. Seeing this performance was an embarrassment of riches.

In the ninth, Lincecum retired Infante on a grounder, fanned Heyward for the second straight time and froze Lee on a fastball, completing the game with his 14th strikeout. That matched the fourth-highest total in a postseason game and equaled the most ever by a pitcher in his postseason debut. The Franchise obliterated the franchise postseason record of 10.

"It just felt like things were in place," Lincecum said.

It was a typical understatement. Start to finish, he directed the game with the finesse of a classical composer and the power of overwhelming force. It was one of the greatest postseason pitching performances by any Giant—New York or San Francisco—in the team's 128-year history.

In reaching that level, Lincecum demonstrated exactly what Aubrey Huff had noticed in seeing The Franchise pitch for the first time in the regular season: His ability to "step it up" as challenge stepped up, too—the mark of a true master.

This being 2010, however, Lincecum's transcendence almost wasn't enough. Derek Lowe and the Braves were able to hand the zeroes right back to the Giants but for one—and even that one required assistance.

In the Giants' half of the fourth, Buster Posey led off with a single off Lowe. Posey broke for second base as Pat Burrell struck out on a full-count pitch and was ruled safe, although television replays suggested otherwise. Asked later about the call, Posey couldn't abandon his innate honesty. He winced and said, "I guess it's a good thing we don't have instant replay."

After Posey's steal, Juan Uribe struck out. Braves manager Bobby Cox then elected to intentionally walk Pablo Sandoval. Though first base was open, it was a curious move, given Sandoval's season-long struggles at the plate. Moreover, Lowe had struck him out to end the second inning. The free pass prolonged the inning for Cody Ross, who grounded a 2-0 pitch under third baseman Infante's glove and into left field for an RBI single. Infante appeared to have a play on the ball, but it somehow eluded him.

"We probably got a break," Bochy said. "In a game like this, you take it."

The apparent mistake was cashed in for a critical run—the only run of the game in yet another 1-0 Giants win. It was an early omen that breaks were set to fall the Giants' way.

Brilliance Overshadows Brilliance

One of the most amazing things about Lincecum's pitching performance was that, although it stood up to any in the team's 128-year history, it wasn't even the best postseason pitching performance of the past two days. The night before, Roy Halladay had christened the Phillies' own playoff run with a no-hitter against Cincinnati in Game One of the other Division Series—only the second no-hitter in postseason history, following the perfect game thrown by Don Larsen of the Yankees against the Dodgers in 1956. Brilliance overshadowed brilliance.

On the *Post-Game Wrap* for Game One, Dave Flemming said the story of the playoffs was Lincecum, Halladay and Cliff Lee—three pitchers transcendent in the openers. It was a more prescient comment than even Flemming knew, although Lee had already distinguished himself with one of the greatest records of postseason dominance in history and Halladay had just achieved baseball immortality with his no-hitter. Surely, Halladay was the premier pitcher in the league, if not all of baseball. Certainly, the Phillies were the team to beat in the postseason. Halladay and Lee would figure prominently in the story yet to be written, even if that story had already been defined.

From Brilliance to Resilience

Things remained in place for the Giants through seven innings of Game Two. They led 4-1, having received Pat Burrell's three-run homer in the first inning and Matt Cain's resolute 6 2/3-inning performance.

Cain allowed only one unearned run while striking out six. Scarcely noticed at first against the dazzling performance of Tim Lincecum, Cain began a playoff run that can only be equaled—and never broken.

Right-hander Sergio Romo—who'd allowed just three hits to the last 31 regular season batters he'd faced—yielded singles to Lee and McCann to open the eighth. Correctly surmising the game had reached a critical stage for the Giants, Bochy summoned Wilson, who secured 11 of his major league–high 48 saves by recording four or more outs.

Third baseman Pablo Sandoval committed a throwing error after fielding Melky Cabrera's grounder, scoring Lee and leaving runners on first and second. Brooks Conrad's sacrifice bunt advanced the runners before Alex Gonzalez, 0-for-6 in the series, drove Wilson's 97-mph fastball to the left-center field gap to tie the score. Wilson was so disgusted with himself that he ripped a towel in half after pitching a 1-2-3 ninth.

Undaunted, the Giants rallied in the 10th. Noticing Troy Glaus had entered the game to play third base, pinch hitter Edgar Renteria dropped a bunt in the defensively challenged veteran's direction and beat it out for a hit. Andres Torres sacrificed Renteria to second base. Pained by a sudden oblique injury, Braves relief ace Billy Wagner left the game. In came Atlanta's sixth reliever, right-hander Kyle Farnsworth, known for his temper and his 5.40 ERA since being acquired from Kansas City at the trade deadline. Farnsworth hit Freddy Sanchez and walked Aubrey Huff to load the bases.

Up came Posey, in position to save the evening for the Giants. All it would take for a victory would be a flyball, a well-placed grounder or any form of hit, walk or hit batsman. A wild pitch, a passed ball—*anything*. AT&T Park was ready to explode, already tasting the victory at hand. Posey grounded a 1-1 pitch to Glaus—the kind of grounder that might or might not get the job done. Rather than seek a force play at home, which would get the sure out but prolong the rally, Glaus went for the inning-ending double play and threw to second base. The peg was neither fully firm nor wholly accurate, but Infante was able to grab it. If he could turn and throw out Posey, it would finish the inning and the Giants' rally. If he couldn't, the game was over.

Infante threw out Posey. The elusive victory remained just out of reach, and the crowd settled in again with a groan. More extra innings.

With one out in the 11th, Braves center fielder Rick Ankiel hit a monstrous homer off Ramon Ramirez to put Atlanta ahead. In the bottom of the inning, the Giants got a runner aboard but couldn't consummate the rally, sending the crestfallen crowd home quiet. The Braves' 5-4 win evened the series out to a game apiece, and it put the Giants in an ominous position. Since Division Series play first began in 1995, teams in both leagues have gained a split on the road 11 times in the first two games. Eight of those clubs advanced to the League Championship Series. The Braves had just gained such a split, and now the series headed back to the home-field advantage of Atlanta. The Giants would have to win on the road if they were to win at all.

The nature of a short five-game series complicated their task. "It's a very paranoid environment in which to play," said Mike Krukow on the air. "Momentum swings back and forth so dramatically. . . . There is no momentum that is safe." The Giants had just squandered theirs.

"The one word that jumps out at you is *urgency*," Krukow continued. "You gotta make things happen! . . . It's completely nerve-racking." But the Giants seemed unconcerned about statistical history and short-series challenges.

"This team's been resilient all year," Aubrey Huff said. "We've lost a lot of tough games like this all year long and came back and got them the next day."

There was no game the next day, though. Urgent resilience would have to wait.

Ankiel

The saga of Rick Ankiel is one of baseball's strangest—and it had now twice benefited the Atlanta Braves in the postseason, each time a decade apart.

Unfortunately, in 2000, Ankiel wasn't playing *for* the Braves—he was playing *against* them as a 21-year-old pitching phenom who'd struck out 194 batters and garnered Rookie of the Year votes as a member of the St. Louis Cardinals. His future appeared bright—until the first game of the Division Series against Atlanta. Cardinals manager Tony LaRussa was forced to start Ankiel in Game One because of injuries to his pitching staff, and Ankiel's third-inning implosion is legendary. After starting the inning by walking opposing pitcher Greg Maddux on four pitches, he proceeded to throw *five* wild pitches in the inning—a modern-day record—alongside four walks and two hits, combining to produce four of the ugliest runs in history, all in the cruel glare of the national spotlight. Ankiel didn't finish the inning, and his implosion continued clear into the next year as he fell through the minors with horrific statistics. In Triple A ball, he walked 17 batters and threw 12 wild pitches in only 4.1 innings before he was demoted all the way back to rookie league ball. After failing to recover from whatever mental quirk had caused his sudden inability to throw strikes, he ceased his attempts to be a pitcher entirely.

But Ankiel didn't retire. He reinvented himself as a power-hitting outfielder—one who, not surprisingly, had a terrific throwing arm as well. It took him six more grueling years to reach the majors again, but after hitting 32 home runs in the Pacific Coast League in 2007, he was rewarded with a return to the St. Louis Cardinals, where he continued to hit home runs at a prodigious rate for a while. He added 11 more to his 2007 totals in the big leagues and 25 more in 2008 as an everyday Cardinals starter. But he still had holes in his swing, and after injuries, he started to falter. His path took him to Kansas City and more injuries in 2010, and then to Atlanta in a deadline-day trade on July 31. That in turn took him back to the playoffs as a hitter.

When Ankiel connected for his crushing 11th-inning homer against the Giants, he placed his name alongside two greats. He became the first since Babe Ruth to both start a postseason game as a pitcher and hit a postseason home run as a position player; he also became only the second player ever to put a postseason home run into the waters of McCovey Cove, following Barry Bonds.

It was a staggering if strange achievement. And it staggered the Giants, who gave up dangerous control of momentum in a game they'd appeared to have all but won.

Crazy Enough

Two days later at Atlanta's Turner Field, the start of Game Three presaged the improbable finish.

The Giants left the bases loaded in the first inning without scoring, failing to capitalize on Brooks Conrad's gaffe. The Braves' second baseman bobbled the ball as he fielded Freddy Sanchez's grounder and prepared to flip it to second base for a would-be force-out on Andres Torres. Play foiled: Conrad error number one.

San Francisco couldn't help but score on Conrad's next miscue. Mike Fontenot christened the second inning with a triple to right field on a drive Heyward struggled to track in the twilight. "I was following the play and thinking, 'Don't catch it,'" Fontenot said. Heyward didn't. Ross then lifted a fly to short right that Conrad simply couldn't hold. Fontenot came home: Conrad error number two.

Forgetting he was supposed to be erratic, Jonathan Sanchez no-hit Atlanta for 5 1/3 innings. Braves right-hander Tim Hudson—who had reached five previous Division Series with teams that advanced no farther—allowed four hits through seven innings.

The Giants clung to that 1-0 lead as Gonzalez, who struck out in his first two at-bats against Sanchez, singled to open Atlanta's eighth. Conrad popped up a sacrifice-bunt attempt, still trapped in his own personal hell.

With right-handed-batting Glaus in the on-deck circle, Bochy followed baseball gospel by inserting the right-handed Romo for the left-handed Sanchez—although Sanchez had allowed only two hits and struck out 11. Atlanta responded by summoning Eric Hinske, a left-handed hitter, to bat for Glaus. The Giants didn't counter that move; Romo remained on the hill. The yelps of second-guessers could almost be heard above the ensuing din as Hinske lined Romo's 2-2 slider up the right-field line and over the wall for his second career postseason homer.

"That put a lot of heads down," Huff said.

Especially Romo's. He'd been brilliantly effective in the eighth inning all year, but now for two games in a row—the first and only playoff games of his life so far—he'd failed at critical moments. The Giants were now losing 2-1 entering the ninth as Romo sat in the dugout, towel over his hung head, tears in his eyes.

His teammates came over in sequence to console him, telling him it would be fine. Still no panic. Still no defeated souls.

Atlanta's choice to replace their injured closer Wagner was Craig Kimbrel, a 22-year-old rookie whose regular season statistics appeared fictitious. In 21 appearances, Kimbrel recorded an 0.44 ERA—that's one earned run in 20 2/3 innings—while striking out 40.

Cody Ross popped out for the first of the last three outs. Travis Ishikawa then batted for Romo, comprehending the odds not only against him but also against the Giants.

"I was very, very nervous. You're already 1-1 in the best-of-five, and I knew if we dropped that game, especially in Atlanta, that would have caused some concern," Ishikawa said. "That was probably the most pressure-filled at-bat I've ever felt in my entire life. Every pitch I was trying to take a step out, take a couple of breaths. I don't know if you guys could see it, but my legs were shaking inside my pants. I was trying to control myself and control my breathing. At that point, I'm just trying to find any way on base."

Almost consumed by these terrible, wonderful sensations, Ishikawa was as alive as he ever had been. As he coaxed a walk on a 3-2 pitch, so were the Giants.

Tension still gripped Ishikawa as he stood at first base. "It didn't get any easier," he said. "I knew what my run meant." Scanning the field, he nervously assessed the outfielders' throwing arms and calculated his chances of breaking up a double play. Baserunning was literally a sore subject for Ishikawa, who'd spent all season healing from torn ligaments in his left foot. "I had the foot thing kind of holding me back all year, and I'm not the fastest guy," he admitted.

Still throwing wickedly, Kimbrel fired a called third strike past Andres Torres. One out to go.

Up next was Freddy Sanchez, defying human nature with each stride he took towards the batter's box. Sanchez was born with a club right foot and a pigeon-toed left foot that forced him into a cast when he was a day old. He had barely finished taking his first breaths on this earth when doctors told his mother he might never walk properly.

A person overcoming that kind of adversity would never cower from the challenges a mere ballgame might present. "Ishikawa battled, had a great at-bat. So I'm thinking to myself, 'I'm not making the last out,'" Sanchez said.

Nevertheless, Kimbrel forged ahead on the count, 0-2. One strike separated the Giants from falling behind in the series.

"I was pretty calm," Sanchez said. "I want to be in those situations. Two strikes or not, you've still got another strike."

Sanchez worked the count to 1-2 before stroking a single up the middle. Ishikawa pulled in at second base.

The Braves called on left-hander Mike Dunn to face the left-handed–batting Huff, who bounced a single into right field. Telling himself, "I've gotta run faster than I've ever run before," Ishikawa scored the tying run. When asked if that was the most important hit of his career, Huff replied, "Shut your mouth! Of course."

Following Huff and facing right-hander Peter Moylan, Posey hit a smash directly to Brooks Conrad. Always finding the one who isn't prepared for it, the ball scooted between the embattled infielder's legs for his third error of the game. It continued on into right-center field as Sanchez dashed in from second base with the go-ahead run. "I thought he was going to make the play," Posey said. "You don't ever wish that upon somebody. That's the way the game is sometimes."

The bottom of the ninth was relatively uneventful for Wilson, who allowed Brian McCann's two-out single but nothing else as he sealed the 3-2 conquest—the third consecutive one-run decision in a series leaving no margin for error. Or errors, in Brooks Conrad's case.

"Everybody was telling me that it was going to be a big day for me," said Ishikawa, acknowledging the vibe of wearing No. 10 on 10/10/2010.

This victory deepened Bochy's sense that more big days awaited the Giants.

"That's when I realized, 'They're crazy enough to win the World Series,'" he said. "They really believed it, and they weren't going to be denied."

Frozen in Agony

To err is to be a second baseman. That is a corollary to the old literary truth of human existence, and Brooks Conrad will never forget it after that game. He wouldn't have even been out there were it not for the Braves' unfortunate run of injuries—they came to the playoffs a battered team, while the Giants were gaining strength—but out there he was, and it will probably haunt his dreams for decades.

It's happened to far more accomplished players—their near-greatness being wiped clean from public memory by the pain of one disastrous moment. Bill Buckner is perhaps the most famous in modern times: His 2,715 hits over a 22-year career were just one of many skilled accomplishments, and in his days as a young Dodger outfielder, he was known for the grace of his diving catches. He never quite reached Hall of Fame status, but he was close—yet most will only remember Buckner for his critical error in the 1986 World Series. The ball that trickled through his legs at first base cost the Red Sox the chance to break the curse that had hung over their own attempts at championship since they'd traded Babe Ruth to the Yankees. It was a rare moment of slippage for Buckner, but it was magnified by the intensity of the moment and frozen into history with a vicious permanence.

Since it was only the Division Series and not the World Series, Conrad's three gaffes may not quite suffer the same curse of national immortality. As part of the swan song of Bobby Cox in Atlanta, however, they surely will. For the rest of his life, Conrad will have to learn how to accept failure as a simple survival tactic.

After his third and final error—during which the ball had scooted through his legs to allow the winning run to score—the camera focused on Conrad's miserably pained face as he unmistakably asked himself the great philosophical question, "*What the f—k?*" Only Brooks Conrad can find the answer. May he someday find peace with it, just as Ralph Branca eventually did regarding his fateful pitch to Bobby Thomson, just as Rick Ankiel did by finding a new path to the majors. It may take decades for Conrad. It may take forever. And the outcome will never change in retrospect. The only option is to live with it—to wear it, as ballplayers say. History is a tattoo.

Relentless Flow

The physical effects of playoff pressure can deeply affect outcomes. Ask Brooks Conrad. Ask Rick Ankiel. Ask Travis Ishikawa.

"The pressure, it can make you stop breathing," Tim Flannery said in the offseason. "It can actually change your breathing and the way you deal with how you perform or not perform." This is where he says Pat Burrell again brought his valuable leadership and experience with the World Championship Phillies of 2008 and the Giants of 2010. "He knew how it gets real heavy . . . Burrell taught those guys: Here's what's going to happen. Here's what to expect." The need to slow down and breathe was one of the things to expect. It's baseball, it's mindfulness, it's the simple core of living effectively, distilled into prominence by the beautiful pressure of the playoffs.

Flannery noted how the positive intensified as the playoff pressure did, remembering how when the Braves had pulled ahead in the eighth inning of Game Three—putting the Giants on the verge of a potentially devastating loss—Mark DeRosa's leadership gave the team a jolt of inspiration. Although he hadn't even played since May and wasn't on the playoff roster, DeRosa remained a key member of the team.

"When Atlanta went ahead, I remember DeRosa came flying out of the clubhouse, just beating on people's backs and saying, 'Quit thinking like that! Quit thinking like that! Stay positive!'" said Flannery. The Giants did, making their miraculous ninth-inning comeback with the assistance of the third error by Brian Conrad, who presumably wasn't breathing fully or thinking positively.

DeRosa wasn't the only one who understood the necessity of a positive outlook, according to Flan. "Javier Lopez called it 'the relentless flow of the positive river.' And Javy would do it . . . the bases would be loaded, and you could hear Javy almost chanting: 'You're *going* to get out of it. . . . *We're* going to get out of it.' There was this positive thing from guys who had been there before [to the playoffs and World Series] who knew: You can't let the genie out of the bottle. . . . You can't let Atlanta all of a sudden get an edge because they'll take off. It's such a different part of the season."

Flannery had experienced it as a player and then as a coach for the San Diego Padres. In 1984, he got a hit in his only World Series at-bat as the Detroit Tigers took out the Padres in five games. He returned to the World Series as a Padres coach in 1998, with Bruce Bochy managing as the Yankees swept the Padres in four.

"I'd been there a couple of times before, but you forget a little bit. And these guys like DeRosa, Lopez, Burrell . . . they didn't even let anybody have a thought of negativity enter their minds. . . . You think about that on other levels—not only with baseball. If you can think about that on every level that you live, it's got to help."

The relentless flow of the positive river. It's an eloquent description of what you must create as well as what you must surrender to. A positive mind helps inspire a positive outcome—with a person, with a team, with the wider world. And if you can open up to it inside as an individual, you'll find the positive river is as vast as the spirit that informs the surrounding entirety. The relentless flow of the positive river is here at every moment—as a source from which to draw strength and to contribute to in the blessing of greater service. If you do it well enough and humbly enough, it just might take you where you wanted to go all along. It just might take you to World Series victory.

The positive river was once described another way by Robert Muller, former assistant secretary general of the United Nations, on the public radio program *New Dimensions.* "We have no right to give up," he said. "Too many people give up too early. We are in a stream of time, and some progress will take longer; some positive things will happen after our lives. If you are really determined to be on the good side of life, the forces of the universe are there to help you."

You're going to get out of this. We're going to get out of this. Whatever "this" is. Without belief, it's far less possible.

Flow Reversal

The Giants got out of it. The relentless flow of the positive river worked, even if it needed the assistance of one of the postseason's most infamous fielding lapses. And when the Giants did succeed in positive creation and surrender, the momentum of the "very paranoid" short-series environment completely reversed. After being one strike from placing the Giants' backs against the wall with a win, the Braves suddenly found themselves in the same position. One more loss, and their final chance to send Bobby Cox to retirement as a winner would forever be ruined. One more critical mistake, and there would be no removal of that historical tattoo from their backsides.

They still had home-field advantage, although the Atlanta crowds had become so used to playoff appearances over the years that many times the games weren't even sold out. The fans could make some hard noise, however, annoying both the Braves' opponents and Native Americans who considered the "tomahawk chop" disrespectful.

Buster Posey had grown up in Georgia as a Braves fan. He dismissed the idea of it as a homecoming, however, since his small hometown of Leesburg was over 150 miles to the south. Posey dismissed the significance of anything that might bring nervousness—and he simply wasn't showing any.

For the critical Game Four, Posey's batterymate was another rookie: Madison Bumgarner, who was continuing to defy modern views about young arm development by still getting stronger and better as the fall progressed.

The list of the youngest pitchers to appear in a postseason game includes names that induce goose bumps: Bret Saberhagen, Fernando Valenzuela, Johnny Podres, Jim Palmer, CC Sabathia, Chief Bender, Babe Ruth. In Game Four of the Division Series, Madison Bumgarner now claimed the sixth spot on that list at 21 years and 71 days of age, following No. 5 Podres (21 years, four days), who was the 1955 World Series hero with Brooklyn. Bumgarner was just ahead of No. 7 Rick Ankiel (21 years, 76 days). Yes, Bumgarner was five days younger than Ankiel had been during his 2000 implosion. And it was only three days since Ankiel's slugging had subdued the Giants.

Game Four was a hefty assignment for Bumgarner and Posey, but both seemed born for the challenge. It was the natural progression of things—exactly what they'd been working towards while honing their physical gifts and mental calm.

Bumgarner dominated without being as spectacular as other accomplished left-handers. He threw hard but didn't possess the blinding stuff Vida Blue or David Price owned. He was deceptive but not to the dazzling extent of Valenzuela or, at their zenith, Barry Zito or Dontrelle Willis. Yet make no mistake: With his combination of youth, skill and determination, Bumgarner was indeed brilliant.

"You go back to early August, and it seemed like every series, we were saying, 'You know, this is a big series.' We were battling to get to this point, and he pitched a lot of big games for us," Bruce Bochy said. "The way he carried himself is beyond his years."

Facing the Braves before a less-than-sellout crowd of 44,532 at Turner Field, Bumgarner maintained his cool and his knack for recording the tough out.

He weathered a bases-loaded, two-out jam in the second inning by retiring opposing pitcher Derek Lowe on a flyball. He yielded three third-inning singles and Brian McCann's sacrifice fly but limited Atlanta to one run.

Normally, Derek Lowe wouldn't have been back out on the mound yet, but with the season on the line, the Braves had to come back with their ace on short rest. Lowe would deal from the mound, and deal he did. While Bumgarner was solid, Lowe was even more in control and appeared confident of the outcome of every pitch. Entering the sixth inning, he had a no-hitter going, threatening to match Roy Halladay's postseason wizardry. The Braves had a 1-0 lead.

To lead off the sixth, Cody Ross stepped in against Lowe's no-hitter. *You're going to get out of this. We're going to get out of this.* Ross lined a pitch over the left-field wall to break up the no-hitter, the shutout and the Atlanta lead in one swing. Tie game.

Unfortunately, there was then a little clog in the positive river's flow: On the very first pitch from Bumgarner in the bottom of the sixth, Brian McCann homered directly over Ross' head on first pitch of the inning. 2-1 Braves. Bumgarner left after six, having fulfilled a pitcher's primary obligation—to keep the score close. Now it was up to others to take over and lead the Giants.

The homer by Ross was still the only hit Lowe had yielded as the seventh inning began. But the Giants had proven capable of seizing upon the slightest lapse, which occurred as Aubrey Huff drew a one-out walk. Posey topped a slow roller towards the ponderous Troy Glaus at third base, who had no play. Displaying the selectivity that made him unique among the free-swinging Giants, Pat Burrell walked to load the bases. Atlanta manager Bobby Cox wanted a fresh pitcher and summoned right-hander Peter Moylan from the bullpen.

Juan Uribe, who was 1-for-13 in the series, grounded a 2-2 pitch to deep shortstop, where Alex Gonzalez lunged for the ball and gloved it. But his throw to second base veered wide and pulled Omar Infante off the bag for an error—the seventh Atlanta error of the series. Huff scored; everybody was safe. 2-2 tie. New game.

Jonny Venters struck out pinch hitter Aaron Rowand to set up a confrontation with Ross, who drove in just seven runs in 73 at-bats in the regular season after joining the Giants.

That modest output didn't dampen Ross' attitude. "Obviously, you want to perform well on the big stage and do what you think you're capable of doing as a person," he said later in the clubhouse. "Everybody in here knows we're capable of being the best. Otherwise, we wouldn't be here. I had all the confidence in the world in myself; I was going to get the job done."

Nor did Ross' numbers diminish the Giants' estimation of him. "I always thought he was the kind of guy who's got a flair for the dramatic," Huff said.

Ross bolstered that reputation by grounding a 1-0 pitch through the shortstop hole to score Posey. Though left fielder Matt Diaz threw on the fly to retire Burrell at the plate, the Giants led 3-2, allowing them to entrust their fate to the bullpen.

First came Santiago Casilla. The right-hander was formerly known as Jairo Garcia, the name he'd used when signing with the A's in 2000. In spring 2006, Garcia's conscience overwhelmed him and prompted him to tell the A's his real name and submit his true birthdate: June 25, 1980. That aged him by nearly three years, since the fictional Garcia's birthdate was March 7, 1983. Instead of reprimanding Garcia/Casilla, A's officials praised him for his honesty.

On this night, Casilla could have called himself Goose Gossage or Mariano Rivera, and nobody would have known the difference. He was that overpowering and dominant. Casilla struck out Diory Hernandez to open the Braves' seventh before coaxing two comebackers. He began the eighth by striking out dangerous Derrek Lee. McCann singled and was replaced by pinch runner Nate McLouth, who moved to second on Gonzalez's groundout.

Jason Heyward advanced to the plate, serving as the cue for Javier Lopez. The trading-deadline acquisition had hastened the Giants' surge as a valuable lefty-on-lefty specialist, known in baseball as a "LOOGY" (Left-Handed One-Out Guy). Lopez was capable of being more than that, but left-handed batters hit a mere .162 off Lopez (16-for-99) in the regular season, including .111 (5-for-45) in his Giants tenure. Heyward went 1-for-5 during the regular season off Lopez, who also struck him out looking in Game Two of this series. This matchup differed only slightly as Heyward struck out swinging.

The ninth inning, as usual, belonged to Brian Wilson. In his last chance for atonement, Brooks Conrad pinch-hit to start the ninth. His three errors would never be forgotten—unless he came through in the clutch here. He received an encouraging ovation from Braves fans. And he hit a deep fly to center—but not deep enough. One out.

His historical tattoo was now permanent at age 30, having finally reached the big time in the big leagues only to become famous for disaster. Surely, his boyhood dreams had never turned out like this.

After Conrad came none other than Ankiel, with his own chance to continue reversing his playoff legacy. The fans' yells turned hopeful as Wilson walked Ankiel and also Eric Hinske, both on 3-2 pitches. Torture again. What else?

But Wilson's walks didn't reflect vulnerability. "He's staying on the corners," Posey explained. "He's not going to make a mistake. That's the way he pitches. He's not going to give in. There's no fear in that guy."

Wilson didn't expect to fail. "I've had runners on first and second with one out before," he said. "You just keep pumping positive energy. It sounds kind of Walt Disney, but it works." *The relentless flow of the positive river.*

This stage of Mr. Toad's Wild Ride concluded happily for the Giants—barely. Wilson struck out Infante. There was one out to go, but the tying and winning runs were still on base. Pinch hitter Melky Cabrera hit a grounder to third, where Uribe was then stationed. Uribe's throw was high and down the line—a potentially disastrous sail of the baseball. But defensive replacement Travis Ishikawa, one of the game's most graceful first basemen, made the difficult look easy as he crossed the line into foul ground in front of the baserunner, deftly keeping one toe on the bag as he snared the ball at the full extent of his reach. Had he failed, at least the tying run would've scored. The game might've been lost. And with momentum shifted, the series might well have been won by Atlanta the next day.

Following the surprise victory, Wilson made his traditional warrior's gesture, honoring his father and his God. It set off a repeat performance of the victory dance the Giants had indulged in eight days earlier. Huff described this one as more "businesslike." The Giants didn't let euphoria cloud their perspective.

The final out painfully ended the career of Braves manager Bobby Cox. Momentarily appearing dejected, he quickly turned towards the tunnel to the clubhouse before bravely returning for a final farewell. As the Turner Field crowd showered one last ovation on him, virtually every Giant stopped and joined the spectators in applauding him.

"He's such a legend in this game," second baseman Freddy Sanchez said. "It was only right that everybody paid their respect to him."

Said Cox, "That was a nice gesture by the Giants. I love Bochy. He's one of the best guys in baseball. If we couldn't win, I'm glad he did."

Fans seeking omens undoubtedly remembered the Giants had ousted Atlanta in the 2002 Division Series en route to their star-crossed World Series appearance, when they collapsed against the Angels five outs from the world championship. Although that Atlanta series had gone the full five games, this one was actually tighter since a single run had decided each game. The Giants were primed for the challenge, having played more games decided by three or fewer runs (115) than any team in the major leagues in 2010. The Giants successfully submerged themselves in the positive river, surviving the paranoid environment.

"They don't know *how* they're going to win," said Mike Krukow. "But they have that confidence. . . . It's going to be a different hero every day—and the pitching's going to make it stand."

It was indeed a different hero every day—in the Atlanta series as it had been all year. There is no official MVP for the Division Series, but Krukow and the other announcers decided to vote anyway. "We'll give the winner a can of Guinness," Krukow joked. ("A *can?!*" came the response.) Krukow amended it to *half* a can, saying in jest that his was already open. It was a tough call, but after discussion, the broadcasters gave accidental outfielder Cody Ross their MVP votes. He'd driven in the game-winning run in two of the three games and had provided the key spark against Derek Lowe. And he'd done it while batting eighth, buried in the lineup.

Despite the team's confidence, even a few Giants might have thought they were achieving the unattainable. Said Bumgarner, "It's surreal. I'm sure it'll sink in sometime in the next few days, but it's pretty unbelievable that we're going to go play for the National League Championship."

They would be playing against the Philadelphia Phillies, the expected victors, where the first game would feature a classic pitching matchup: Roy Halladay vs. Tim Lincecum. "That sounds like a World Series Game One," said Jon Miller.

It's still far from the World Series, though. After winning the Division Series, what has a team won so far? Nothing that public memory will keep. In the paranoid short series, the winners get to keep going is all. And the losers are left with that bitter taste of waste all winter.

"The Phillies are going to be strong, too," Krukow summarized. "There'll be no excuses."

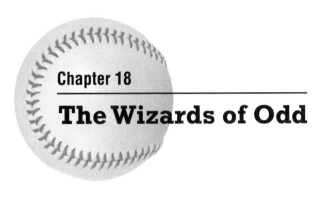

Chapter 18

The Wizards of Odd

Surprising Force

To reach the World Series, the Giants had only one team left to beat—but putting it that way is like saying they only had to slay one grizzly bear with a plastic butter knife.

The skeptics—a group that included virtually everybody who paid attention to baseball except the Giants' most faithful fans and the team itself—figured Philadelphia would handle San Francisco easily in the National League Championship Series. Having won the 2008 World Series and the 2009 pennant, the Phillies were poised to become the league's first team to win three consecutive flags since the 1942–44 Cardinals.

The Phillies had strength up and down the lineup as well as experience with success. Surely, San Francisco would wilt under the stress of trying to wrest four victories from the likes of Jimmy Rollins, Ryan Howard, Chase Utley, Jayson Werth and Shane Victorino.

After the mid-season acquisition of Roy Oswalt from the Houston Astros, the Phillies were perceived to have a stronger pitching rotation, too, led by Roy Halladay, Oswalt and Cole Hamels. Never mind that the Giants had defeated all three during the regular season (*three* times in Oswalt's case). Never mind also that the Giants' starting pitchers had excelled in the Division Series by allowing only three earned runs in 29 innings. Perceptions were still perceptions, and the Giants were perceived as weaker.

This perception was heightened since the defeated Atlanta squad had lacked second baseman Martin Prado and third baseman Chipper Jones, key players sidelined by injuries. The skeptics diminished the Giants' accomplishments. Their NLCS presence was deemed an odd fluke.

On paper, the Phillies were judged a better team—but oneness is rarely rated as the central factor it is, especially by skeptics. The relentless flow of the positive river continued to run with surprising force.

Symbolic Renaissance

The flow brought back the possibility of a fourth seasonal confrontation between Oswalt and his dominating nemesis, Tim Lincecum. The pitching rotations didn't align that way, however. In Game One, Lincecum would face Roy Halladay instead.

Halladay had been canonized as some sort of uber-ace since no-hitting Cincinnati in Game One of the Division Series, complementing the perfect game he threw May 29 at Miami. But the Giants still approached the NLCS opener filled with confidence.

After all, they had the revitalized Lincecum pitching.

Madison Bumgarner summarized the Giants' faith in Lincecum when he was asked how he maintained his composure in the Game Four Division Series clincher at Atlanta.

"There wasn't a whole lot of pressure. We would have had Timmy going [in Game Five]," Bumgarner said. Giants fans shared that faith. His success lit fires of hope, and those blazes reached Burning Man proportions as this game approached.

"His starting this game is more than a fortunate turn of the calendar," said Brian Murphy, cohost of the *Murph and Mac* morning show on KNBR, the Giants' flagship station. "It's the symbolic renaissance of a franchise that has had some great runs."

Early in 2011, Lincecum—who looked like he should have been skateboarding to his driver's education class—would be selected by *GQ* magazine as one of the 25 coolest athletes of all time. It wasn't always thus. Overwhelmed by self-imposed pressure, Lincecum had practically hyperventilated on the Busch Stadium mound when he started the 2009 All-Star Game. But he's a quick learner. That experience installed an internal thermostat that enabled him to cope with hype.

"Obviously, it's a big game," Lincecum said on the eve of Game One. "But I don't want to get too over-amped." He didn't.

The Illusion of Control

Halladay appeared to be in control as Game One began, retiring the first seven batters he faced—continuing his no-hitter from Cincinnati into the next game.

Then Cody Ross stepped into the right-handed batter's box. Ross had every reason to feel comfortable, even with Halladay staring him down. Not only was Ross coming off a powerful, clutch performance in the Division Series finale, but he had also thrived in the cozy environs of Citizens Bank Park, where he'd homered seven times in 116 plate appearances. Moreover, with 13 homers in 241 lifetime plate appearances against Philadelphia, Ross should have made the Phillies wary—not the other way around.

Although Ross was again batting eighth—"hidin' in the weeds," as Mike Krukow put it—he was anything but insignificant. He maintained his simple goal of trying "to get something going for my team, whether it's drawing a walk or hitting a home run. Anything that you can do to spark your club."

Ross lit that spark on a 1-1 pitch, whipping a home run into the left-field seats. With one swing, he ripped the cloak of invincibility from Halladay's shoulders by collecting the first hit of the postseason off the Phillies ace. Ross had still been with the Florida Marlins when Halladay recorded his perfect game against them and went 0-for-3 that day. "He's got the potential to do that every night he pitches," Ross said. Obviously, Ross didn't let that conviction blind him to the possibilities of his own skills.

As if angered, Halladay struck out the next two batters. The Giants' minimal lead vanished when Carlos Ruiz homered off Lincecum to open the bottom of the third. The Phillies threatened to take down Lincecum right then and there. Halladay singled, and Victorino bounced into a double play, but Placido Polanco doubled and Chase Utley walked. Lincecum would have to regain his equilibrium against Ryan Howard, who'd doubled in his first at-bat one inning earlier. Five pitches later, Howard struck out swinging.

The Giants' fifth inning virtually duplicated the third. Again, Ross batted with one out. Again, he lined a home run off Halladay, his drive landing in seemingly the same spot as the first. Ross' wizardry conjured wonder everywhere except the Giants' dugout. "It's not a surprise," manager Bruce Bochy said after the game. "We got him for a reason. He's coming through big-time for us." It marked only the second time all year that an individual had homered twice off Halladay. Ross also became just the fourth player to hit two homers in an NLCS opener. Any longtime Giants fan can identify the last one who did that: Will Clark, who mauled the Cubs in 1989.

This time, the Giants built on their lead, although some Phillies fans will swear to this day that it should have never happened.

Buster Posey's single prolonged the sixth inning with two outs and nobody on base. Halladay thought he had Burrell struck out on an 0-2 pitch—the right-hander started to stride off the mound—but umpire Derryl Cousins called it a ball. Even Giants announcer Mike Krukow agreed with Halladay after watching the replay. But the game of inches continued to fall in the Giants' direction as Burrell capitalized by doubling off the glove of left fielder Raul Ibanez, who appeared to have a shot at making the catch but missed a leaping attempt at the wall. Running freely with two outs, Posey scored. So did pinch runner Nate Schierholtz when Juan Uribe then singled up the middle.

To his credit, Halladay handled the disappointment like a pro. Asked if he thought the fateful pitch to Burrell was a strike, he said, "Yeah, I did. But that's part of it. There were obviously calls that they wanted, too. It's part of the game. If you don't get a pitch, you have to make a pitch on the next one." No excuses.

The Giants needed those runs to offset Jayson Werth's two-run homer in the Phillies' half of the sixth. Lincecum obviously wasn't at his sharpest. He fell behind 2-0 against eight of the first 14 hitters he faced and fed first-pitch strikes to only 12 of the 29 Phillies he confronted. But he also struck out the side in the sixth and fanned Victorino during a 1-2-3 seventh. That hiked his October strikeout total to 22, matching Bob Gibson for the most in a pitcher's first two postseason starts.

Lincecum deserves further credit for maintaining his concentration and sense of humor. Taunting Lincecum for his long hair, Phillies fans wolf-whistled in derision each time he batted. "I was thinking, 'I must have a really nice butt,'" Lincecum said.

On this night, the best-looking back end belonged to the Giants' pitching staff, following their front-end starter.

Relievers Javier Lopez and Brian Wilson didn't allow a Phillie to reach scoring position in the final two innings. Lopez, the lefty-on-lefty specialist, retired lefties Chase Utley and Ryan Howard. Wilson then entered the game and weathered mild trouble while securing the final four outs. He yielded Werth's single upon relieving Lopez but struck out Jimmy Rollins. He finished his third postseason save by striking out the side in the ninth, although he put the tying run on base with one out by grazing Carlos Ruiz with a pitch.

Wilson increased his degree of difficulty by falling behind on all four of his strikeout victims. Obviously, none of this fazed him.

"I'm not going to give in," Wilson said after San Francisco's 4-3 victory. "You're going to work. I'm going to work. It's a battle. I'm not going to lay one in there. They know that. And you know what? I've got three chances to get you out on strikes. I've got four chances to walk you. I like my odds. And if I can't get that guy, I'll get the next guy. The last thing I want to do is throw 15 strikes in one inning and blow the game. I think percentage of strikes helps, but at the end of the day, unless it says 'W' next to the team, it doesn't matter."

It said "W" next to the Giants. It mattered. The Giants had beaten another master pitcher, just as they'd done all year.

Missing Targets

The Giants had played seven consecutive one-run postseason games—five in 2010, plus the final two in their ill-fated 2003 Division Series against Florida. Game Two against the Phillies upset this balanced tension. It also left the Giants pondering lineup alternatives—playing the lineup game again even now.

Philadelphia's four-run seventh inning doomed San Francisco to a 6-1 loss, tying the series at a game apiece.

"It wasn't a pretty game for us, all around. Defensively, offensively, everything," Ross said. "This is one when we came off the field in the ninth [and] you walk up those [dugout] stairs, you have to forget about."

Jonathan Sanchez mostly maintained his late-season effectiveness. He struck out seven, permitted five hits, lasted one batter into the seventh and left the game with the Giants trailing only 2-1.

Some things didn't change. Ross homered to break up a no-hitter for the third game in a row, connecting against Oswalt to tie the score 1-1 in the fifth. Ross' latest round-tripper proved he wouldn't be intimidated, since Oswalt played him "chin music" in the form of a high, inside fastball during his first at-bat.

Ross nearly homered again in the seventh as he drove Oswalt's 1-0 slider to deep left-center. That happened to be a recessed portion of the outfield, giving Victorino an easy play on the ball.

"When I'm seeing the ball well, good things happen," Ross said. "I'm just trying to get something going for the team. Tonight wasn't enough."

The Phillies' seventh inning was more than enough for them. Oswalt's leadoff single chased Sanchez, who was replaced by Ramon Ramirez. Victorino sacrificed Oswalt to second base, and Utley drew an intentional walk. Polanco's single scored Oswalt, who disobeyed third-base coach Sam Perlozzo's stop sign and slid home while Huff caught Torres' throw instead of allowing it to bypass him.

"I made a bad decision there on the cutoff," Huff said. "As I'm getting by the mound, I glanced at the third-base coach, and he had his hands up. So I cut it off. . . . The throw was on the money, it nails him. I have to let it go."

Out went Ramirez; in came Jeremy Affeldt. He struck out Howard and intentionally walked Werth to load the bases. Santiago Casilla confronted Rollins, who doubled off the right-field wall to score Utley, Polanco and Werth. It was essentially over.

The Giants met the goal of any team that opens a series on the road: They broke even. But after their rousing Game One victory, it somehow didn't feel like enough.

"You come into a place like this, when you first start the series, your goal is to go 1-1," Huff said. "But when you get that first one, you want to come out and get this one."

Pundits began to write the Giants off. This was the expected result at last.

Dominant Purity

For any baseball purist and Giants fan, the postseason setting culminated with Game Three of the NLCS. The convergence of the starting time (1:20 p.m. Pacific) and the calendar (Oct. 19) bathed AT&T Park in a wondrous, natural chiaroscuro that recalled classic photos and newsreels of postseasons past.

Fans of a certain age recall when the postseason consisted solely of the World Series and, if your grade-school class behaved nicely enough, the teacher would cart in a television so everyone could watch the drama unfold. That was the theatre of the sublime, seeing Bob Gibson, Mickey Lolich or Tom Seaver stare at the catcher's sign.

In the years since the Giants had won a World Championship, not only had baseball migrated from East Coast to West, it had also migrated from sunshine to darkness. With the advent of powerful lights and ubiquitous television, the game had slowly shifted to primarily being an evening affair. Even the Cubs at Wrigley Field, the last fully daytime holdout, had given in to the inevitable and installed light standards.

Still, baseball is classically an affair of the warm sunshine, and no setting beats a perfect blue afternoon.

The Giants were gifted with such a perfect day upon returning home for Game Three of the NLCS—the only true daytime game of the series. Afternoon temperatures were in the ideal sixties, with only slight breezes. Nothing but blue brilliance reflected off the diamond's pure green, the glinting waters of McCovey Cove and its teeming assemblage of boats. If ever there was to be an advertisement for the beauty of San Francisco and its baseball climate, this was it. Even before the game, the entire neighborhood was magical: At the Ferry Building down the block, the black metal statue of Mohandas Gandhi was adorned with Giants orange, while the farmer's market below buzzed with life. Pedestrians swarmed the neighborhood in their own orange and black, enjoying the orange sun and dark shadow of one of the world's great downtowns. From young kids wearing Lincecum and Posey T-shirts to grizzled old fans donning ancient Giants caps covered with Croix de Candlestick pins, evidence of Giants allegiance clearly overshadowed the minimalistic smattering of Philadelphia gear dotting the sunshine.

There were new Lincecum T-shirts, too, bound to cause the front office more consternation and rebellious San Francisco fans more glee. After the final clinching game of the regular season, The Freak had put shivers in the hearts of FCC-fearing broadcasters. Asked by Comcast's Amy Gutierrez, "Are you ready for your champagne shower?" On live television, he succinctly and loudly replied, "F—k yeah!!!"

Naturally, this became another rallying cry for the fans in its fully uncensored form. The phrase could be heard echoing in the stands as well as throughout the neighborhood before and after the game. It was available on unofficial T-shirts, some of which featured Lincecum's silhouette in motion as the "K" in the first word.

It all blended well with the crowd of false beards, the privately worn thongs, the stalwart Panda hats, the orange rally towels and all of the other adornments worn by San Francisco's famously individual fans. All in all, it was a superb day to be at AT&T Park. And it was an even better day to be a Giants fan.

Looking like the ideal successor to past heroes, Matt Cain stood atop the mound amidst the dramatic mixture of light and shadow only baseball's elite get to experience. He was facing Cole Hamels, the MVP in both the NLCS and the World Series for the 2008 champion Phillies.

Cain asserted himself immediately by retiring the first seven Phillies he faced, including three on strikeouts.

But Hamels appeared Cain's equal. He set the Giants down perfectly through the first three innings, leaving the team facing yet another no-hitter early on.

It was Edgar Renteria who finally broke it up this time, leading off the fourth. Strange that Renteria—who'd appeared in only 72 regular season games and endured three trips to the disabled list—emerged as the face of the offense by being installed at the leadoff spot. Even now, he was playing with a completely torn bicep he had suffered in the Atlanta series and was reputedly considering retirement at season's end. "It's hard. It's hard," he said, referring to the adversity he'd weathered. "But it's not time to think about that. It's time to think about how we can win ballgames." Thinking about that is what inspired Bruce Bochy to place Renteria there, and, as with most of Bochy's postseason moves, it worked.

Renteria singled to lead off the fourth inning. He advanced on a sacrifice bunt before the ever-patient Burrell drew a two-out walk. Then Cody Ross—who else?—stepped in to do damage. After homering three times in the previous two games, Ross showed he could torment the Phillies with more than just long-distance hitting. He deftly poked at a 2-1 fastball that couldn't have been more than eight inches above the ground and lashed it into left field. Ross' bat control amazed Hamels. "I don't know too many guys who can lift that up over a third baseman," Hamels said. "Most guys normally hit it into the ground."

Said Ross, "For the most part, it's about confidence, going up there and knowing you're going to get the job done or do something to help your team." It's about the relentless flow of the positive river. Aubrey Huff kept that flow going with another RBI single, and the Giants held a 2-0 lead.

Aaron Rowand, another veteran who left the bench to start, doubled to open the fifth and was still on second base with two outs. Freddy Sanchez then hit a 1-2 pitch to Utley at second, who was torn over whether to charge the low, looping liner or play it on a bounce. He chose the latter approach. The ball short-hopped him and caromed towards second base as Rowand, running unimpeded with two outs, scored easily to make it 3-0.

Two-out scoring was the afternoon's theme for the Giants, who scored all of their runs that way. "That's the way it's going to have to be in this series," Aubrey Huff said of the Giants' economical offense. "The pitching's so dominant."

In that regard, Hamels was strong with eight strikeouts. It wasn't enough as Cain continued to dominate the Phillies in the team's seventh consecutive postseason quality start. Philadelphia batters went 0-for-5 against him with runners in scoring position, hitting the ball out of the infield only once. Cain entered the game 0-3 with a 6.23 ERA in five regular season starts against Philadelphia, but that might as well have been ancient history as he subdued past tormentors. Chase Utley (previously 7-for-15 against Cain with three home runs) went 0-for-3 off him. So did Jimmy Rollins (previously 6-for-10). Ryan Howard had been only 2-for-10 against Cain, but both hits were home runs. Cain limited him to a harmless 1-for-3. Overall, Cain only allowed two hits in seven masterly shutout innings, keeping his postseason ERA at a perfect 0.00.

"When [Cain] was in trouble, he got even better," said Phillies manager Charlie Manuel.

"I think the biggest thing was really making sure the location was better than the previous times," Cain said. "The main goal today was to try to keep the ball closer to the knees and stay at the bottom of the strike zone."

In doing so, Cain led the Giants to their second home postseason shutout. (Tim Lincecum's two-hit, 14-strikeout performance against Atlanta in the Division Series opener was the other.) A mere 93 years had passed since the Giants had last done this, when Rube Benton and Ferdie Schupp blanked the Chicago White Sox on back-to-back afternoons in Games Three and Four of the 1917 World Series.

In the present moment, the Giants' 3-0 victory gave them a 2-1 series lead. That was all that mattered now. It was back to the twilight shadows as the series continued in a game that will never be forgotten in San Francisco.

Epic and Delicious

Game Three was for purists. Game Four had more mass appeal, featuring three hours and 40 minutes of relentless drama. It was a blockbuster instead of an art film. Some even called it an instant classic, perhaps because it could be viewed through a variety of prisms.

The first view was through the prism of surprise, given both teams had been led by their least-heralded starters. For the Phillies, it was Joe Blanton, who'd face Giants rookie Madison Bumgarner. (Speculation had been that the Phillies would bring back Roy Halladay on short rest, but they were still confident of their series position.) No one expected a classic.

Another prism through which to view the game—and perhaps the best vantage point for observing it—was atop the sturdy shoulders of Buster Posey. Entering the game batting .091 (1-for-11) with four strikeouts in the series, Posey carried the San Francisco side with a 4-for-5 effort, his hits driving good pitches all over the field.

Posey gave the Giants a 2-0 lead with a pair of two-out, run-scoring hits—a first-inning single and a third-inning double. He proceeded to become the second rookie to collect four hits in an NLCS game—Derek Jeter of the Yankees being the first—and the seventh to accomplish this feat in any postseason game. Asked in a postgame news conference whether he understood that he had manufactured an "epic night," the unassuming Posey prompted laughter by replying, "Well, thank you."

Posey's "epic" defense also bolstered the Giants. In the fifth, he deftly grabbed center fielder Aaron Rowand's strong but tricky short-hop throw to tag out Carlos Ruiz as he tried to score from second base on Shane Victorino's RBI single.

"Looked like a shortstop," Duane Kuiper said of Posey on the air, admiring his ease in making an exceptionally difficult play look fluid.

Since the Phillies scored four runs in that inning, Posey's play denied Philadelphia a bigger outburst. It was Bumgarner's only tough inning after beginning with four strong shutout ones, but one bad inning can mimic one bad apple. There was a rotten smell about the 4-2 hole it put the Giants in. Bumgarner was gone.

The goggles of Pablo Sandoval provided another prism through which to view the drama. In the sixth inning, Sandoval came to the plate after Pat Burrell had walked and Cody Ross had doubled, putting the tying and go-ahead runs on base in what was now a 4-3 game. Sandoval smoked a line drive down the right-field line that umpire Ted Barrett ruled foul, although replays showed the ball might have grazed the white stripe. As an agonized Sandoval returned to the batter's box, Bochy was in the closing stages of a colorful yet futile argument with the umpires. Sandoval seized upon the brief delay to calm himself. "Count to 10. Breathe," he said. "Get a pitch you can hit a flyball [on] or try to hit to the middle. Don't try to do too much."

The free-swinging Sandoval followed his own advice, lashing Durbin's 1-2 fastball to left-center field for *another* double—his second one of the same at-bat in some viewers' eyes. It gave the Giants a 5-4 edge.

"It's what you dream of, when I was a little kid in the backyard," said Sandoval, who flapped his arms in unison with the crowd's rhythmic cheers as he reached second base.

"I don't think anybody enjoys celebrating more than him," said Duane Kuiper on the *Post Game Wrap*, mentioning that Sandoval loved to celebrate *everything*, from a fine meal to a beautiful woman.

But Sandoval couldn't celebrate the Giants' failure to hold the lead as Ryan Howard and Jayson Werth doubled to tie the score in the eighth. The teams entered the ninth inning tied 5-5.

At that point, Juan Uribe gained the ultimate perspective on the game. He'd spent all game on the bench, nursing soreness in the wrist he'd injured while sliding into second base in Game One. But now he entered on defense to begin the ninth as part of a double switch that brought Brian Wilson to the mound.

Uribe immediately prevented a rally before it started. He was challenged as pinch hitter Ross Gload smashed a grounder in his direction, catching him between hops, deep in the hole towards left. Uribe backpedaled, picked the hard hop cleanly and somehow threw out Gload while falling backwards—a difficult feat made nearly impossible by coming in off the bench, cold and injured.

"That was an awesome play," Aubrey Huff said. "I didn't think there was any chance he was going to throw it. [But] he made a strong throw, and it was pretty accurate." Wilson closed out the ninth without further issue. Still tied.

With the season's momentum on the line, the Phillies decided to pull out all the stops and brought in Roy Oswalt, Philadelphia's starter in Games Two and Six. Roles matter less in the postseason. "That's what winners do," an admiring Brian Wilson said. "They ask for the ball."

Oswalt asked for it and got it. But Huff singled with one out and dashed to third on Posey's single to right, which followed a pair of opposite-field fouls in that direction.

Up came Uribe, who later admitted that given his injury, he couldn't handle Oswalt's fastball. Uribe acknowledged the discomfort in his wrist. "It hurt, but when I hit, I didn't want to think about it being hurt. I wanted to focus on my swing," Uribe said. "Before the swing I wasn't thinking, 'Oh, easy swing now.' I was thinking, 'Swing like normal.' "

One unhittable heater came in on Uribe with the count 1-1. Uribe insisted to umpire Wally Bell that the pitch hit him. Manager Bruce Bochy even left the dugout to argue briefly. Again, the argument was to no avail. Again, losing the argument benefited the Giants. Two pitches later, Oswalt sent Uribe a friendlier delivery.

"*Cambio*," Uribe said, employing the Spanish word for changeup. "Something low."

Uribe transformed it into something high, a flyball to medium-deep left field. He flipped his bat and raised his arm triumphantly as

Huff tagged up and scored easily with the winning run, raising his own arms in triumph as the stadium and dugout erupted.

"It seems like he's always in the right situation at the right time," Huff said of Uribe. As many as 11 of Uribe's 24 regular season home runs had either tied the score or put the Giants ahead. This one hiked the Giants' series lead to 3-1, putting them one win shy of the World Series.

"Every victory's just as tasty, but tonight's was really delicious," Wilson said.

Mike Krukow described one reason for its epic deliciousness. "There is not one guy in there thinking about a personal stat," he noted at game's end. "We are bearing witness to one of the great *teams* that's come along in a long time."

But that team wouldn't be remembered so well if they couldn't get that last NLCS win, followed by the World Series' four. The last wins can be the hardest ones. And this one, with its extended drama, was exceptionally taxing.

"I need a nap," summarized Duane Kuiper.

Wrong Mayhem

If this LCS was anything like most previous ones, the Giants were World Series–bound. Since the LCS had gone to a seven-game format in 1985, 24 of the previous 30 teams to grab a 3-1 lead advanced to the World Series. Moreover, the prospect of securing the National League pennant at home was intoxicating.

"I hope it's mayhem," Brian Wilson said.

But while history stoked the Giants' hopes, urgency wouldn't let them relax.

"We have to try to win it as soon as possible," right-hander Sergio Romo said. "Those guys [the Phillies], they want it, and they're going to give it their best as well. One win is kind of hard to get at times."

Said center fielder Aaron Rowand about the Phillies, "They're capable of catching fire and doing things that a lot of other teams in baseball can't do, and that's why they're here. So you can't take that for granted. When it's over, then you can relax."

Although the Giants had Tim Lincecum's reassuring presence on the mound for Game Five, the Phillies—as was the case in Game One—countered with the redoubtable Halladay.

"I'd say if we like to play with our backs against the wall . . . I think we're standing right there now," Phillies manager Charlie Manuel said. It was do or die for them.

Led by the speed of Andres Torres—back at leadoff in the lineup game—the Giants leapt to a 1-0 lead in the first and had Halladay further on the ropes, but they couldn't capitalize when Ryan Howard's diving stop stole a potential key hit from Aubrey Huff. Halladay was further on the ropes after pulling a groin muscle in the second inning, but—no excuses—he stayed on effectively despite not having his best stuff.

Lincecum was effective, too, but that was of no help as the Phillies' odd three-run third inning spoiled his otherwise fine effort. Still trailing 1-0, the Phillies began a strange surge with a single by Raul Ibanez—who was batting .130 in the postseason at the time—one of only four hits allowed in seven innings by Lincecum. The Franchise then nicked Carlos Ruiz with a pitch, putting two runners on.

That called for a sacrifice-bunt attempt from Halladay. His modest contact yielded significant results. The ball landed nearly at Halladay's feet in the right-handed batter's box, spun across home plate and began to trickle off the dish—clearly foul. His view perhaps blocked by catcher Buster Posey, umpire Jeff Nelson ruled the ball fair. Posey pounced on the ball and fired it towards third baseman Pablo Sandoval. But the sluggish, overweight Sandoval had charged for the bunt and couldn't retreat to third in time to retire Ibanez, although he tried to step on the base with his right foot. Sandoval did manage to throw out Halladay at first base, but only because the Phillies ace hadn't immediately run, having seen the ball was clearly foul. Somehow, in the end, the sacrifice worked. Second and third, one out.

Undaunted, Lincecum induced Shane Victorino's grounder to first baseman Aubrey Huff. "I wish it wasn't right at him," Victorino said. That didn't matter, because the ball, which had taken a mildly tricky hop, struck the heel of Huff's glove and caromed towards second base for an error. Ibanez and Ruiz raced home. Victorino, who'd reached second on the play, scored on Placido Polanco's single, leaving the Giants with a 3-1 deficit.

This was not the sort of mayhem Brian Wilson had envisioned.

Although Cody Ross did manage to drive in yet another run off of Roy Halladay, there was little mayhem in the rest of the long game. After three hours and 15 minutes of baseball, the Phillies remained standing as the Giants lost a quiet and clear 4-2 decision. It denied San Francisco a wild celebration, returned the series to Philadelphia and left the Giants pondering their own mistakes.

The botched third inning bunt play particularly rankled. Bruce Bochy forced himself to consider the squandered chance. "We're inches away from getting a double play, and the bunt was right in front of home plate," he said, generously accepting the umpire's interpretation. "At that point, the third baseman goes back to the bag, and we had a force there and [Halladay] wasn't running. So that's a missed opportunity for us not getting the double play, and it came back to haunt us."

It haunted Sandoval, too. "I tried to get back quickly to the bag," he said. "I missed the base. It's one of those mistakes you don't want to make. You practice that every day." He sat glumly at his dressing stall after the game, perhaps fearing he had started his last postseason game at third base. The Kung Fu Panda was not bringing peace to the valley this time. Others would have to take over.

Aubrey Huff was no happier with his own error, although it was one of the few he'd made all year. That Huff had successfully rewritten his defensive reputation was of little consolation now.

There was nothing to do but wear it and head back to Philadelphia, serenaded by the pundits, who again cried of the Giants' imminent demise. Philadelphia can be a cruel place for the opposition (and sometimes for the home team), and momentum had swung in the Phillies' favor.

Optimists, Pessimists

The Phillies had every reason to feel optimistic as the series returned to Citizens Bank Park. Their 54-30 regular season home record, combined with their status as two-time defending NL champions, indeed made their 3-2 deficit look manageable—especially with Roy Oswalt scheduled to pitch Game Six.

In the hours before the game, Philadelphia manager Charlie Manuel essentially predicted his team would force a seventh game the next day. Manuel wasn't being cocky; he was merely expressing the confidence in his players that anybody in his position should exude. Asked whether he'd use Roy Halladay as a reliever in either of the series' final two games, Manuel said without a hint of bravado, "If we get to tomorrow, we'll see. We're *going* to get to tomorrow. I don't want to say *if* we get there, because we *are* going to get there."

The Sequel to *Braveheart*

Errors on the field are obvious, but sometimes critical errors are made by those who never touch the diamond. The night of Game

Six, the Phillies organization unknowingly used their video board to make one.

Giants third-base coach Tim Flannery recalls it. "They played that [*Braveheart*] clip on their scoreboard of Mel Gibson firing up the troops. And we all looked at each other and said, 'Oh, they just made a mistake!!!'" The Phillies had unwittingly fired up the wrong team by tapping into the Giants' own private lore, recalling the critical team meeting in Los Angeles that had turned the tide. *Freedom! This is our time!* Even chance events were favoring San Francisco.

For all intents and purposes, Game Six didn't truly begin until the third inning, with the score tied 2-2. Jonathan Sanchez, who'd allowed a pair of first-inning runs only five batters into the game, opened the third by walking Placido Polanco. Struggling badly with his control, Sanchez then hit Chase Utley in the back with a 2-0 pitch.

That was throwing down the gauntlet. It was obviously unintentional, but history must be cited to provide context. In a July 30, 2009, game at AT&T Park, Sanchez had launched the feud by hurling a pitch over Utley's head.

This time, Utley responded en route to first base by picking up the ball and underhanding it disdainfully towards the mound, where it struck the rosin bag. Touché.

Once Utley reached first, Sanchez looked over and scolded Utley for his lack of manners. At least that's the sanitized version of events. Utley retorted before dismissing Sanchez with a wave of his arm and turning away. Both benches emptied, emotions on edge, ready for more mayhem.

Martial arts masters know that oftentimes the most important fight is the one you do not enter. Readiness and preparation in a warrior's world serve the purpose of knowing *when* to fight before they serve the purpose of *how* to fight.

In the case of the Giants vs. the Phillies, it was bullpen coach Mark Gardner who knew this warrior's lesson best at that key moment. It was he who held Jeremy Affeldt back from exiting the bullpen to enter the fray—if "fray" is the proper term. (It proved to be more milling around than anything—in the grand baseball tradition of gathering to look fierce but avoiding unnecessary and potentially injurious idiotic punches.) Affeldt was warming up, and the Giants wanted him to keep throwing so he'd be sharp on entering the game. He was needed to pitch far more than he was needed to mill around in a mob. Gardner kept him in the bullpen, and thus kept Affeldt in the great place of readiness, letting the rest sort out the scrum.

Naturally, the spectators gathered around the Giants' bullpen didn't understand why Affeldt remained a conscientious objector. "The fans were calling me some not-so-nice names for not going out there," he said. "But they can call me names all they want as long as we do our jobs."

Bruce Bochy and his coaches knew Affeldt would have to enter the game. Sanchez, who hadn't pitched well anyway, would likely be a mess after experiencing this emotional interruption. With the season on the line, the Giants couldn't take that chance. Sanchez would have to be removed. Usually full of bravado, Sanchez later acknowledged his poor outing by saying, "I didn't have it today . . . I was all over the place."

In contrast, Affeldt's readiness paid off with one of the best, most important performances of his career.

Having recorded a 4.14 regular season ERA—up from 1.73 the previous year—Affeldt was hardly a lock to shut down the Phils, who had their best hitters coming up, two runners on with nobody out and suddenly all the momentum. But this wasn't the same Affeldt who had struggled through most of the season. *Freedom! This is our time!* Beginning his stint by striking out Ryan Howard, Affeldt also retired Werth and Victorino to strand the Phillies runners. He was on his way to working two perfect innings.

"For whatever reason, mechanically, I was as good as I could be," Affeldt said. "I felt exactly like I felt in 2009. I felt like I was in total command of my pitches, command of the game, command of the situation."

Pitching coach Dave Righetti heaped praise on Affeldt. "That game was going to get out of hand," Righetti said. "Whatever superlatives you write, to me, he was the game." And the game was again the season.

Affeldt begat a succession of relievers that limited Philadelphia to five hits in seven innings. Next came Madison Bumgarner, who'd worked 4 2/3 innings in his Game Four assignment three days earlier—not enough rest to start again but enough to fortify him for a relief appearance. The rookie pitched two dicey but effective innings, coaxing a Shane Victorino comebacker to leave the bases loaded in the fifth before striking out pinch hitter Ben Francisco and retiring Rollins on a flyball to strand a runner on third in the sixth.

With left-handed batters Utley and Howard due up in the seventh inning, Bochy summoned Javier Lopez, who had limited lefties to a .162 batting average—the lowest among the league's left-handers with a minimum of 85 at-bats accumulated. First Lopez had to skate past Polanco, a right-handed hitter, and he did so by inducing a fly-ball. Utley grounded out and Howard struck out, preserving the 2-2 tie into the eighth.

The Giants put runners on second base in the fifth through seventh innings but failed to score. Ryan Madson, Philadelphia's excellent setup reliever who'd thrown a scoreless seventh, retired the first two batters in the eighth. Towards the batter's box strode Juan Uribe—batting .111 (3-for-27) in the postseason and .154 (2-for-13) in the series—but always a dangerous hitter in the clutch.

Uribe's futility didn't curb his aggressive approach. He punched Madson's first pitch, a "cut" fastball that didn't cut much, towards right field. The drive initially didn't appear deep enough to carry into the seats. But the ball cleared the barrier and gave the Giants a 3-2 edge.

"It's a big one, like me," Uribe said of his round-tripper as he lifted himself up on his tiptoes. The team rode on Uribe's back once more.

As memorable as Uribe's homer promised to be, attention switched to the bullpen. Who would Bochy entrust with this lead before giving the ball to Brian Wilson? There, warming up, was a slender right-hander with long hair sprouting from the back of his cap and an impossibly long stride, repeatedly firing firm-looking pitches with an unmistakable sense of urgency.

Lincecum.

Bochy, an aficionado of card games, was playing his ace. This would have been Lincecum's day to throw off a bullpen mound for his between-starts workout under normal circumstances; he might as well channel that energy into a more meaningful situation.

"I swear when I tell you this: He orchestrated that before the game," general manager Brian Sabean said, praising Bochy's use of the bullpen. "This all was premeditated."

But the results weren't as well-orchestrated. Lincecum tried his best to assume his temporary role. He pitched from the stretch position as if he were a full-time reliever. Lincecum struck out Jayson Werth, but Victorino and Raul Ibanez singled. For all the faith the Giants had in Lincecum, this was Brian Wilson's time.

"It's been a while since I've been in a situation like that," Lincecum said. "I don't have a lot of experience doing it. I was just coming in to do what I could, whether it was getting an out or leaving it the way I did. We've got guys in the bullpen to back us up."

The Giants received a fleeting scare as Carlos Ruiz connected solidly with a 1-1 pitch. But he lined it directly to Huff, who snared it cleanly and threw to second base to double off Victorino.

"I've never squeezed the ball harder and never lobbed the ball softer to second base," Huff said.

Torture? The ninth inning provided a substantial dose.

After Wilson walked Jimmy Rollins with one out, Polanco tapped a grounder to third base that forced Rollins at second but wasn't hit hard enough for the Giants to turn a double play. Working carefully to Utley, Wilson walked him on five pitches.

That left the tying and winning runs on with two out for the embattled Howard. He was batting .333 (7-for-21) in the series but hadn't driven in a run while striking out 11 times. The pro-Phillies zealots in the crowd of 46,062 whipped their white towels as the count went to 3-2. No matter what came next, high drama was in store.

Wilson threw a knee-high cut fastball past a staring, motionless Howard. Umpire Tom Hallion twisted his torso to his right, fists clenched. Strike three.

Whatever hitting advice Barry Bonds had previously given Howard, it surely wouldn't have included taking a called strike three to end the season, with the tying and winning runs on base.

The Giants thus ended their National League season as they'd begun it—by winning despite Roy Oswalt's mastery on the mound. They began celebrating the fourth pennant in their San Francisco-era history on the field, their joyous howls breaking the silence that suddenly enveloped Citizens Bank Park (well, since this was Philadelphia, there was *some* booing).

The Giants had reached the goal that had united them all season. Once again, they did it the hard way—on the road. Once again, they did it with humor, personality and perseverance. They were the Wizards of Odd, and they were going to the World Series.

"This is what you dream of when you're little," said 6-foot-3-inch, 230-pound Matt Cain, who's tough to picture as a little kid.

Players knew they'd be underdogs in the Fall Classic against the American League (AL) champion Texas Rangers. Wilson had an answer for that, just as he had an answer for everything.

"When you come this far, you have a chance to win," he said. "We like our odds, even though not many do. We're the real deal. We just won the pennant. It's time to start believing."

Sabean, who'd constructed this team, also tasted others' skepticism along with the beer and champagne that cascaded through the visitors' clubhouse. He echoed what that clear-eyed Phillies official had said the night before.

"We *deserved* this because we pitched really well," Sabean said. Philadelphia actually outscored the Giants 20-19, but San Francisco, in its typical fashion, recorded three of its four NLCS victories by one-run margins. "Everybody's saying the Phillies didn't hit, but they didn't hit because we pitched this well. That's why we really won the series. *It's our time.* You can't pick the time. For some reason, the time is now for us, and we'll see what happens in the next round."

Freedom!

Castoffs and Champions

Cody Ross was in the midst of the Giants' clubhouse celebration, waiting to receive the trophy for the NLCS Most Valuable Player. Ross was in a celebratory but reflective mood. "Two months ago, I thought I was going home," Ross said, speaking of his release by the Marlins. "And I was going to sit on the couch and watch teams celebrate."

Instead, he was smiling a broad, brilliant and slightly dazed smile as Bill Giles handed him the NLCS MVP trophy, his teammates chanting like fans in the background. His three NLCS homers were etched in San Francisco legend now, his .950 slugging percentage for the six-game series was historically unsurpassed and his .350 batting average was another fine high.

"Not bad for a garbage pickup," Aubrey Huff said, with his usual outrageous mix of truth and humor.

Chris Rose from Fox Sports said to Ross: "You embody what this team is all about. Florida didn't want you." Referring to Ross' nickname ("Smiles"), Rose asked, "How long you going to be doing that?"

"For a long time," Ross said quietly, still smiling. His wasn't the only smile.

"We had such a diversity of contribution from everybody," Bochy said, then sounding a bit like Huff as he added, "Not bad for a bunch of castoffs and misfits." Bochy also said that night, "I've never had a club with more heart. I've maybe had a little more talent."

His smile at that jibe matched that of Ross and the others. He joined owner Bill Neukom, president Larry Baer and general manager Brian Sabean on the podium for the trophy presentations. Sabean admitted to being "choked up" and "weak-kneed," but he found voice to praise the "unique group" the 2010 Giants were. Baer was asked how much hair he'd lost watching the "torture," and he skillfully deflected the question with an answer about how "they play 100 percent *for each other,*" noting the successful application of service over self-interest in this year's Giants Way.

Somewhere in the champagne spray, Chris Rose found Brian Wilson. Rose reported that Texas Rangers pitcher C.J. Wilson (no relation) had just tweeted, "See your beard real soon."

"Sounds delicious," answered Brian, using his favorite word.

This wasn't enough for Rose, who prodded him dangerously. "You don't have anything to tweet back to him? You're a pretty creative guy."

Getting the best of Rose again, Wilson took the bait with a straight face. "I think The Machine will say all he needs to say when he makes an appearance again."

"We *don't need* to take The Machine on national TV!" Rose said emphatically, with suddenly wide eyes, thereby driving untold numbers to YouTube to find out what Rose and Wilson were talking about and why Rose had reacted with such electricity. Too late, anyway: The Machine had already gone national. TV didn't matter in quite the same way anymore in a day of new technological avenues.

And yet TV did matter. East Coast baseball fans—who often can't catch West Coast night games because of the time difference—were finally waking up to the Giants as a national force. And they would now do it in the World Series, like it or not.

"I know America probably wants to see the Phillies and Yankees," Huff said. "But you know what? It's time for new blood."

The World Championship blood would be new either way. While the Giants were trying to end their 56-year drought, the Texas Rangers had just reached the World Series for the first time in their 49-year history—and they had done so under the ownership and leadership of Nolan Ryan, one of Brian Wilson's role models. As a matchup, it was an underground classic. The castoffs and misfits, again predicted to lose, would have to subsume themselves in the relentless positive flow once more.

Hijacking

First the Giants had to return home, where they would begin the World Series on Oct. 27. Virtually everybody anticipated an arduous flight. The previous weekend, when the Giants had played Games One and Two of the NLCS in Philadelphia, players were allowed to bring wives or significant others. So were the franchise's investors. This multiplied the traveling party and created cramped conditions on both legs of the cross-country flight. Nobody appreciated the humor when, after Game Two in Philadelphia, the driver of the lead bus in the Giants' entourage began to pull over alongside an enormous 747 that would have given the passengers plenty of room. One problem: It was the Phillies' plane! The buses kept moving towards the smaller jet that would transport the Giants and their legions of guests back West.

After celebrating their Game Six triumph, the Giants and another cadre of guests again bused to the airport. Once again, the driver took the lead bus towards the same jumbo jet the Phillies had occupied. Nobody got excited. They weren't about to get fooled again! This time, however, the plane really was reserved for the National League champions and their VIPs. Those who had already begun to develop hangovers were especially grateful for the extra room.

As the passengers boarded, Aaron Rowand stopped and made an unscheduled announcement. "That's right," he declared. "We kicked their asses, we drank their beer and now we steal their plane."

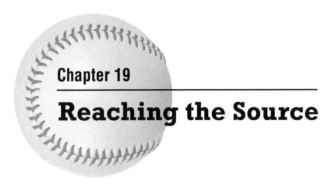

Chapter 19

Reaching the Source

Strange Currents

With the singular focus of salmon swimming back to their place of birth, baseball players spend their lives fighting against the currents to reach that ultimate source: World Series victory. It's an exhausting run, even in the best of careers and times. Few ever reach it. Even then, reaching it without winning can induce permanent heartbreak—haunted memories of what almost was.

Now Texas and San Francisco were next to each other in the currents, two elegant teams swimming in the same positive river, trying to stay in their flow for the final mile. The transition from October to November would determine who would attain victorious permanence in history, shattering their club's long records of falling short of their ultimate quest. It would decide whose fingers would wear championship rings—except in the case of one man beloved by both teams.

Bengie Molina was in a unique, bittersweet position. The outcome of the World Series would not determine whether he would wear a championship ring but only which team that ring would represent. There was no question that he was a key reason the Giants were in the Fall Classic: His past leadership of the team remained foundational, his mentorship of the Giants' homegrown pitching staff an essential element of their brilliance. Yet, after the advent of the Posey Era and the Giants' trade of Molina to Texas, Bengie had contributed his strengths and personal presence to the Rangers' sweet run, too. In an unprecedented way, he was a key reason *both* teams were in the World Series. Whichever team won, he would rightfully wear a victor's ring.

Settling in behind the plate for the Rangers against the Giants, Molina was now assigned the task of beating the very team he'd given his soul for during the past four years. He knew in intimate detail the pitching staff the Rangers would have to solve. From behind the plate and on the bench, he was to mastermind the attempt to take down his brothers, his friends. He was playing against family, from within the context of new family, and the emotions were complicated.

Before the first game, Molina and the Giants greeted each other warmly across that strange divide. There were hugs all around, the affirmation of love and bonds, the permanent respect of those who had accomplished beautiful things together. And there was also a tinge of bitterness for Molina, an inevitable feeling of betrayal and rejection—a feeling that would only increase during the offseason, when Brian Sabean admitted the Giants' signing of Molina for 2010 had been done with the unspoken knowledge that a mid-season trade was likely. The currents and eddies were poignantly swirling in strange directions.

Molina wasn't the only catcher for whom the currents were swirling strangely. Eli Whiteside, who had struggled for many years in the minors before hooking on with the Giants as Molina's backup, was now Posey's backup instead. He, too, had struggled a lifetime to reach this moment: And now his odd fate was to be the only Giants player on the active World Series roster not to appear in a game. He had successfully risen to the ultimate arena of baseball accomplishment while being destined never to make an on-field appearance there—yet he was deservedly poised to wear a championship ring. A long way from his Mississippi roots, Whiteside had quietly contributed to San Francisco's championship presence. He would later admit he hated not playing in the World Series, yet he—like Zito, Rowand, Sandoval, DeRosa and all Giants who had to contribute less than their expected roles—was never once heard to complain.

This lack of complaint was particularly impressive given the unusually grueling route the team had taken to the World Series.

"I remember when the World Series started," Tim Flannery later said. "I looked at Eli Whiteside, and I go, is this our 61st playoff game? That's kind of what it felt like." The path there wasn't what turned Whiteside's hair prematurely gray, but it could have been. The sweet taste of the ultimate victory was finally within reach—in a way that had eluded more than 1,500 Giants players since the team had moved West in 1958.

For Zito, silence in grueling service even had to transcend baseball. Not only was he left off the active roster for the entire playoff run, but his father was hospitalized with a serious heart condition the day after the Atlanta series had ended. To keep it from being a potential distraction, Zito kept it a secret until months later. The news wasn't publicly disclosed until shortly before spring training in 2011. Meanwhile, Zito kept throwing and working out hard, keeping his readiness intact in case the Giants needed him because of injury to another starter. They didn't. But to the end, the team stayed in service as one, and the result of service was transcendent success.

Absurd Projections

Those who want to project their own personal and political agendas onto convenient situations—such as those wearing *Let Tim Smoke!* T-shirts during the Proposition 19 campaign—were quick to draw the Texas/San Francisco match in political and cultural terms. After all, Texas is portrayed as a conservative state, and none other than former President George W. Bush had owned the Texas Rangers in another troubled administration. (He and his fellow ex-president father would be in the stands for this World Series.) And San Francisco is portrayed as the liberal bastion of all things permissive to the point of kinky—yet the classically tolerant city was also the place least likely to tolerate Bush's views.

The projections were ridiculous. In the first place, baseball at its purest is a refuge from politics, not an allegorical expression of it. The Giants and Rangers were not playing to see if red states were better than blue states or vice versa. Secondly, such stereotypical portrayals are grossly inaccurate, anyway. Texas has areas and residents with liberal leanings, just as San Francisco has many conservative citizens—including some Giants owners and investors. And the conservative element of the current Texas team was far better represented by the fiscal and baseball discipline exuded by Rangers owner, baseball legend and banker Nolan Ryan, who was admirably leading the Rangers away from weak teams and failed finances. This was a Rangers organization to be respected.

The players' presence as representatives of Texas or San Francisco had nothing to do with their political and cultural views—or even their place of residence. Despite the increase in player freedom from the "reserve clause" slavery that preceded free agency, the harshness of baseball realities still limits most players from freely choosing their career cities. Most of them live in different cities—and even countries—from the names stitched across the fronts of their uniforms. The 2010 Giants were not alone in employing players from several countries.

No one exemplified this better than Bengie Molina: Born in Puerto Rico, he came up through the North American system, playing for several minor league teams in the United States and Canada before enjoying major league tenures with the Angels in California and the Toronto Blue Jays in Canada. Eventually, Molina landed in San Francisco, where he remained until his reluctant trade to Texas. His path had nothing to do with politics or international relations, culture or personal beliefs. It was just *baseball.*

This World Series properly extended only to that game of baseball, undiluted by other issues. Even if it was expected to draw low television ratings simply because of the absence of a major market East Coast team, it was a great and refreshing matchup—and George W. Bush should've been able to sit right next to a Haight Street hippie as they enjoyed the beauty of the game together, without interference. This was a place for common appreciation—not political squabbles. End of story.

Moveable Parts

The World Series was also the beginning of the final chapter of a great story. Against a Texas team that had led the majors in hitting and largely had a set lineup, Bochy would still need to play the lineup game down to the wire. By this point, he had surrendered to and embraced this reality.

"We have so many moveable parts," he said before the series began, ignoring the challenge of constant change and presenting the flexibility as a positive. "You can be creative with these guys."

Bochy did admit what had become obvious, however: "We don't do things easy here," he said with a slight smile. And the Texas juggernaut was heavily favored to make it hard, if not impossible.

Another Hijacking

Game One of the final chapter was to begin at wildly rocking AT&T Park in San Francisco with yet another classic pitching matchup. First as a member of the 2009 Phillies and now as part of the 2010 Rangers, left-hander Cliff Lee had established one of the greatest postseason pitching records of all time. As the World Series began, he had a lifetime 7-0 record in the postseason, with a miniscule 1.26 ERA. Even more astonishing, in his 3-0 playoff record for the Rangers in

2010, his statistics included 34 strikeouts against only one walk, his ERA a ridiculous 0.75. He was as unhittable as Roy Halladay—perhaps even more so.

If Lee was the immovable object, he was matched against the unstoppable force: Tim Lincecum. The Freak was well-rested and ready for the resolution of that ultimate conflict—a conflict that, naturally, was everything except what it was expected to be.

If anything, the teams were *too* well-rested. It had been nine days since Cliff Lee had last pitched, and the Giants had also played a waiting game.

The Giants abandoned their usual style of play while falling behind early.

Typically smart and precise, the Giants were neither at the outset. With one out in the first inning, runners on the corners and a run already in, Tim Lincecum fielded Nelson Cruz's comebacker and then noticed Michael Young had strayed too far from third. Lincecum properly ran him back towards third base, where Juan Uribe and Edgar Renteria stood like sentries, figuring Lincecum would toss the ball to one of them for a key out. Instead, the ball inexplicably remained glued to Lincecum's hand, enabling Young to return to third safely and loading the bases.

Luckily for Lincecum and the Giants, his self-described "brain fart" proved irrelevant as Ian Kinsler grounded into an inning-ending double play. But the Giants weren't done goofing around. Freddy Sanchez lined a broken-bat, one-out double off Cliff Lee but broke for third base on Buster Posey's very catchable pop-up to second baseman Kinsler in short right field. Easy double play.

Leading off the second inning, Lincecum now faced the man he often credited with his own success: Bengie Molina. Molina, who knew Lincecum's pitching style as well as anyone, singled and scored. The Giants fell behind 2-0—previously a death sentence against Cliff Lee in playoff conditions.

The Giants considered it no such thing. In the third, they climbed back to a tie after back-to-back RBI hits by Sanchez and Posey. Lee worked a 1-2-3 fourth but was taxed in that inning by Juan Uribe, the notorious free swinger who chose that moment to metamorphose into a disciplined hitter. Although Uribe fanned, he elevated Lee's pitch count by fouling off five two-strike pitches.

Lee had thrown 75 pitches as he entered the fifth with the score still tied 2-2. Andres Torres and Sanchez broke the deadlock with back-to-back doubles. Posey struck out looking, but Burrell wouldn't let Lee escape as he drew a full-count walk. Cody Ross and Aubrey Huff then lashed RBI singles. That finished Lee, who looked somewhat dazed as he sat in the dugout.

The Giants' 5-2 lead wasn't insurmountable, but three pitches after Lee was removed, Uribe's three-run homer off Darren O'Day essentially finished the Rangers, widening the lead to 8-2. Asked about the 2-0 delivery he'd crushed, Uribe said through an interpreter, "Look for that fastball, take each pitch one at a time and when the ball's in the strike zone, be ready to connect." It was a good basic strategy—if less poetic than his usual creative English.

Uribe's bolt finished the six-run outburst and enraptured the 43,601 AT&T Park patrons. They came expecting a Giants victory, but few fans if any expected Lee to go down this hard. Certainly few baseball "experts" did.

One person in the shrieking crowd wasn't surprised at all, though, and he happened to be loitering in the concourse in front of the press box while fans were still buzzing over the Giants' uprising. "It's a free-swinging team, and the guy threw too many strikes," said J.T. Snow, the elegant former first baseman who continued to work for the Giants as a special assistant.

The widely anticipated collision of Cy Young Award winners—the seventh such matchup in a postseason series opener—had been hijacked by the hitters. The teams combined for 11 extra-base hits, seven by San Francisco. Lee was charged with seven runs (six earned) and eight hits in 4 2/3 innings; Lincecum allowed four runs and eight hits in 5 2/3 innings, ultimately getting the win despite surrendering another hit (an RBI double) to his former mentor Molina.

Even after the departure of the battered masters and the widening of the Giants' lead, mild torture returned. Entering the ninth inning leading 11-4, the Rangers rallied and forced the Giants to bring in Brian Wilson as their seventh pitcher of the night. Wilson allowed three inherited runners to score before finally retiring Ian Kinsler to close out the messy, unpredictable 11-7 victory.

"You [bet] 100 bucks in Vegas, you're probably a millionaire, aren't you?" Aubrey Huff said, "That's what's funny about the postseason, man. You never know what's going to happen."

That included the Giants' offense. Their nine hits with runners in scoring position during Game One matched their total for the entire National League Championship Series against Philadelphia.

As so often happens with the Giants, the past intersected poignantly with the present that night. Sanchez's four hits tied a franchise record for a World Series game. The last player to accomplish this, Monte Irvin, was on the premises, still waiting at 91 years old for his final wish: to see the Giants win the World Series. Sanchez also became the first player ever to hit doubles in his first three World Series at-bats. "Obviously, for no one to have done that yet, it's something special," Sanchez said. "It's also special for just a little guy like me to go out there and be able to do it." To hit all three off of Cliff Lee made it even more special.

Although offense was the story for the Giants, Edgar Renteria provided one of the evening's most breathtaking moments by ranging to his left to snare Kinsler's fourth-inning grounder up the middle, then whirling to make the throw for the first out. Appearing at shortstop in his third World Series with his third different club, the man had announced his revitalized presence. Perhaps on the verge of retirement, Renteria desperately wanted to go out a winner, and he got his last chance to redeem the unfulfilled promise of his Giants contract, set to expire when the World Series did.

However messy, it was a win. The Giants were now only three more from the source.

More Magic Inside

The entire neighborhood around Third and King in San Francisco started screaming long before Game Two began. The crowd had gathered in the streets around the stadium hours before the game started, tasting the hopes of a victory more than half a century in coming. As Mike Krukow reported, "The buzz here, I don't even know how to describe it. It's giving me chicken skin!"

Eventually, the gates opened, and the electric celebration moved into AT&T Park.

How could the Giants top Game One's ceremonial first pitches by five franchise legends—Hall of Famers Irvin, Willie McCovey, Orlando Cepeda, Juan Marichal and Gaylord Perry? By reviving and honoring the memory of the most important home run in the club's history. They invited the daughters of Bobby Thomson—Megan Armstrong and Nancy Mitchell—to make the ceremonial tosses.

The triumphant second act would have to be delivered on the field in the present moment, however. Having won the highest-scoring game of the 2010 postseason, could the Giants deliver again?

If so, they'd have to do so against C.J. "See your beard real soon" Wilson, another tough left-hander who'd had a breakout year for the

Rangers. But the Giants might not even need their bearded bullpen ace if Matt Cain—the "horse" of the Giants rotation—maintained his Secretariat-like run through October and if the inspired Giants offense could continue its sudden resurgence.

Cain maintained his steady tempo early on, but so did Wilson. It was scoreless through four—the classic pitching duel that had been expected the night before.

Then Ian Kinsler christened the fifth inning by driving Cain's 0-2 pitch deep to center field. On the mound, Cain already began cursing himself with the ball in mid-flight, knowing a home run when he allowed one. But the ball landed exactly on top of the wall in dead center, and instead of continuing on over, mysteriously caromed back to Torres. On the replays, the ball appeared to violate the laws of physics by doing so. But it did what it did. Kinsler settled for a double.

"Things happen for a reason," said Torres, referring to Kinsler's fickle double. "I was like, 'Wow, how'd that happen?' Sometimes there are things you can't explain. I just said, 'This is for us,' and not just this play. We've been playing like that, and we're going to continue to be positive."

"We definitely got a break there," Bruce Bochy added.

Cain took advantage of the break. He escaped as David Murphy lined out, Matt Treanor grounded out and, following an intentional walk to Mitch Moreland, Wilson bounced to first base. The scoreless tie remained, entering the bottom of the fifth.

It didn't remain scoreless for long. The suddenly youthful Edgar Renteria strode to the batter's box and planted one in the bleachers.

"I've kept myself ready for anything that can happen in this game, and I was ready for that pitch," Renteria said of the 0-1 fastball he hammered to left field. The Giants had a 1-0 lead, which they extended to 2-0 on Juan Uribe's seventh-inning RBI single off Darren Oliver.

Meanwhile, Cain again displayed his resolve in the sixth. Michael Young singled, and so did Josh Hamilton, the American League's most fearsome hitter. Playing right field, Cody Ross dove for Hamilton's one-hop liner and managed to keep it in front of him. Had it skipped past, Young probably would have scored, and Hamilton might have reached third. Given this reprieve, Cain coaxed popups from Nelson Cruz and Kinsler to keep the shutout intact.

Cain maintained the shutout again in the seventh—*and* in the eighth. He blanked Texas on four hits through 7 2/3 innings, hiking his postseason innings total to 21 1/3 without an earned run allowed. He left only because, with two outs in the eighth, Bochy had called in lefty specialist Javier Lopez to get Josh Hamilton. Lopez induced a harmless flyball to end the inning.

Cain thus became only the eighth starting pitcher not to allow an earned run in three consecutive postseason starts and the fourth to accomplish this feat in his first three outings. He negotiated a challenging path to reach that summit by holding the Rangers hitless in seven at-bats with runners in scoring position. That was something he'd frequently accomplished in 2009–10—holding opponents to a .193 batting average with runners in scoring position, ranking second-best in the majors during that span. On this night, Cain also capitalized on AT&T Park's spacious outfield dimensions with his tendency to make hitters send his pitches harmlessly aloft. Texas recorded 13 outs against him on flyballs or pop-ups.

The self-effacing Cain attributed his success to simple concentration and Posey's heady direction behind the plate. Since the postseason began, Cain said, "I really tried to make sure that I made every pitch count from here on out." His 0.00 ERA was the perfect testament to his success. It will never be bested.

Even after Cain's unblemished brilliance, the game's outcome was still uncertain. It was 2-0 entering the bottom of the eighth—hardly a safe lead against the best-hitting team in baseball.

Temporarily recovered from the night before, Darren O'Day struck out Andres Torres and Freddy Sanchez to open the inning, but Posey's single prolonged the inning. With left-handed–batting Nate Schierholtz due up, Rangers manager Ron Washington summoned lefty Derek Holland from the bullpen. Like a desperate boxer, the Rangers started flailing as Schierholtz drew the first of four walks in a row from Holland and Mark Lowe. Pulling a minor Ankiel, Holland only managed to throw one strike in 13 pitches before being removed, and Lowe wasn't much better. The Giants then stepped forward and landed authoritative, consecutive knockout punches: Edgar Renteria's two-run single, Aaron Rowand's two-run, pinch-hit triple and Torres' RBI double.

The Giants' six-run fifth in Game One had been their highest-scoring World Series inning since their six runs in Game Four against the Yankees in 1937. After waiting 73 years to equal it, the Giants had now outdone themselves in one day by amassing seven runs in the eighth. Doing so after having two outs with nobody on base marked only the second time in World Series history a team had scored that many runs under those circumstances, according to the Elias Sports Bureau.

The headbanging crescendo hastened the conclusion of what would be only the sixth shutout defeat of the season for Texas—a 9-0 crushing that had actually been a pitchers' duel until its final acts.

The Giants set an unexpected, all-time World Series record: 20 runs in the first two games had never been accomplished before. And the Giants had launched that offense against the pitcher with one of the greatest postseason performance records in history.

Mark DeRosa, the injured veteran leader who continued to offer teammates advice and support from the bench, referred to the Giants' season-long marketing slogan for his take on what was unfolding.

"I think the PR guy who came up with 'There's Magic Inside' should get a pretty good raise," DeRosa said.

As it does following every Giants win, the voice of Tony Bennett serenaded the departing AT&T Park fans with "I Left My Heart in San Francisco." The neighborhood party got even wilder as the taste of victory drew even closer. And statistics—those lying little devils—backed up the odds. Of the previous 51 teams to grab a 2-0 lead in the World Series, 40 proceeded to win it. The Giants' long-awaited goal seemed more attainable than ever. But now they would have to make magic in Texas—in the Rangers' raucous, hitter-friendly park. The closer the goal got, the harder it seemed to get there.

Screaming and Hungry

After waiting 49 years without their team winning a single postseason series—let alone the World Series—fans of the Texas Rangers (and their earlier incarnation, the Washington Senators) were bound to be screaming and hungry.

As a native Texan who'd grown up attending Rangers games, Aubrey Huff knew what awaited the Giants at Rangers Ballpark in Arlington. "We're going to their place. They're going to be fired up," Huff cautioned. "Their fans have been waiting a long time for this, too. They're going to be loud. . . . All they have to do is win the next one, and they're right back in it."

The situation and momentum were volatile, especially with Jonathan Sanchez on the mound. He wasn't a weak point in the rotation as much as a flashpoint—still an unpredictable point of light or wild trouble. Sanchez had every reason to be tired, too. Including the postseason, he'd worked 213 1/3 innings, far exceeding his previous high of 163 1/3 in 2009.

Sanchez benefited only marginally from his six-day rest after his short outing in Philadelphia. He pitched adequately overall but lost a nine-pitch standoff in the second inning to Mitch Moreland. Had Sanchez survived Moreland's challenge, the entire evening might have been different. But Moreland fouled off four 2-2 pitches before planting a drive into the right-field seats for a three-run homer and a 3-0 lead. Sanchez later allowed another run on another homer, authored by Josh Hamilton with two outs in the fifth inning. Those long balls revealed Sanchez's fatigue. He had allowed just five homers to the 167 left-handed batters he'd faced before encountering the Rangers pair. He had thrived down the stretch (4-1, 1.03 ERA in his last seven starts) and in his first postseason start (7 1/3 innings in a 3-2 Division Series triumph at Atlanta). But in Sanchez's final three outings, he recorded a 5.68 ERA while allowing 14 hits in 12 2/3 innings. He had helped get the Giants there, but he didn't have enough left to finish it off.

The Giants' failings didn't all belong to Sanchez. They also couldn't generate scoring opportunities. Rangers starter Colby Lewis held them hitless in two at-bats with runners in scoring position after they went 13-for-26 in those situations during the World Series' first two games.

The face of the Giants' offensive futility bore Pat Burrell's distinguished features. San Francisco threatened Lewis immediately as Freddy Sanchez lined a one-out single and Buster Posey drew a two-out walk in the first inning. Burrell struck out to end the inning and proceeded to whiff in each of his four plate appearances. That extended his World Series–long hitless streak to nine at-bats, eight of which had resulted in strikeouts.

To Burrell's credit, he sugarcoated nothing.

"That's not exactly how you draw it up when you get your pregame routine going," Burrell said. "I've just picked a bad time to struggle. There's no way around it. I'm getting pitches to hit, but I'm just not doing anything with them. I'm chasing some balls off the plate." He was not exactly hitting like a Machine.

Lewis, who surrendered five hits in 7 2/3 innings, lapsed only briefly as Cody Ross and Andres Torres clobbered one-out homers off him in the seventh and eighth innings, respectively. Darren O'Day and Neftali Feliz retired the four batters they faced to preserve Lewis' third consecutive postseason triumph. In the end, it was a quiet 4-2 loss in a game that didn't seem that close.

Although the Rangers had secured a much-needed victory, their highly respected third baseman Michael Young refused to call it essential. "I really never bought into that must-win stuff," Young said. "Every game is big. The only time it's must-win is when the other team has three wins."

The Giants only had two. If Texas won the next day, the series would be even.

Playing the Other League's Game

Bochy had to shift strategies in a new way in Texas: Since they were playing in an American League park, they would play under American League rules. That meant having a designated hitter (DH), giving the Giants potentially more offense but hampering traditional National League strategies. Bochy chose the struggling but potentially explosive Pablo Sandoval as the DH for Game Three, with the grand result of nothing—the same result he got from the rest of the bottom of the lineup that night. He'd have to try something else again the next night, when (ironically) the Giants had their best-hitting pitcher going: Madison Bumgarner, who wouldn't get the chance to demonstrate his prowess with the bat.

Halloween

By starting Madison Bumgarner in Game Four, the Giants became the first World Series team in 24 years to employ a completely homegrown pitching rotation. (Take that, Mat Latos.) Furthermore, with equally homegrown catcher Buster Posey starting, Bumgarner and Posey became the first rookie battery to start a World Series game since 1947, when catcher Yogi Berra had launched his long brilliant career for the Yankees, along with pitcher Spec Shea, who'd launched his short career of being forgotten.

That night was Halloween, too. This was mostly significant because Matt Cain showed up at the team bus dressed as a giant whoopee cushion. At 6 feet 3 inches tall and 245 pounds, Cain was undoubtedly the largest whoopee cushion in World Series history. The Giants were setting records all over the place.

Cain's lighthearted contribution was important because it kept the team loose.

"The reason it worked is he's not that funny of a guy," said Duane Kuiper. When people laughed, Cain kept a straight face, asking them what was so funny.

Bruce Bochy might have had a similar response to people who laughed about his lineup. Playing it "backwards," he used the designated hitter to allow him to place his best *defensive* team on the field from the beginning—notably Travis Ishikawa at first base and Nate Schierholtz in right, both of whom would normally be late-inning replacements. Aubrey Huff moved to DH and a slumping Pat Burrell moved to a corner of the bench. It was another creative combination of the moveable parts.

Bochy needed to be creative. With Texas' victory over the Giants and Sanchez in Game Three, Rangers hitters had hung a 5.24 ERA on opposing left-handed starters in six postseason games, roughing up such estimable figures as Tampa Bay's David Price and the New York Yankees' CC Sabathia. Now the Rangers would face lefty Bumgarner, the fifth-youngest pitcher ever to start a World Series game at 21 years and 91 days of age. Surely such a callow youth also would struggle against Texas.

Surely you jest.

Watching Bumgarner work in the World Series, it was hard to conceive he was the same pitcher who'd been explosively wild in spring training—and explosively angry in a minor league incident. This Bumgarner was utterly cool and in control.

"I just keep telling myself to relax," he said. "And I've told myself [that] so much that it's starting to become second nature. It makes it a lot easier on me and the players, I think, to see somebody that's relaxed out there throwing."

Easier said than done. The Mad Bum walked leadoff batter Elvis Andrus on four pitches to start the game, but even then, he said nerves were not the issue. "I was relaxed and just happened to throw four balls. I felt fine." After that, he allowed only three harmless singles in eight innings and didn't permit a runner to reach second base until the seventh inning. He dealt 22 of 28 first-pitch strikes and kept the Rangers' offense utterly shut down with surgical precision, inning after inning. Barely 21, Bumgarner was dealing a game as masterly as any World Series pitcher had thrown—against a hitters' team, in a hitters' park, on the road and in front of screaming, hungry fans—including both Presidents Bush and Nolan Ryan.

Bumgarner's unruffled expression throughout summarized it all this way: *Whatever.*

Aubrey Huff admired this in Bumgarner. "He's fearless, man. He came to the yard today, and you could see he was just chilling. Nothing really bothers him. Put on some David Allen Coe on the playlist and let him go to town."

A nonstop defensive effort helped Bumgarner's calm as much as anything else on the playlist. Second baseman Freddy Sanchez soared to snare Jeff Francoeur's second-inning line drive. Sanchez also started two double plays and adroitly handled Josh Hamilton's fourth-inning smash off Bumgarner as he whirled to tag Michael Young and barely missed throwing out Hamilton for another double play. That didn't matter, though, because catcher Buster Posey apprehended Hamilton on a stolen-base try. Then Cody Ross in left made a diving catch on Kinsler's one-out liner in the fifth. Posey led the effort from behind the plate all game, with Bumgarner's complete confidence. "I trust him 100 percent; whatever he puts down, I want to throw. Besides that, he's a great catcher."

Of course, this being the 2010 Giants, great pitching and defense guaranteed nothing. The Giants would still have to score, and they faced a worthy adversary in Texas right-hander Tommy Hunter, who was 13-4 during the regular season. But Hunter cracked in the third inning, with a little help from the baseball gods. The gods also bestowed their gift upon Andres Torres, who hit a smash that might have been playable had it not caromed off first base. It went for a double.

Huff batted one out later and drove Hunter's first pitch deep into the right-field seats. It was a meaningful, memorable trip around the bases for Huff, recalling how he'd rooted for the Rangers as he grew up in nearby Mineral Wells, Texas.

"I remember as I hit second base running to third, I looked up at the section I always sat in when I was a kid," said Huff. He had once stuffed himself there on Dollar Hot Dog Nights at the ballpark, watching his idol Nolan Ryan. Now it was Ryan who sat in the stands watching Huff—an ideal and surreal turnaround.

Huff's homer gave the Giants a 2-0 lead, rarely enough in Texas. The Giants needed to keep the pressure on—and they did. Edgar Renteria continued his resurrection when he singled for his third hit of the night with one out in the seventh, then scored with relative ease on Torres' long double to right-center field.

In the eighth, with Bumgarner still holding the Rangers scoreless, all that remained was for Buster Posey to gain a little revenge against Darren O'Day. The Texas reliever had coaxed a groundout from Posey with one out in the eighth inning of Game Three, when Posey had represented the potentially tying run. Now Posey again faced O'Day with one out in the eighth in Game Four. This time, he lofted a fly to center field that didn't stop carrying until it plummeted to earth beyond the wall, making Posey the youngest catcher to hit a World

Series home run since Cincinnati's Johnny Bench in 1970. This was fitting, since Posey had earned the Johnny Bench Award—given to the nation's top collegiate catcher—in 2008, his final year at Florida State. The thoughtful kids who pounced on the ball later presented it to Posey, who was again graced with generous fans, just as he had been after hitting his first major league homer.

Brian Wilson closed out San Francisco's 4-0 win with a perfect ninth, striking out the heart of the Rangers' order—Michael Young and Josh Hamilton—to end it. The Giants thus became the first team to record two World Series shutouts since the 1966 Baltimore Orioles had shut out the Dodgers for a third time, beating Sandy Koufax during his last game in the majors.

"How could the team of black and orange lose on Halloween?" Asked Jon Miller, who answered his own question. "They couldn't."

They didn't. Blame it on the human whoopee cushion.

While being grilled about his performance, Bumgarner remained cool and in the moment. When he was asked to name the toughest hitter he'd faced in the ferocious Texas lineup, he replied, "Whoever was up at the time, I guess."

After the storybook poignancy of returning to his boyhood stadium to homer in the World Series, Huff was asked a moving question about . . . whether he was wearing his thong.

Affirmative. "It hasn't left my body since . . . 30 games [to go] in the regular season. It's something you get quite used to after a while. I always wonder how women do it, but it's really not a big deal anymore." Except in Giants lore, where it will never die.

More importantly, the Giants had widened their lead in the Fall Classic to 3-1. They were now only one win away from reaching the ultimate baseball destination.

That wasn't nearly enough, and Posey knew it. "For me and probably everybody in this locker room, we're going to come in with the attitude that it's a must-win game," he said. "I think you have to approach it that way and come out ready to go because you've got one of the best on the other side throwing at us."

Posey was referring to Cliff Lee. Although the Giants had roughed him up in Game One, his playoff track record still stood behind him, and Lee seemed unlikely to remain vulnerable. He'd be opposed by Lincecum, who was seeking his 20th win of the year (including the postseason). It was master against master, one more time, with Lincecum facing off in the rematch to try to seal down the World Championship.

"Two of the best pitchers going at it," Cody Ross observed. "Last time, we won 11-7, which was weird. But I doubt that's going to be the case."

It wasn't. This time, the expectations of a brilliant duel were fulfilled.

Erasing the Ghosts

Seated behind the desk in the visiting manager's office at Rangers Ballpark in Arlington, Bruce Bochy seemed as calm as ever as he chatted with the quartet of Giants beat writers for around four hours before Game Five. Noting that the previous night had been Halloween, Bochy joked about how one of his nephews had gone trick-or-treating at the team hotel with other youths.

"He loaded up," Bochy said with a grin. "They probably went to 10 rooms and had more stuff than when I used to go around and work it for two hours. We used to change costumes and go back."

The reporters roared with laughter. Bochy probably barely heard them. He later admitted he hadn't slept the night before, agitated over trying to engineer the one victory that would give the Giants the first World Series triumph since moving to San Francisco in 1958.

Another protagonist was purely relaxed. Tim Lincecum awoke that day in his hotel room feeling energized and confident. "I was just bouncing around, playing my music and probably eating something I shouldn't," said the man who would strive to become the first Giant to win four games in a postseason.

Unlike Bochy, Lincecum slept soundly. "It wasn't one of those nights where I laid awake and wondered if I ever was going to fall asleep," he said. "I tried to treat it like any other game. Obviously there was more at stake, but I never want to put that kind of added pressure on myself."

Lincecum's dance party continued after the team arrived at the clubhouse. "We had some pretty good music going," he said. "I can't remember what we were playing, but it was going pretty good. It was a pretty relaxed atmosphere as far as the clubhouse goes, but that's just obviously us."

As gametime approached, Lincecum concentrated less on iTunes and more on the task at hand. "I knew what was at stake," Lincecum said. "You kind of just zone in and go into a different kind of mindset where it's like, okay, I know I'm going against Cliff Lee, I gotta be pretty fine with myself. I know he's going to keep the game close."

That proved to be an understatement.

Through six innings, nobody on either team—*nobody*—advanced as far as second base. Lincecum had allowed two hits; Lee three. Lee's breaking pitches, which had rolled lazily towards home plate in Game One, darted wickedly past Giants hitters. Lincecum was Lincecum, piling up strikeouts in bunches—six in a span of 10 batters from the third through fifth innings.

In one of the radio broadcasting booths sat a man who understood more than almost anyone what was developing on the diamond. After all, he had wielded such mastery hundreds of times himself. Juan Antonio Marichal was ostensibly an impartial observer in his role as a commentator for ESPN Deportes. But the greatest pitcher in San Francisco Giants history did not hide his sentiment.

"I tell everybody that I left my heart in San Francisco," Marichal said before the game, gleefully pirating Tony Bennett.

Elsewhere in the press box, media relations assistants hurriedly distributed information sheets telling reporters what they had been witnessing: "Tonight's game is the first World Series game to be scoreless through 6.0 innings since Game 4 of the 2005 World Series. ... The Ranges [sic] have not scored a run in 18.0 consecutive innings beginning with the sixth inning of Game 3."

The final item on the legal-sized sheet began, "MEDIA INFORMATION IN EVENT OF POTENTIAL GIANTS CLINCH."

As if on cue, Cody Ross singled to open the Giants' seventh, completing his remarkable postseason run. Juan Uribe also singled. Lee, who had struck out five, had two-strike counts on both hitters but couldn't capitalize.

Up came Aubrey Huff, dropped to sixth in the order against the left-handed Lee. Having given himself the thrill of his baseball life with his homecoming homer the night before, Huff provided an equally compelling sequel: He dragged an exquisite bunt between the mound and first base to record the first sacrifice of his major league career. For a power hitter to give himself up for the first time in a decade—in the World Series, in a spot where another homer would make him the classical hero? Perfect. Beautiful. Unexpected.

Huff's bunt was so well-executed he nearly beat it out for a hit.

Third-base coach Tim Flannery had flashed him the bunt sign. "But I was going to do it, anyway," said Huff, who attributed his expert manipulation of the bat to bunting daily in batting practice. *Be ready.*

Rested in Game Four to ease his mind and fix his stroke, Pat Burrell struck out. Again. Given his World Series–long misery, that was nothing new.

Up came Edgar Renteria—also nothing new.

This was the man whose single in the bottom of the 11th inning of Game Seven had won the 1997 World Series for the Florida Marlins. Having implored his teammates to send him out a winner, Renteria now faced a priceless opportunity to repeat history, carry his team and achieve his desire on his own.

Twice before the game, Renteria approached Andres Torres and predicted he would hit a home run that night. "I was joking," Renteria said later.

Of course, humor has its basis in truth. As Renteria said after homering in Game Two, "I told you I was a power hitter."

Pitchers make mistakes, but it's incumbent upon the hitter to capitalize on them. That's why the first piece of advice given to everyone who steps in a batter's box—from Little League to the majors—is, "Get a good pitch to hit." A big leaguer since 1996, Renteria had lived by this credo.

With the count 2-0, Lee served up the pitch Renteria wanted. "I got lucky," Renteria said. "He threw a cutter inside. The ball didn't cut."

It dangled there for Renteria, who lined it towards left-center field, where it carried past outfielders David Murphy and Josh Hamilton until it cleared the wall.

The Giants erupted with joy in their dugout, as did vast numbers of their far-flung followers—even some in the stands in Texas, where a surprising amount of orange and black could be found so far from home. Edgar "Smoothie" Renteria returned to the dugout, where he was nearly pounded onto the disabled list by exuberant teammates.

Renteria wore a smile, but he was hardly jubilant. "I didn't forget that we were playing a great offensive team like Texas," he said. "That's why I told my teammates, 'Keep playing,' because we know they can tie the game right away."

Indeed, Nelson Cruz lined a one-out homer off Lincecum in the Rangers' half of the seventh. Kinsler walked on a 3-2 pitch to bring the tying run to the plate. A Texas rally seemed possible, if not imminent. But Lincecum never considered such notions.

"I was just like, if something happened, I have to bounce back, and my team would expect me to," he said. "I can't really make any excuses. Just leave it out there on the field. It's my last start of the year."

Up came Murphy, who had drilled a pinch-hit RBI single off Lincecum in Game One. He struck out on five pitches.

Next was Molina, Lincecum's former battery mate who had rocked Lincecum for a pair of Game One hits. But he, too, went down swinging on five pitches, finishing off the strange story of brothers battling each other. Barring a last-minute Texas rally, Molina would have to wear a San Francisco ring.

The ninth inning arrived. Although Lincecum had enough left to finish the game, Bochy beckoned for Wilson, giving his eccentric, effective right-hander an opportunity to protect the 3-1 lead and surmount the challenge of the final three outs. After leading the majors in saves, he'd also closed out the last the series against Atlanta and Philadelphia. Win or lose, this ninth inning was again his to own.

"It was like any other ninth inning, except it was the final one of the year," Wilson said later.

Back in the taverns of San Francisco, the crowds were shouting: *Fear the beard!*

Wilson would again have to face the hardest part of the vaunted Texas lineup to get it done—probably the way the warrior Wilson would script it if he could. Josh Hamilton took a called third strike to start the inning. Vladimir Guerrero, a hacker to the end, grounded to shortstop on the first pitch. Nelson Cruz now represented the final obstacle between the Giants and history.

Wilson forged ahead on the count 1-2 but then missed with his next two pitches, bringing him back to his "standard" 3-2 count. To the end, it was never easy for the Giants.

If Wilson walked Cruz, the tying run would come to the plate. But he didn't issue a single walk in his first two World Series appearances, and he didn't intend to start now. His next pitch was a vicious 90-mph cutter that might have sawed Cruz's bat in half had he made contact. He didn't. *Strike three!*

The Giants erupted as Wilson turned his back to the plate to make his warrior's gesture, honoring his father and his God one more time. Players and coaches raced from the dugout and the left-center field bullpen, some tackling each other before happily smothering Wilson. Bochy and his coaches enjoyed their own triumphant moment in the dugout before joining the mayhem on the field. One of baseball's proudest franchises, whose greatness ranged from Cooperstown to Candlestick, from one coast of this nation to the other, had scaled a peak it hadn't reached since 1954. The San Francisco Giants had won the World Series.

The legends who had ennobled the Giants despite their lack of championships still loomed large. As broadcaster Duane Kuiper said in the immediate aftermath of Wilson's final strikeout, "You can't help but think that this group is celebrating for the Say Hey Kid. For

Will the Thrill. Celebrating for No. 25 [Barry Bonds]. And celebrating for all you Giants fans, wherever you are. Giants fans, *this party is just getting started!!!*"

Indeed, that's exactly what Wilson, still on the field, had in mind. When asked on camera what he was feeling, Wilson said, "I'm ready to rage. *Right now!*"

Back home, the city was ready to rage, too. And it did, the streets everywhere filling with orange-clad revelers throughout the nearly riotous night. This was a team that had united the city not just in victory but in the *spirit* of that victory—in the wild laughs and beauty with which it had been accomplished. San Francisco was somehow forever different now, and the city knew it.

As Wilson said amidst the flowing beer and champagne, "It's been storybook the whole year. We gotta win this one for the guys who come in our locker room all the time who never got to experience one. Willie Mays, McCovey, all those guys coming in our locker room who we get spoiled to see on a daily basis. This one's for them."

Aubrey Huff would reflect on that as well, come spring 2011. "It's really humbling. It's nuts, to be honest with you. . . . So many Hall of Famers, so many unbelievable players have come through here, and a bunch of jackasses like us win the World Series. It just doesn't make sense! We won it after all these class acts and Hall of Famers? We're just a bunch of rejects—castoffs and misfits, like everybody says. It just was a perfect storm of team chemistry and camaraderie that willed us all the way to the top."

Yet the power of that chemistry and camaraderie *made* it make perfect sense, as Huff himself then said. "Whoever thinks that team chemistry's overrated is an idiot. It really does mean a lot. We probably weren't the best team on paper in the big leagues at all. But with chemistry, we were the tightest."

It all went back to Mike Murphy in the Giants clubhouse during spring training, observing to Jimmy Davenport and Joe Amalfitano that it was the closest team he'd ever seen. Of all observers, Murphy had perhaps seen the most Giants teams from the most inside perspective. His observation was as perfect and prescient as Renteria's predictions of his own World Series home run. In becoming truth, it not only gave Murphy a ring, too, but it assuaged deep historical wounds.

"This erased a lot of ghosts, right?" said J.T. Snow, a Giants special assistant who had played first base for the star-crossed 2002 team.

It did. And Snow wasn't just talking about Halloween.

As usual, the Giants' pitching made the difference. During the season, they compiled a major league–best 3.36 ERA—and they improved on that in the postseason, against three great teams no less. In the postseason, they dropped their ERA to 2.47 and allowed only 94 hits in 135 innings while finishing 11-4. San Francisco was especially stingy in the World Series, limiting Texas' second through sixth hitters to a .167 batting average (15-for-90) and a .267 slugging percentage. Overall, the Rangers hit just .179 (5-for-28) with runners in scoring position. The Giants might have struggled at many points during the year, but when it came time to play the best, they rose and beat the best—just as they had from the season's first game.

"They just outpitched us the whole series," Cliff Lee said. "Their pitchers did an unbelievable job."

But the Giants were proud of more than just their pitching. "Every single guy we put on the field made a huge impact on where we are now," Wilson said.

That was true all the way down to the nearly unknown players—people such as Matt Downs, who delivered his only big hit of the year in extra innings against San Diego, breaking a critical curse. And Darren Ford, who never even got an at-bat all year, yet as a pinch runner scored a daring, crucial game-winning run against Colorado—his only run of 2010. With such a constantly changing lineup, the list of key contributors was far longer than even the final roster of players. With the Giants only winning the division by one game on the last day, even one fewer run—one fewer play by one fewer man—and the entire outcome of the season might have been different. In the annals of baseball, there may never be another team in which every member in the shadows as well as the light would be essential to overcoming all odds against securing the championship. *Every moment mattered.* It was one of the most beautiful, selfless, timeless sights—the year everything turned orange.

Behind the scenes and off the field as well, the invisible Orange and Black Ops team of scouts, managers, assistants, secretaries, minor league bus drivers and everyone from the top of the front office to the bottom rung made it possible to bring those people to the field—and to dare to let them *be themselves* in the process. Thus, the last word belonged to the architect who had created the winning blueprint.

"The group that we have going wild in this room showed a lot of determination and a lot of will, and they weren't going to be denied," general manager Brian Sabean said amidst the final spray of champagne.

The entire organization had shown the same determination, and so had the fans, not only in San Francisco itself but in other cities, where they had traveled to scream their support in ways most players had never experienced. The Giants won every playoff series *on the road.* The fans took it *on the road.* Even the staff took it *on the road* at the end. Cognizant of the support staff's vital role, the Giants had gracefully and gratefully flown nearly the entire organization to Texas to watch the World Series games in person. What more of a Giants Way could there be than to do it all *on the road* with edge and joy? What more of a San Francisco style? Jack Kerouac would be proud.

In keeping with the mantra of Javier Lopez, the Giants stayed in the relentless flow of the positive river to the end. With Edgar Renteria carrying the World Series MVP trophy home to finish his Giants career and with Mike Murphy packing the team trophy for the flight, the Giants fulfilled 91-year-old Monte Irvin's last wish. The championship was secured, along with the legend of the Rally Thong, the weirdness of The Machine and the mysterious color of the burgeoning bullpen beards.

"We just laughed all year long," Huff said. But the Giants were all business on the field—and they were in the business of service over self-interests. They were in the business of *trusting each other.* It was a classic, beautiful year, with its intangible mix of humor, grace and triumph. It will echo through the institutional memory of baseball for decades. It deserves to.

Chapter 20

Afterglow and Afterburn

The Best Answer

It's the simplest and most complete sentence in the Giants' Good Book: Torres wept.

Andres Torres did so the night before FanFest in February 2011, when Mike Krukow asked at a Comcast Town Hall gathering what the championship year had meant to him.

"You waited a long time," Krukow noted. "You paid a lot of hard dues in your career. And at age 32, you got to climb the mountain and plant a flag. What did this season mean to you professionally?"

Torres couldn't speak a word in reply and simply looked down, tears instantly flowing as Krukow put a supportive hand on his shoulder.

From the other side of the stage, Duane Kuiper broke the poignant silence. "That's a pretty good answer," he said.

"Best answer I've ever heard," Krukow softly agreed, emotional himself.

The audience went compassionately wild for Torres' tears, and tears were shed by other Giants as well.

"They got all choked up about it," Tim Flannery said a few days later, praising the team's openly emotional spirit. "They're not afraid to just sit and cry right in front of the world. . . . When [Torres] started weeping, Krukow started weeping, our whole team is sitting in the first three rows, we're all weeping. It is so beautiful that it happened again."

On the surface, perhaps it's victory that brought those tears. But in the inner personal depths, it's more than that. It's persistence, it's the core belief in self and dreams despite all odds; it's the resilient dedication and diligence in doing the grinding hard work an unlikely dream requires. It's an affirmation of the essential nature of doing that work *together as one*, with the spirit of service over self-interests the Bochy Paradox had laid out back in spring. And it's an embodiment of the Giants Way Bill Neukom had in mind when he wrote that memo at the beginning of the year. Those tears are the central essence of the Giants Good Book and the oneness that defines this team's story.

Torres wept. It was a beautiful coda for the 2010 season.

Pray, Cry, Vomit

Those February tears were hardly the first ones shed. Mere minutes after the World Series ended, with the on-field celebration still raging in Texas, the first man in a Giants uniform to quietly turn and walk away from it all was third-base coach Tim Flannery.

"It was very emotional, the whole thing. Not to mention . . . you haven't slept in a month or two months," he said. By the end of the World Series, "You're totally living on this adrenaline hit." At the conclusion of each victorious celebration during the playoffs, he would vanish first to the clubhouse to get a few precious minutes of privacy before the players arrived. "I never felt any of the pressure when I was down there in the moment. But afterwards, I would pray, I would cry and I would vomit. I didn't want anybody to see it. And then I'd be the guy, first guy to grab the champagne, and when [the players] came rushing in, I'd let them have it!"

After that, he says the coaches took transient space from the players each time. "All of us coaches would just go to our coaches' office and shut the door and look at each other, and our wives would come in and sit on our laps and drink champagne and we would laugh and all of a sudden—"

All of a sudden it would get weird in that unique 2010 Giants Way.

". . . all of a sudden, Aubrey Huff would come in with just his red thong on and let all the wives take a photograph of him . . . and then [player name withheld], oh I can't say [same dude], because no one knows he's The Machine, right? So The Machine would also come in . . . and I'd say, 'See, honey? I *told* you I was the normal one.'" Flannery laughed at the memory. "It was pretty heavy. It was really an amazing ride."

264 This is Our Time!

Close Encounters of the Third-Base Kind

From his coaching box, Tim Flannery enjoyed a unique vantage point from which to experience that wild orange ride. His appointed station offered a clear position from which to see and be the action—directly on the field, involved with happening plays, mere feet from fair territory and ever observant of each game's detail. Yet the job also lends just a touch of observer's remove, allowing him to assist with the architecture and design of the artful team.

Considered by some to be the best third-base coach in the business, Flannery is also the most passionate—often chasing runners most of the way home on close plays, guiding and exhorting them with complete physicality and even spirituality. And Flan has done it while also capably handling a surfboard and a guitar, bringing that guitar with him on every road trip. By 2010, he'd put out 10 CDs as a singer/songwriter, playing with everyone from Garth Brooks to Jackson Browne and accomplishing a greater achievement along the way: to love not only baseball but also people and life itself with a joy not fading with youth. His story is another one of human spirit that transcends victory.

Looking back at the season through the frame of his eyes, there's more than just a line of vanquished teams to be seen.

"This shows that we can also beat a computer," he said, speaking of the sport's invasion by complicated statistical metrics and analysts far removed from the field. Although the Giants invite those modern perspectives in to a degree, he says the Orange and Black Ops team remains unique behind the scenes. "Everybody's willing to think a little bit of a different way," he says of Brian Sabean and the crew behind him, "but this is the last place of old-school guys I've been around." They rely more on deep personal baseball experience and honed intuition than the impersonal instructions of statistics and electronics.

Flannery and Bochy—who had worked together in San Diego throughout their careers before coming to the Giants together five years prior—came to San Francisco specifically for that reason. "We came up to work for *him*," Flan says of Sabean, mentioning what a wild pleasure it was when they'd first arrived and had all gone out to drink wine and talk baseball. He joked, "This is like signing up with a bunch of pirates on a pirate ship!"

It had been different in San Diego, where new-school analysts pestered Bochy with computerized lineup recommendations on a daily basis. As a radio analyst then, Flannery dared to differ. "I said,

'If you can't play catch, if you've not played catch one time in your life, you can't be an expert. That's the way it is.'" He recalls, "I said, 'Take your computers and your fractions and go ruin another sport.' These guys in San Francisco are anything but that."

The players the Giants assembled for 2010 were anything but mechanistic, no matter the precision and discipline of their conditioning. According to Flannery, "They're all a bunch that's perfect for San Francisco. Most of them are artists and musicians in their own way. . . . They all definitely have their own music in their own mind and their own natural rhythms behind it."

Flannery's rhythms turned baseball into music during the offseason. Responding to the strange side effects of winning—the breaking of vast numbers of hearts in all of the losing cities—he wrote a song called "Breaking Things." Introducing it on stage, Flannery tells the story of beating division rivals Colorado, San Diego and Los Angeles—before also breaking the hearts of people in Atlanta, Philadelphia and Texas. "We beat the Dodgers . . . nobody gives a s—t if we break their hearts or not," he laughed. "And then Texas . . . I'm not really concerned about breaking George W. Bush's heart, but Lyle Lovett . . . We broke Lyle Lovett's heart!" Not to mention Nolan Ryan, Bobby Cox back in Atlanta and hordes of fans along the way who had all hoped their own team was destined for victory.

Flannery also borrowed a song written by Gregory Page in honor of Andres Torres. "I've been singing it all year: 'One thing for certain/I promise you will see/It's never too late to be the person/You were meant to be.' It sure did apply to Torres."

There were so many Giants stories with equal persistence and beauty. On the day after the celebratory FanFest in February, Flan talked about the stories that had rippled through the 2010 team and beyond as well as what those stories and their unified outcome had healed.

"It's not even just the players [who had those stories]. It wasn't just the coaches. . . . It was the city of San Francisco." In previous years, he pointed out, "[The fans] only have experienced teams with big superstars. . . . And I kind of believe that they were healed as well, because they saw that *they* can come together as a team and win. They've *all* had their stories. I saw it yesterday [at FanFest]. We've all heard them wherever we've gone, their stories."

Flannery even heard one while on a surfboard in the Pacific Ocean. "Not too long ago, I was surfing down in San Diego, and a guy paddled over to me and said, 'You know, your team, they made me love baseball again.'" Not because of the victory, but because of the *spirit* of the victory, the beautiful and fun and selfless way the victory was accomplished in an age where ego rages.

"This is a team that will be remembered," Flannery continued, mentioning the fiftieth anniversary of another such team—the underdog 1960 Pittsburgh Pirates, who knocked off the Yankees in a seven-game classic that included a key home run by Flannery's uncle Hal Smith. "They're *still* talking about that team." There had just been a team reunion and a national television special commemorating the team. Recently discovered game footage once thought to be lost had heightened the celebration.

Yes, the 2010 Giants are one of those teams, their memories to be kept alive in memories and books, photographs and movies, laughter that echoes across the ages. This was that one seamless motion in which imperfection and struggle coalesced into magic inside—in a way that can never be repeated or forgotten. Since time never repeats itself, everything that happens is unprecedented, but these Giants were unpredictably unique, destined for their own distant reunions of celebration.

There was no better place to experience that living history than at the third-base line or on a surfboard—or within the melody of a song.

Ghosts at Rest

Freedom! This is our time! The game of sweet inches had indeed gone San Francisco's way at last. At every juncture, just enough had fallen favorably to allow the Giants' hands to raise trophies and champagne for the first time in 56 years.

That erased a lot of ghosts, as J.T. Snow said—or at least it balanced them. Either way, it allowed rest in a plethora of orange-and-black hearts.

The 2010 victory assuaged the ghost of the 1962 World Series Game Seven, when the Giants were scant inches away from the World Championship, with two outs in the bottom of the ninth as the screaming line drive off Willie McCovey's bat was snared by Bobby Richardson of the Yankees at second base, leaving the tying and winning runs stranded at second and third in a 1-0 loss. *Just a foot or two higher*, some had lamented for 48 years.

It released the ghosts of the five consecutive second-place finishes from 1965 to 1969, when the collective Hall of Fame mastery of

Mays, McCovey, Marichal, Perry, Cepeda and others couldn't even *get* them to the World Series. Many had lamented that for decades, too.

It soothed a bit of the ache from 1989, when the Oakland/San Francisco World Series was rendered insignificant by the Loma Prieta earthquake as it ravaged the region moments before Game Three was to start. The drama, the meaning, the spirit and the championship were gone. The whole heart of the region was broken.

It softened the memories of 2002, when the Giants were six outs from the World Championship and had a 5-0 lead in Game Six but couldn't hold it, unraveling in Game Seven before watching the Angels drink their champagne.

The 2010 championship even took the hard edge off the memories of the entire Bonds Era, with its glory and shadows. His monumental presence and performance had created the possibility of AT&T Park—truly The House That Bonds Built—and all the beauty that followed. Yet his dark shadows and the allegations that followed him—including his tainted chase of Henry Aaron's home run record—had done damage that took years to recover from. That ghost, too, needed healing.

All the Giants ghosts were now at rest, laid there by Bochy's Dirty Dozen, as he called them, by the castoffs and the misfits and the ones who didn't even fit within those labels. This was the year that painted San Francisco history in that bright, beautiful shade of Giants orange.

Ride Down Market Street

The most amazing ride of all occurred two days after the champagne haze had faded, after the Giants had taken their last victorious flight home from the road, after a night of sleep had begun to reveal upon waking that it hadn't been a dream, after all.

The tradition of a victory parade is as ingrained in baseball as a champagne shower, and the Giants chose to honor their deep history by repeating the 1958 team's ride down Market Street as they were welcomed to the city, with Willie Mays riding out front. A Giant as much as ever, Mays now rode out front again, this time in celebration of a championship he had contributed deeply to by leading San Francisco's major league beginnings.

That day along Market Street, the high seas of orange and black crested in ways the city had never seen. The estimated one million people—more than the entire population of San Francisco—traveled to cram themselves in along the route and down in the plaza in front of Civic Center, where the parade would collapse into speeches. It was the largest gathering of any form the city had ever experienced, throughout all of its years as a center of culture, celebration and protest.

This spoke volumes. The parade outdrew the previous day's election in popular interest—the Giants were much easier to root for than most candidates and ballot initiatives (including the failed cannabis initiative that didn't *Let Tim Smoke!*). In the team, there was hope, not gridlock. There was unity in greater purpose, not self-serving special interests. There was lightness and honest humor, not hidden agendas. The leaders were people who remained grounded in success, who did not take it for granted after surviving the bitter taste of failure for enough years to create permanent gratitude. There were no warring political parties, just a true jubilant party of outrageous scale. There was a surreal sense of time slowed down, stretching into heightened territory, where it only goes in moments of transcendence or crisis. This party was everything politics was not.

Even the million there physically were but a fraction of the ones watching, taking in the perfect blue day San Francisco was blessed with that particular Nov. 3. The entire parade was simulcast to the Internet and the MLB TV network, inviting the world to see the sights (if not inhale the smoky smells). The world was able to watch Brian Wilson ignore police instructions to stay on his appointed faux cable car (authorities were afraid of the team causing a riot) as he ran down Market Street to lead the cheering on—without ensuing riot. It could watch a line of fine young women, whose bare midriffs deliciously spelled out "P-O-S-E-Y." It could see Aubrey Huff hold up his thong in triumph along the route, stashing it once more before pulling it out, *Zoolander* style, in front of Willie Mays at the podium. It could see pitching coach Dave Righetti wearing a "Fear the Beard" T-shirt on the dais—a man highly responsible for why the pitchers behind the bullpen beards were worth fearing. The world could witness Jon Miller blessing the crowd in the name of the Giants' greats and hear Brian Wilson and Arnold Schwarzenegger honor The Machine. It could watch Tim Lincecum reach out to celebrate all those Giants fans who had taken the show *on the road.*

"Well, like Brian [Wilson] and The Machine, I'm a man of not many words at all," said Lincecum. "I don't talk very much . . . [but] seeing black and orange everywhere was so awesome. . . . It made it so much more comfortable for us to play in there," he said, recalling the castles of the vanquished teams, where the fans had made the Giants feel at home.

Duane Kuiper listed the vanquished with an adapted version of his traditional home run call. "The San Diego Padres, the Atlanta Braves, the Philadelphia Phillies, the Texas Rangers. They are all OUTTA HERE!" Kuiper recalled his own long Giants history, waiting for the championship that never came. "I came to this organization in 1982, and I only knew a couple of things about it. One, it had a really bad ballpark [Candlestick]. It used to have a centerfielder by the name of Willie Mays. Its current center fielder was a guy named Chili [Davis]. I also knew that it had never won a World Championship. So my torture started in 1982. And I'm happy to say, thanks to these gentlemen here, *the torture is over!!!*"

Before Mike Krukow brought out the Vicar of the Bearded Ones, he had one more thing to add. "Before Brian Wilson comes up here, I do want to say one thing. Before the last game, we were having coffee in Texas. He [Wilson] looked at me and said, '*This story's been written.*'"

It's been written now in the Giants Good Book as the ultimate Giants Way. And it was written in a manner that allowed Wilson to become the elite closer he'd said no one could ever be without getting the last out of the World Series. Wilson did that—and he got the clinching out of the regular season, the National League Division Series and the National League Championship Series as well. It doesn't get more elite than that.

"I'm still waiting for the tears," Tim Lincecum said, when the parade was over, after having returned to the stadium and the clubhouse via the players' usual pregame walking route from left field to the dugout.

He wasn't the only one. History takes time to sink in.

Rings

Receiving that World Championship ring symbolizes the sport's pinnacle of achievement. Yet a symbol is all it is. Unlike, say, a red thong, it's not the kind of adornment that can be easily worn while pursuing the very championship that earns it.

Who are those rings for? Not just the core 25 players on the roster at the time of playoffs and the World Series. At the first level, they're for everyone who had service time on the team's major league roster during the championship season—and for the Giants in 2010. That alone was a long list. It even included outfielder Fred Lewis, who'd entered the season on the Giants roster but also on the disabled list and was traded to Toronto before making even one on-field appearance. He received a ring. So did the array of coaches so essential to the team's success: Dave Righetti, Hensley "Bam Bam" Meulens, Ron Wotus, Tim Flannery, Mark Gardner, Billy Hayes and Roberto Kelly.

Regardless of whether the ones behind the scenes receive actual rings, the championship rings represent them as well. They're for Mike Murphy. They're for Dave Groeschner and his training staff. In the front office, they're for Bill Neukom, Larry Baer, Brian Sabean, Bruce Bochy and the corporate cast of hundreds, if not thousands. They're for the scouts, the minor league organizations, the peanut vendors, the parking lot attendants and the ticket-takers. They're for the accountants, the staff of the Giants Community Fund, the Junior Giants and more. Many of the players would tell you they're for the fans as much as for anyone. And in 2010, there were more than three million fans pouring through the Giants turnstiles, making the Giants one of only four National League teams to reach those levels. And for every fan who came to one game or many, there were countless others who followed from a distance—on televisions and radios and through newspapers and word-of-mouth.

The rings are also for all the Giants players—great or forgotten—who toiled during the 56-year championship drought. Of course, they're for Mays and McCovey and Marichal, but they're also equally for Rod Beck and Robb Nen, Mike McCormick, Johnnie LeMaster and Dave Dravecky. They're for everyone who ever passed through the Giants family as the relentless quest for excellence continued (and continues still). They're all revered names in the Giants Good Book, men who did their imperfect best to practice their own Giants Way before it was ever called that.

Those 2010 rings reflect the deeply embedded faces of the great, the obscure and the missing. Those tiny rings encircle the enormity of decades of baseball history.

Offseason Scatter

The baseball quiet of November inevitably arrived, the forces of change already reshaping the Giants. The same forces that make a championship team so difficult to assemble make it equally challenging to keep one together. After the exhaustion and exhilaration of the

World Series win, the team's front office found itself a month behind where it normally would be, due to the extension of the season by the playoffs. The revised contract with the players' union provided that eligible players would become free agents five days after the World Series ended—meaning Aubrey Huff, Pat Burrell, Juan Uribe and Edgar Renteria would be free to leave less than a week after earning their coveted rings. Others eligible for arbitration might not be tendered contracts by the Giants and could become free agents as well.

For Aubrey Huff, leaving was not a desirable possibility, even though he had initially come to San Francisco only by default. "Why go and gamble somewhere else? I love the guys here, I love the staff. Everything stayed intact—why not come back? To be able to come back and try to defend the World Championship—I've been in dead last my whole life. Why would I want to go anywhere else? I know it's not a conducive park for me to hit left-handed, but who cares? I just want to win. Believe me, I got a lot of catching up to do." His leadership was rewarded with a handsome contract.

Huff's college pal and coleader Pat Burrell also chose to stay—eschewing more lucrative offers to return to the area of his youth and a team that meant more than money ever could. As he said upon signing, "At this point in my career, being a part of something special is more important to me."

Juan Uribe, who had been so significant to and so beloved by the team and fans alike—with a family history reaching back into the Giants family tree—made a different choice. Uribe raced to sign a three-year deal with the Dodgers—the *Dodgers,* of all teams—so quickly he gave the Giants no chance to re-sign him, despite their desire to do so, and despite the fact that the Giants had previously given him a chance to resurrect his career not only once but *twice.* Two years in a row, they had signed him to contracts when there was little other interest in his services. The sense of betrayal was immediate and palpable, and in spring training, he was booed upon return.

Edgar Renteria was cheered instead. Inspired by his World Series revival, he chose not to retire. The Giants, however, showed faint interest in keeping him—the minimal offer he received was not enough to keep his services—so he moved on to Cincinnati with his usual grace, and the Giants signed Miguel Tejada to replace him. Renteria was warmly welcomed by Giants fans in Arizona when the Reds and Giants met, and he visited the Giants clubhouse to an equally warm reception from his former teammates.

The offseason scatter was minor compared to many teams in many years. The major pieces of the team remained intact, led by the core of the homegrown pitching staff and the bullpen behind them. They would return to defend their title and the spirit of loose laughter behind it all. They would try to paint another year orange, this time with raised expectations—no less than Hank Aaron predicted a Giants/Red Sox World Series for 2011—and the target of the baseball world upon their backs.

Double Handicap

One side effect of winning the World Series (or even losing it) is that as the schedule is lengthened by success, the offseason is equally shortened. Workload is increased, and time off to recover is lessened. It's a double handicap—one factor in explaining why there are so few repeat champions.

Sergio Romo was asked at FanFest in February what he did in the offseason after the victory. "*What* offseason?" Romo asked in reply.

At the same event, Brian Wilson mentioned that he usually began his offseason workouts on Nov. 1—about a month after the close of the regular season. But on Nov. 1, 2010, he was still closing out the final game of the World Series. No rest for the victorious.

This double stretching is a modern challenge the previous championship Giants didn't have to contend with. The season was shorter in 1954—154 games instead of 162—and the playoffs were *far* shorter, with no Division Series or League Championship Series preceding the World Series. Even with a World Series appearance, there was still sufficient time for a normal offseason.

The Giants entered camp in 2011 knowing this, particularly watching the strain on the pitching staff's young arms. Many had thrown more innings than ever before, and vigilance would be required as the end reached the beginning again, and the quest for another championship started anew.

Inevitably, a few things shifted. Aubrey Huff retired the Rally Thong, for example, much to the visual relief of Bruce Bochy. "It wasn't easy on the eyes," Bochy half-joked. "I can go in the clubhouse a little more now."

Meanwhile, Pablo Sandoval did stellar conditioning work over the winter, dropping 38 pounds in an effort to return to form, and he immediately showed renewed quickness. Brian Wilson, after a bizarre television appearance dressed as a sea captain, showed up with a beard of overwhelming magnitude—again unnaturally black and now reaching ZZ Top proportions. Despite arriving in his usual phenomenal physical shape, Wilson injured an oblique muscle during spring training and began the year on the disabled list. Almost everyone on the team showed up *early* and in terrific condition for the defense of their title. This time, Tim Lincecum's only offseason brush with the law was to be nearly arrested for attempted mustache: He spent a month before camp trying to grow something that was barely visible. "Fear the Fu?" He asked at FanFest, before making the feeble facial hair vanish again and claiming his dog had licked it off. The stories went endlessly on, and the jovial striving continued.

Would it be one year or another 56 before championship again? Only the residents of a future time would be able to answer.

The End Is the Beginning

To reach the source, to taste the ultimate baseball victory, brings completion and satisfaction. Yet it doesn't often bring complacency. For the competitive athlete, triumph instead brings a renewed hunger to reach it again. Just ask Aubrey Huff.

"I always said to myself I'll take one World Series ring in my career, and I'll be happy," Huff said in spring. "I'm happy. But it was such a fun rush last year, being able to play in those intense, fun playoff games—that's what's so exciting about baseball. I never knew that's the kind of rush it was. Now it's an addiction for me to get back there." After briefly pondering retirement before joining the Giants, he said he now felt reinvigorated for another five to 10 years ahead.

Reinvigorated and newly inspired himself, Tim Flannery again summed it up. "If you get a taste of it and you get an opportunity to do it again—that's why these guys are playing and why they're preaching the religion of the relentless flow of the positive river." That river's flow never ceases, and the desire to merge with it can have the urgency and depth of a spiritual quest. It continues with the constancy of the passing years as baseball annually returns to almost exactly where it began. The baseball season's rhythms and timing truly align with the seasons and their forces, changing only who dips into the positive river and how.

Does baseball matter in the grand scheme of things? In a world with poverty and war and *real* forms of torture rampaging on, is it important that an eccentric bunch of athletes continues to chase a little white sphere?

Yes. Absolutely. Not only because it offers respite and refuge from all the raging trouble within the larger, all-encompassing sphere, but also because the human hearts that pursue it can mirror the best of humanity. When the players honor the game with integrity and passion, there is as much depth of spirit as within any noble pursuit.

That sacred depth exists between the foul lines as well as in the stories of the fans who follow the game. "If you've not experienced it, you hear somebody talk about it, you think they need to go to the loony farm," Flannery concludes. "But I think that the game is bigger than what we've ever imagined."

At least, it is when there's magic inside—when there's laughter, grace, humility and selflessness merged with talent, discipline and triumph. No team has exemplified that better than the Giants of 2010. Thus their journey will live on in memory and in history. Yes, what a long, strange trip it has been. What a long, *orange* trip it has been. And what a long, strange, orange trip it will still be. Let the trip begin again. Let legend upon legend coalesce into new echoes of selfless triumph and laughter.

This Is Our Time! Supports the Junior Giants Program of the Giants Community Fund

Junior Giants, the flagship program of the Giants Community Fund, is a free, non-competitive and innovative baseball program for boys and girls ages 5-18 years old.

In 1994, the Fund sought a program that would give at-risk kids a meaningful partnership with community-based organizations and provide an alternative to drugs, gangs and crime. The Junior Giants Program was therefore established and now serves more than 17,000 children in 85 leagues across California and into Nevada and Oregon. The Community Fund provides all of the uniforms, equipment, and training necessary to run a league as well as tickets to select Giants games so the youth can experience a Major League Baseball game.

But more important than the fundamentals of baseball, Junior Giants focuses on the four bases of character development—Confidence, Integrity, Leadership and Teamwork—and offers programs in Education, Health and Violence Prevention. This framework is integrated into the Junior Giants handbook distributed to all of the kids and parents.

This program welcomes kids from all backgrounds and encourages them to live healthy and productive lives by getting outside and playing baseball!

A portion of This Is Our Time! sales goes to support the Junior Giants program of the Giants Community Fund.

What makes Junior Giants Baseball unique?

> It's a free program!
>
> The league is non-competitive
>
> It's a program for girls and boys
>
> Higher value placed on character than on wins and losses
>
> Programs in education, health, and violence prevention
>
> Pitching machines are used
>
> Professional training by the Giants and other experts is provided to the coaches

For more information about the Junior Giants program, please visit jrgiants.org or call 877-JR-GIANT.

About the Authors

Rich Draper

CHRIS HAFT is MLB.com's beat writer for the San Francisco Giants, and has been covering the team since 2005, after growing up as a Northern Californian worshipping in the Giants' cold, windy temple. He's been covering Major League Baseball full-time for most of the past twenty years.

Michaela A. Begg, Core Photography Group

ERIC ALAN is author of *Wild Grace and Grace and Tranquility*. He wrote the biographical material accompanying the CD *Travelin' Shoes* by Giants third base coach/professional musician Tim Flannery; and his photograph "The Inner Giant" has hung in the Giants' broadcast booth in recent years.

For more information about the book and authors, visit: www.this-is-our-time.com.